Data-Driven Decision Making for Effective School Leadership

Anthony G. Picciano

Hunter College and Graduate Center
City University of New York

PEARSON

Merrill
Prentice Hall

Upper Saddle River, New Jersey
Columbus, Ohio

To my grandson, Michael Anthony

Library of Congress Cataloging in Publication Data
Picciano, Anthony G.
  Data-driven decision making for effective school leadership / Anthony G. Picciano.
      p. cm.
  Includes bibliographical references and index.
  ISBN 0-13-118722-8 (alk. paper)
  1. Educational indicators. 2. Education—Mathematical models. 3. Educational planning—Mathematical models.
  4. School management and organization—Mathematical models. I. Title.
  LB2846.P53 2006
  379.1'58—dc22

                            2005019466

Vice President and Executive Publisher: Jeffery W. Johnston
Executive Editor: Debra A. Stollenwerk
Assistant Development Editor: Elisa Rogers
Editorial Assistant: Mary Morrill
Production Editor: Alexandrina Benedicto Wolf
Production Coordination: nSight
Design Coordinator: Diane C. Lorenzo
Cover Designer: Terry Rohrbach
Cover Image: Corbis
Production Manager: Susan W. Hannahs
Senior Marketing Manager: Darcy Betts Prybella
Marketing Coordinator: Brian Mounts

This book was set in Times New Roman by Laserwords. It was printed and bound by R.R. Donnelley & Sons Company. The cover was printed by R.R. Donnelley & Sons Company.

Pearson Education Ltd.
Pearson Education Singapore Pte. Ltd.
Pearson Education Canada, Ltd.
Pearson Education—Japan

Pearson Education Australia Pty. Limited
Pearson Education North Asia Ltd.
Pearson Educación de Mexico, S.A. de C.V.
Pearson Education Malaysia Pte. Ltd.

10 9 8 7 6 5 4 3 2 1
ISBN 0-13-118722-8

Preface

This book provides a theoretical background and practical considerations for planning and implementing data-driven decision-making processes in schools and school districts. Systems theory serves as the theoretical framework for examining how effective data-driven decision making requires planning, developing efficient and reliable data resources, and sharing knowledge among all stakeholders in our schools. Basic concepts of educational research to help administrators gain a conceptual understanding of data analysis, allowing them to choose and develop appropriate analytical approaches, are presented. By tying these methods to practical decision processes, links to information in the education literature are provided, which promote intelligent consumption of research by the professional school administrator.

Emphasis is placed on the *total* development and application of data-driven decision-making processes, not on any single or isolated component. Most important, the book establishes a foundation from which educators can move forward using the powerful potential of data to meet the diverse needs of students.

TARGET AUDIENCE

This book is written primarily for aspiring school leaders: assistant principals, principals, superintendents, and other district level administrators. It is designed as a supplemental text for K–12 educational administration courses, as well as a resource for practitioners who want to become knowledgeable about data-driven decision-making concepts and techniques. Readers who are familiar with research methods, information systems development, statistics, and quantitative techniques will understand the material easily. The Technical Support section provides reference information.

How much are school leaders really expected to know about data and information resources and management? Are they expected to be the producers or the users of data for decision making? Surely superintendents in large urban districts rely on staff to provide data. However, there are more than 15,000 school districts in the United States, most of which are relatively small. In these districts, educational leaders are expected to have a broad range of managerial and technical skills. Educational leaders primarily need to understand how to use data. Nevertheless, they would be well served in developing an understanding of the effort, resources, and techniques used in generating timely and accurate data.

Rationale

Various factors have led to a strong focus on data-driven decision making, and ultimately motivated the development of this book: the shift toward data-driven approaches to school reform, the No Child Left Behind legislation, and new requirements for certification in school administration.

In the 1990s, new terms such as *data-driven decision making, data warehousing*, and *data disaggregation* began to appear in the school reform literature. These terms and the approaches to which they referred were connected to research methods and information systems development. However, they were also a call to action that would be integrated into teaching and learning. A connection has formed between the data-driven school reform approach and collaborative action research projects that involve administrators and teachers. As a result, subtle but real changes are occurring in educational research methods courses to reflect more data-driven decision-making concepts.

In 2001, when President George W. Bush and the U.S. Congress reauthorized the Elementary and Secondary Education Act (ESEA), better known as No Child Left Behind, the importance of data-driven decision making became fully apparent. Federal funding for education would be contingent on monitoring and demonstrating student progress as measured by quantifiable outcomes—clearly a task facilitated by data-driven decision making.

In addition, many states began to rethink the requirements needed for academic programs leading to certification in school administration. In 2003, the New York State Department of Education issued new guidelines for these programs with specific references to the need for administrators who could plan, develop, and implement and who were "informed by data." Higher-education teachers of education began to revise their programs to comply with these guidelines; many developed required courses that included data-driven decision making. Few textbooks, however, provide the three major components necessary for such courses: reliable data resources; the connection to research methods, especially action research; and the techniques needed to implement data-driven decision making. This book fills these needs and facilitates compliance with No Child Left Behind, thereby helping educators analyze data, harness the power of data, and make data work in improving teaching, learning, and the overall condition of schools.

ORGANIZATION OF THE BOOK

Section I provides the basic concepts needed to understand the major issues related to developing data-driven decision-making processes. Planning and development of information management systems are fundamental for any effective data-driven decision-making activity. Section I stresses the development of all aspects of the information system, including hardware, software, and most importantly, people. The section includes a chapter on educational research methods and concludes with a discussion of projects designed to improve teaching and learning in schools.

Section II concentrates entirely on data-driven decision-making applications. It offers practical examples in the areas of enrollment management, budgeting, professional development, and instruction to illustrate concepts introduced in the previous section. Readers are encouraged to work through the examples using an electronic spreadsheet program, such as Microsoft Excel, or a statistical package, such as the Statistical Package for the Social Sciences (SPSS).

The Technical Support section provides reference information related to statistical concepts, software tools, and other resources for developing effective data-driven decision making. These resources facilitate the organization, development, collection, and analysis of data.

FEATURES

Case Studies. Most chapters have case studies that can be used to present material and as exercises to develop expertise in data-driven decision-making approaches. The case studies are excellent for group problem solving in a traditional class and for initiating discussions on electronic bulletin boards in an online course. Although the case studies are fictional, they are based on real-life situations.

Key Terms. Readers can refer to the Glossary for definitions of key terms, which are italicized in each chapter.

Chapter Summary. Each chapter concludes with a summary designed to help the reader understand and focus on the key concepts introduced.

Technical Support. The Technical Support section provides additional information and resources. Readers may wish to review some of the material before reading the chapters, or refer to the material when they encounter new routines or procedures.

- Part A introduces statistical concepts. It is not a replacement for an educational statistics course, but it does provide a basic review of the key concepts used in this book.
- Parts B and C introduce two relevant software packages, Excel and SPSS. Most college computer facilities provide these packages as part of the normal suite of software programs available to faculty and students. The decision to use these two packages was important. Although Excel and other electronic spreadsheet programs do many of the basic tabular summary statistical routines well, they are not at all graceful or powerful enough to do other forms of statistical analysis (e.g., correlation, means

analysis, and crosstabulations). The case materials in this book have been taught with various groups of students, including recently appointed data analysts, and I have found that a combination of software approaches (Excel and SPSS) works best.

- Part D summarizes database management terminology and presents a sample database file outline recommended by the U.S. Department of Education, National Center for Education Statistics.
- Part E lists a number of Internet resources pertinent to data-driven decision making.

COMPANION WEBSITE

The Companion Website (http://www.prenhall.com/picciano) provides readers with access to the major data sets used as examples in Section II. These data sets are formatted for Excel or SPSS software and are explained in Chapters 6 through 10. They make excellent resources for class discussions, and can be used for hands-on student activities and assignments.

Wherever a data set is first presented in the text, readers are directed to the Companion Website to view the data being discussed.

Technical Support D is available on the Companion Website as a printable document. The websites in Technical Support E are available as clickable hot links.

Anthony G. Picciano

Acknowledgments

I gratefully acknowledge the guidance and assistance provided by the staff at Merrill/Pearson Education, especially Debbie Stollenwerk, Elisa Rogers, and Alex Wolf. I also acknowledge the fine work provided by Stephanie Levy and the staff at nSight. I would like to thank the following reviewers for their feedback: Irwin Blumer, Boston College; Bryan R. Cole, Texas A&M University; Michael Copland, University of Washington; Jeanne R. Fiene, Western Kentucky University; Margaret Grogan, University of Missouri, Columbia; Larry W. Hughes, University of Houston; Ellen Jane Irons, Lamar University; Dale Johnson, Tarleton State University; Stanley A. Schainker, University of North Carolina, Chapel Hill; Jan Walker, Iowa State University; Will Weber, University of Houston; and Harold Wenglinsky, Baruch College.

In addition, I have benefited significantly from my professional associations with a number of colleagues, specifically the faculty in the Educational Leadership Program in the Department of Curriculum and Teaching at Hunter College; the faculty in the Ph.D. Program in Urban Education at the City University of New York Graduate Center; colleagues at the Alfred P. Sloan Consortium for Asynchronous Learning Networks; and all of the school administrators who provided source material and who are truly leading their schools in creative uses of technology.

Especially important to my efforts were the students in the Educational Leadership Program at Hunter College. They are an industrious group of future leaders who will make many fine contributions to their schools for years to come.

Lastly, my gratitude to Michael and Dawn Marie who have helped me to be a better person. And Elaine, more than a wife, a friend, and companion, she cares for me and about everything I do.

Anthony G. Picciano

About the Author

Anthony G. Picciano is a professor in the Educational Leadership Program at Hunter College, and in the Ph.D. Program in Urban Education and the Program in Interactive Pedagogy and Technology at the City University of New York Graduate Center. His teaching specializations are educational technology, contemporary issues in education, educational policy, organization theory, and research methods. He is the author of six books, including *Educational Leadership and Planning for Technology*, Fourth Edition (Merrill/Prentice Hall, 2005); *Educational Research Primer* (Continuum, 2004); and *Distance Learning: Making Connections Across Virtual Space and Time* (Merrill/Prentice Hall, 2000), which extensively covers the field of online learning.

Dr. Picciano has served as a consultant for various public and private organizations including the Commission on Higher Education/Middle States Association of Colleges and Universities, the New York City Department of Education, the New York State Department of Education, New Leaders for New Schools, the U.S. Coast Guard, and Citicorp. He has received numerous grants and awards from the National Science Foundation, the Alfred P. Sloan Foundation, the U.S. Department of Education, and IBM. He currently serves on the board of directors of the Alfred P. Sloan Consortium of Colleges and Universities.

His articles and reviews have appeared in *The Teachers College Record*, *The Urban Review*, *Journal of Asynchronous Learning Networks*, *Journal of Educational Multimedia and Hypermedia*, *Computers in the Schools*, *Equity and Choice*, and *EDUCOM Review*. Dr. Picciano lives in Pocantico Hills, New York, with his wife, friend, and companion, Elaine.

Prologue

In June 2001, I had the pleasure of being part of a group of 30 Americans who visited the People's Republic of China to participate in a 2-week exchange dedicated to sharing ideas and educational approaches. The discussions centered on technology, teaching English as a second language, and corporation–university relationships. Most of us were affiliated with colleges and universities, but several members of the group were businesspeople. Much of our time was spent in the northwestern provinces, a rural, mountainous region rich in Chinese culture, history, and tradition. We traveled approximately 1,500 miles in China, all by bus, to visit colleges; primary, middle, and secondary schools; and cultural centers. Our days were filled with meetings and seminars. We had communal meals with our Chinese hosts who could not have been more gracious, friendly, and helpful with every aspect of our travels.

In the evenings, after dinner, we went for walks in whatever village, town, or city we happened to be in. Frequently I walked with three Chinese-American members of our group (Ken, Oscar, and Y. C.). One evening, as the four of us returned to the visitor's center at a college in Taiyuen, Shanxi Province, we stopped for a nightcap in a small bar area set up just for us. The young man who served us was a 17-year-old student. When he was not waiting on our table (there were only three tables in the bar area), he was reading his books. Ken asked his name, where he was from, and what he was reading. The student explained that he was from a mountain village and was studying for the national examination—the centuries-old Chinese system that determines whether he would be admitted into college. Ken asked him a few more questions, including what he would do if he did not pass the examination. Without any hesitation he answered that he would have to go back to his village and do what his father does: work in a coal mine.

Only about 8% of the Chinese population of 1.3 billion people can go on to higher education, and the competition is incredibly keen. Those who pass the examination continue their education; those who do not must find an occupation that does not require a high level of educational training. During our visits to the colleges and universities, we saw hundreds of students studying at all hours, memorizing pages of notes and texts, and preparing for the examinations, which, in the end, would exclude many of them from moving on. Our Chinese colleagues indicated clearly that they would like to change the system but that resources are not yet available to open more higher educational facilities. They greatly admired the American educational system that allows so many students to go on to college.

The American educational system casts a wide net of opportunity that allows students to pursue an education and, ultimately, an occupation of their choice. We know well, however, that not all students have the same opportunities. The poor, minorities, and children with special needs have less opportunity than others. Nevertheless, the American educational system is the major pathway that enables our children to be what they want to be and to do what they want to do.

During the past two decades, public school reform has concentrated on accountability, standards, and testing. Unfortunately, this call for reform has become so tangled in the web of American politics that it is no longer clear whether the intent is to reform education or to trumpet the party line. American education is not all bad, and much of it, as our envious Chinese colleagues brought home, is remarkably good. Can it improve? Can our legal system improve? Can corporate America improve? Can our mass media and press improve? Of course. All major institutions need to improve and reform as society changes and progresses.

Data-driven decision making should play an important role in effecting school change and reform; it should not be viewed or used only as a tool to enforce standards. We want to continue to provide opportunities to our children and to their children. We do not want a system that limits young people's choices simply because they fail an examination. We want a system based on multiple assessments that consider the whole child objectively and subjectively. We want a system that provides first-rate instruction, well-trained professionals in classrooms, vibrant curricula, and cost-effective facilities and environments capable of providing a plethora of educational opportunities. To reach these goals, we must not tolerate ill-informed, poorly informed, or uninformed decisions at any level of education.

Data-driven decision making is a mode of operation with which educators must become familiar, and which should be used in all of our schools. This book provides insights into using this tool to support instructional activities, to aid in the development of professionals, to assist in designing vibrant curricula, and to provide cost-effective approaches for providing educational opportunities for all.

Anthony G. Picciano

Brief Contents

Contents

Section I

Concepts and Foundations of Data-Driven Decision Making

This section introduces the fundamental concepts for developing and implementing data-driven decision making. It emphasizes the importance of planning and building reliable information resources. Educational research concepts are also presented to próvide an understanding of the techniques used in data-driven decision making.

1   Introduction to Data-Driven Decision Making

2   Planning and Developing Information Resources

3   Hardware, Software, and People

4   Educational Research Methods and Tools

5   Teachers and Administrators as Researchers

Chapter 1

Introduction to Data-Driven Decision Making

Deborah Meir (2004), a well-respected educator and urban school reformer, in a letter to the next president listed eight things that should be done to improve education in the United States. After the need for smaller schools and for local decision making, number three on her list was the need for "good" information. Meir commented that (1) policymakers, teachers, parents, and even children need to know what is going on in their schools; (2) educational decision making relies on the quality and accessibility of good information; and (3) too often data rest "in mammoth databases that obfuscate truth" (p. 22).

In an article titled, "Accountability Policies and Teacher Decision Making: Barriers to the Use of Data to Improve Practice," Ingram, Seashore Louis, and Schroeder (2004) reported the results of a 7-year, longitudinal study on teaching practice and decision making in nine public high schools. Using both qualitative and quantitative research methods, the authors attempted to learn more about the culture of data-based decision making and its implications for teaching and accountability policies. One of their conclusions was that most teachers reported serious barriers to their ability to use data effectively in improving instruction. The study suggested that although teachers considered the concept of data-driven decision making and its relation to school improvement as ideal, they thought it was unrealistic under their current working conditions. Ingram, Seashore Louis, and Schroeder identified seven cultural, technical, and political barriers to using

3

data effectively in decision making; among them were time commitment (i.e., the time it takes to access student data, analyze the data, and prescribe remedial action), lack of agreement on student outcomes, and mistrust of the reasons given for data collection activities.

The Association for Supervision and Curriculum Development is one of the leading professional organizations for school administrators in the United States. An entire issue of its monthly publication, *Educational Leadership,* was devoted to the use of data in improving student achievement. In her introduction, Margaret Scherer (2003), the editor, framed the topic with four questions:

1. How will we use the data?
2. Where did the data come from?
3. Where do we start?
4. What do the data really say?

These basic questions indicate that the use of data for decision making in American education is in its beginning stages, especially in respect to guiding instruction. Although some schools have begun to move forward in establishing data-driven decision-making processes, many administrators are still seeking answers to the basic questions posed by Scherer.

The three references just cited suggest that major stakeholders in American education have observed difficulties in implementing decision-making processes that take advantage of accurate, timely, and useful data. In response to the issues and questions posed, this book will provide the fundamentals needed to implement data-driven decision-making processes in schools.

RATIONALE FOR ADOPTING DATA-DRIVEN DECISION MAKING

In many organizations, corporations, public agencies, hospitals, and medical service associations, the use of data to support basic decision-making operations is a foregone conclusion. The computer-information-knowledge age has been evolving for more than 50 years; digital technology now permeates all aspects of organizational life. Writing in the 1980s, Rockert and DeLong (1988) devoted an entire book to the art of corporate decision making based on information-based executive support systems. O'Brien (1988) likewise observed that "for many firms using computers for information processing is an absolute necessity" (p. 33), for a number of reasons, but especially managers' demands for more kinds of information to support their operations. Streifer (2002) commented that corporate America has been using data-driven decision making for decades, but he concluded that in education administration it is an emerging field.

In American education, the information requirements being placed on schools by funding agencies, state education departments, and local boards of education have accelerated in recent years. Linda Darling-Hammond (2004) commented that there are at least five conceptions of accountability in American education:

1. Political accountability: Legislators and school board members must answer to their constituents.
2. Legal accountability: Schools must adhere to laws.
3. Bureaucratic accountability: Schools must operate within rules and regulations promulgated by government agencies.
4. Professional accountability: Teachers are expected to uphold professional standards of good practice.
5. Market accountability: Parents and students have options and choices in some communities.

These demands for accountability have forced many administrators to take a more aggressive position on integrating data-driven processes into all aspects of their operations. Certain administrative operations such as financial accounting, course scheduling, and inventory control have depended on information systems for many years. Instruction, on the other hand, has for the most part avoided data-driven processes and has depended on the intuition, skills, and expertise of educators to prescribe the techniques for working with students. Although resources have been devoted to integrating technology into the classroom, the focus has been on learning activities such as basic skills development, research projects, and multimedia rather than on managing instruction.

In the 1990s, various education agencies and the federal government put an emphasis on standards and testing. The reauthorization of the Elementary and Secondary Education Act, better known as No Child Left Behind, requires all schools to expand the testing of students and to monitor their progress. Compliance with these new requirements, which is critical to educational funding, will be almost impossible without an efficient and accurate data delivery and data analysis support system. Even though concern exists about the increasing tendency of policymakers to link funding to student and school performance, our schools are responsible for the education and maturation of our children, their future, and ultimately the future of our society. Policymakers at all levels are demanding that school administrators modernize the way in which they plan, monitor, and evaluate instruction and learning. Integrating data and information into these processes will empower administrators and help them take command of their school's progress and destiny.

PURPOSE OF THIS BOOK

This book provides the theoretical framework and presents practical considerations for planning and implementing data-driven decision-making processes in schools and school districts. Systems theory is used as the overall framework for examining how effective data-driven decision making requires planning, developing efficient and reliable data resources, and sharing knowledge among all stakeholders in our schools. Basic concepts of educational research methods are presented to help undergird a conceptual understanding of data analysis and to enable school administrators to choose and develop correct analytical approaches. Furthermore, tying these research methods to practical decision processes serves two other purposes: (1) it provides educators with a link to information that has been published in education literature, and (2) it promotes intelligent consumption of research by the professional school administrator.

Throughout this book emphasis is placed on the total development and application of data-driven decision making processes, not on any single or isolated component. Most importantly, this book is meant to provide a foundation from which educators can look to the powerful potential of data as they move forward to meet the diverse needs of their present and future students.

DEFINING DATA-DRIVEN DECISION MAKING

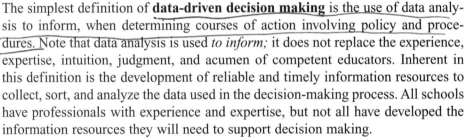

The simplest definition of **data-driven decision making** is the use of data analysis to inform, when determining courses of action involving policy and procedures. Note that data analysis is used *to inform;* it does not replace the experience, expertise, intuition, judgment, and acumen of competent educators. Inherent in this definition is the development of reliable and timely information resources to collect, sort, and analyze the data used in the decision-making process. All schools have professionals with experience and expertise, but not all have developed the information resources they will need to support decision making.

Decision making may be simply defined as choosing between or among two or more alternatives. In a modern school organization, however, decision making is an integral component of complex management processes such as academic planning, policymaking, and budgeting. These processes evolve over time, require participation by stakeholders, and most importantly, seek to include information that will help all those involved in the decision-making process.

Fundamental to the definition of data-driven decision making is an assumption of a rational model that is directed by values and based on data. However, it is well recognized that a strictly rational model has limitations. A review of the literature on organization behavior shows that the concept of the limitations of rationality has dominated decision-making theory for several decades. An individual commonly associated with this concept and whose work is highly recommended for further reference is Herbert Simon (1945, 1957, 1960, 1979, 1982, 1991). Simon was awarded the Nobel Prize for economics in 1978 for his research on decision making in organizations. His theory on the limits of rationality, later renamed "bounded rationality," is based on this principle: Organizations operate along a continuum of rational and social behaviors mainly because the knowledge necessary to function strictly according to a rational model is beyond what is available to administrators and managers. Although first developed in the 1940s, this theory has withstood the test of time. Now it is widely recognized as a fundamental assumption in understanding organizational processes such as decision making and planning (Tyson, 2002; Carlson & Awkerman, 1991; Senge, 1990; Luthans, 1981; Peters & Waterman, 1982).

Regardless of the limitations of the rational decision-making model, modern computerized information systems are facilitating and instilling a greater degree of rationality in decision making in all organizations, including schools. Such systems support the concept of organizations that are able to adjust, adapt, and learn (Dibello & Nevis, 1998). These systems are not replacing the decision maker; instead, they are helping to refine the decision-making process.

Figure 1-1 illustrates the basic data-driven decision-making process. It assumes that an information system is available to support the decision process, that internal and external factors not available through the information system are considered, and that a course of action is determined. Preferably, the information system in Figure 1-1 is a computerized database software system capable of storing, manipulating, and providing reports from a wide variety of data. The details of database software systems will be discussed in Chapter 2.

Terms related to data-driven decision making that have become popular include **data warehousing**, **data mining**, and **data disaggregation**. Data warehousing is essentially a database information system that is capable of storing and maintaining data **longitudinally** (i.e., over a period of time). Data mining refers to searching or "digging into" a data file for information to understand a particular phenomenon better. Data disaggregation refers to the use of software tools to break data files down into various characteristics. For example, a software program may be used

Figure 1-1   Data-driven decision-making process.

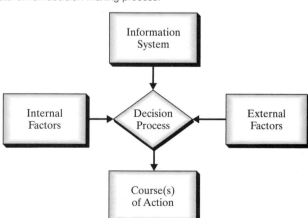

to select student performance data on a standardized test by gender, by class, by ethnicity, or by other definable characteristics.

AN OLD IDEA: KNOWLEDGE IS POWER

The previous section reviewed recent developments in information technology and decision-making terminology, but the need for leaders to know about and understand their organizations' structures and activities has always existed. History abounds with examples illustrating that knowledge is power, for example, the conquest of disease and the development of the atomic bomb. In organization theory as well, the power of knowledge has been well recognized. French and Raven (1959), in a series of studies on administrative management, were among the first theorists to identify "expert power" as a requisite for successful leadership among managers. They defined expert power simply as having access to critical information about one's organization and environment.

The concept that knowledge is power should not be viewed negatively. Because of public control and the number of constituents, schools generally require their administrative leaders to have expert, or information, power. Parents, teachers, staff, school board members, and the media seek out and rely on administrators to help them understand issues and events in schools. The experienced and accomplished administrator is willing and able to share freely her or his knowledge with others. Administrators who invest in and develop their information resources are better able to lead and manage their schools in all activities, be they program evaluations, budget presentations, or curricular improvements. Making good judgments in these areas requires accurate information about what is going on both inside and outside the schools.

Furthermore, given the extensive reporting requirements of various government agencies at all levels, school administrators must have access to and provide critical data about their schools. Lack of accurate information can jeopardize budget requests, grant applications, and overall credibility with government officials. The data-driven decision-making approach is basically a modern extension of the concept of knowledge-based power, emphasizing the efficient use of information resources to inform action.

NEED FOR PLANNING

Developing data-driven decision-making approaches is intimately tied to other information and decision processes within the school organization. Planning at several levels, but especially at the school district level, is critical and starts with the development of reliable information resources. This might be easier said than done. Figure 1-2 illustrates 12 steps necessary for designing and implementing an automated student information system. Note that the first 10 steps concentrate

Figure 1-2 Steps for designing and implementing an automated student record system.

> **Step 1:** Determine the desired uses of the student record system.
>
> **Step 2:** Identify federal, state, and local regulations affecting the maintenance of student records.
>
> **Step 3:** Select the overall contents of the student record system.
>
> **Step 4:** Select the data elements to be kept in the student record system.
>
> **Step 5:** Select a system for assigning a unique identifier to each student.
>
> **Step 6:** Determine the physical design of the student record system.
>
> **Step 7:** Identify the format for the data within the student record system.
>
> **Step 8:** Determine how you will enter or import data into the student record system.
>
> **Step 9:** Determine your procedures for providing access to the system.
>
> **Step 10:** Plan ways to ensure the integrity of the data in the student record system.
>
> **Step 11:** Plan procedures for doing standard and ad hoc analysis and reporting.
>
> **Step 12:** Develop procedures for appropriate reporting of student data.

Source: From *Building an Automated Student Record System,* National Center for Education Statistics, 2000. Washington, DC: Office of Educational Research and Improvement, U.S. Department of Education. NCES 2000-324. Retrieved July 15, 2004, from http://nces.ed.gov/pubs2000/building/

entirely on the development and maintenance of the information system; accessing data is only considered in Steps 11 and 12. Experienced information analysts support this approach, because the time and energy invested in the front end of an information system reap significant rewards in the form of efficient and accurate data delivery and reporting at the back end.

In addition to developing resources, school administrators need to examine how information will be integrated into decision processes. Although planning and development of an information system start at the school district level, effective processes that provide pathways and access to data at all levels—school, department, and classroom—need to be developed. Sharing data and developing strategies for using data regularly to drive instructional and administrative decisions are at the heart of an effective process.

THE SYSTEMS APPROACH

In presenting any topic, a basic framework for study needs to be established. Systems theory is the most appropriate major topic of this book using data in decision processes in primary and secondary schools. The major components of a **system**, input, process, and output—and their interrelationship—are generally accepted as fundamental to all aspects of information system development, as well as to decision processes. The basic data-driven decision-making process presented in Figure 1-1 is a systems model: Note how the information system and internal and external factors provide input to a decision process, which results in an output in the form of a course of action.

The systems approach has been used for many years as a framework for demonstrating and understanding processes and other phenomena in subject areas such as biology, sociology, education, economics, and technology. The dynamics of the systems approach should not be underestimated as a way of thinking about and approaching complex organizational processes (Senge, 1990). Furthermore, a systems approach yields more than simply the sum of its components or parts; rather, the components interact. The interaction generates a synergy that can have profound consequences and influences on a host of activities and processes (Watts, 2003). Successful leaders understand how to use the dynamics of the systems approach by integrating people and information in decision processes, thereby creating a synergy that moves their organizations forward.

In education, the systems approach is most appropriate for studying various types of schools and school processes. Many social scientists and sociologists would describe and analyze schools as social systems. The basic concepts of input, process, and output are regularly applied to communities, students, teaching, curriculum, and outcomes in describing school "systems." Use of systems theory to present the technical aspects of information systems and decision processes allows a consistent, integrated presentation of the material in this book. It would be difficult and perhaps impossible to identify another framework that would work as well.

ORGANIZATION OF THIS BOOK

This book is organized into two major sections and substantive appendixes that provide technical support. Section I focuses on the basic concepts needed to understand the major issues related to developing data-driven decision-making processes. The planning and development of information management systems are established as fundamental for any effective data-driven decision-making activity. This section also stresses the development of all aspects of the information system, including hardware, software, and most importantly, people. The section concludes with a chapter on action research, which includes a discussion of projects designed to improve teaching and learning in schools.

Section II concentrates entirely on data-driven decision-making applications. Practical examples in the areas of enrollment management, budgeting, professional development, and especially instruction illustrate the concepts introduced in Section I. Readers are encouraged to work through the examples using an electronic spreadsheet program such as Microsoft Excel or a statistical package such as the Statistical Package for the Social Sciences (SPSS).

Technical Support Sections A through E provide information related to statistical concepts, software tools, and other resources for developing effective data-driven decision-making processes. These resources are integral to the processes themselves because they facilitate the organization, development, collection, and analysis of data.

SUMMARY

Education in America has had difficulty in implementing decision-making processes that take advantage of accurate, timely, and useful data. The purpose of this book is to provide the theoretical framework and practical considerations for planning and implementing data-driven decision-making processes in schools and school districts.

Data-driven decision making is the use of data analysis to inform when determining courses of action involving policy and procedures. The data-driven decision-making approach is basically an extension of the concept of knowledge-based power, an extension that emphasizes the efficient use of information resources.

Effective information delivery systems need to be timely, reliable, and available throughout the school community. The systems approach (input, process, output) is recommended as the overall conceptual framework for studying schools and the information systems they need to establish effective data-driven decision-making applications.

The first section of this book focuses on the basic concepts of developing data-driven decision-making processes and stresses all aspects of the information system. The second section concentrates on data-driven decision-making applications. The third section provides substantial technical support.

References

Carlson, R. V., & Awkerman, G. (Eds.). (1991). *Educational planning: Concepts, strategies and practices.* New York: Longman.

Darling-Hammond, L. (2004). Standards, accountability, and school reform. *Teachers College Record, 106*(6), 1047–1085.

Dibello, A. J., & Nevis, E. C. (1998). *How organizations learn.* San Francisco: Jossey-Bass.

French, R. P., & Raven, B. (1959). The bases of social power. In D. Cartwright (Ed.), *Studies in social power* (pp. 150–167). Ann Arbor, MI: Institute for Social Research.

Ingram, D., Seashore Louis, K., & Schroeder, R. G. (2004). Accountability policies and teacher decision making: Barriers to the use of data to improve practice. *Teachers College Record, 106*(6), 1258–1287.

Luthans, F. (1981). *Organizational behavior.* New York: McGraw-Hill.

Meier, D. (2004). Creating schools we can trust. In C. Glickman (Ed.), *Letters to the next president* (pp. 18–26). New York: Teachers College Press.

O'Brien, J. A. (1988). *Information systems in business management.* Homewood, IL: Richard D. Irwin.

Peters, T. J., & Waterman, R. (1982). *In search of excellence.* New York: Harper & Row.

Rockart, J. F., & DeLong, D. W. (1988). *Executive support systems.* Homewood, IL: Dow Jones-Irwin.

Scherer, M. (2003, February). Blind data. *Educational Leadership 60*(5), 5.

Senge, P. M. (1990). *The fifth discipline: The art and practice of the learning organization.* New York: Doubleday Currency.

Simon, H. A. (1945). *Administrative behavior.* New York: Macmillan.

Simon, H. (1957). *Administrative behavior.* New York: Macmillan.

Simon, H. (1960). *The new science of management decision.* New York: Harper & Row.

Simon, H. (1979). Rational decision making in business organizations. *American Economic Review, 69,* 493–513.

Simon, H. (1982). *Models of bounded rationality.* Cambridge, MA: MIT Press.

Simon, H. (1991). *Models of My life.* New York: Basic Books.

Streifer, P. A. (2002). *Using data to make better educational decisions.* Lanham, MD: Scarecrow Press.

Tyson, C. (2002). *The foundations of imperfect decision making.* Stanford, CA: Stanford Graduate School of Business Research Paper Series. Retrieved march 15, 2004, from http://www-gsb.stanford.edu/facseminars/events/economics/pdfs/101002.pdf

Watts, D. J. (2003, February 14). Unraveling the mysteries of the connected age. *The Chronicle of Higher Education,* B7–B9.

Chapter 2

Planning and Developing Information Resources

The 20th century saw major developments in mankind's activities and endeavors. The most important of these are characterized as a period of time, such as the age of the airplane, the atomic age, and the space age. The past 50 years are referred to as the computer age or the information age, an era marked by the use of digital technology to collect, sort, manipulate, and report data. Corporations, government agencies, and schools have made significant investments in order to take part in the computer-information age through the development, expansion, and improvement of their computer-based information systems.

Now the computer-information age is evolving into the age of knowledge. Educated people and their ideas, facilitated and augmented by information technology, have become the key to our social well-being and a driving force for creating great changes in all social institutions (Duderstadt, 1997). Peter Drucker, world-renowned writer and consultant, has called knowledge, more than capital or labor, the only meaningful economic resource of the postcapitalist or knowledge society. For Drucker, one of the most important roles of management is to ensure the application and performance of knowledge, that is, the application of knowledge to knowledge (Drucker, 1993). Success and progress will depend on the ability of institutional leaders to harness and convert information resources into knowledge about what is happening within an organization, while monitoring the forces that influence it from the outside. In this chapter, the building of information resources is examined as the foundation for developing data-driven decision making in a school or district.

SCHOOL DISTRICTS TAKE THE LEAD

The development of information resources is one of the more complex activities faced by most school administrators. A good deal of planning is required to determine hardware, software, and staff development needs. Defining the data requirements for a school enterprise requires hours of discussion and thinking about how data will be accessed, integrated, and used effectively in day-to-day administration. In addition, developing information resources can be an expensive proposition, especially if basic hardware and software systems are not in place. Also, the technology must be upgraded continually and the staff kept current. For these reasons, the planning for the information resources needed to support data-driven decision making should start at the highest level of the school organization.

The school district administration is in the best position to initiate, to plan, and to fund the development or upgrade of a major information system. An assessment of the current capability of the information delivery system is critical. School systems that have old or poorly designed information systems may have to consider a major overhaul; others may have to modify or adjust their systems to support more extensive data-driven decision-making processes. In making the assessment, district leadership should look to principals, assistant principals, teachers, and other educators at individual schools to provide insights into the district's needs.

In designing information systems, a school district would be wise to standardize its operations. Certainly basic financial operations such as budgeting, accounting, and purchasing need to be common across the school enterprise. Activities such as student attendance, personnel procedures, and capital projects funding are generally common across a school district as well. Likewise, the information systems that support these activities need to be standardized. Increasingly school districts as well as state education departments want the ability to compare activities across schools. Student performance and achievement, costs for certain operations, and teacher performance and credentials are some of the types of data that are sought by agencies in comparing schools regionally and statewide. Reauthorization of the Elementary and Secondary Education Act (No Child Left Behind), which was mentioned in Chapter 1, has resulted in the federal government making greater demands on school districts and states to provide data profiles and comparisons of schools. Having a common information system for all schools in a district will make this activity more efficient.

DEFINING INFORMATION NEEDS

Figure 2-1 shows how educational information systems in a state or region might interact with one another. Information flows back and forth throughout the diagram from state education agencies to and from school districts, to and from school buildings, and to and from classrooms. Although it might be desirable to

Figure 2-1　Information system flow.

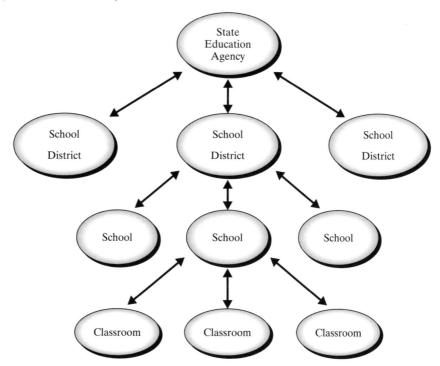

have a single system supporting all the information needs of all school districts and schools throughout a state, in most states this is not the reality. School districts generally assume responsibility for developing information systems to meet operational as well as decision-making needs. Some state education agencies have begun to provide important guidance by developing standard reporting formats for critical data elements. The federal government's No Child Left Behind legislation requires all schools, districts, and states to publish annual school report cards for the public. These report cards focus especially on student performance and include test scores and graduation rates. Skinner and Staresina (2004) reported that 47 of the 50 states and the District of Columbia provide disaggregated student performance data in the form of individual public school report cards. The same data are shared in electronic form with all schools and school districts. Nevertheless, harnessing data for planning and decision making will require the development of additional, more comprehensive data resources.

Figure 2-2 represents the key components of a school district information system and illustrates the major database applications. Each database application area has a unique role in contributing to the overall information resources of a school. The student database applications tend to be the most complex because of the amount of data that needs to be collected. In addition, student data are volatile and subject

Figure 2-2   School district information system.

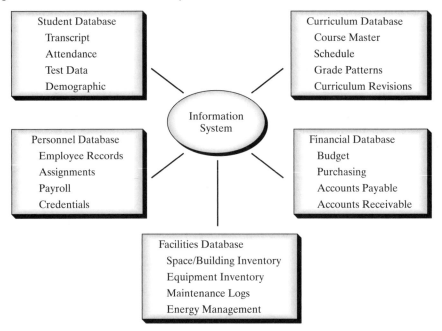

to frequent change. Applications such as attendance reporting and scheduling require extensive data collection efforts and careful coordination. Accurate and timely student database applications are also important because certain areas, such as achievement and outcomes, receive considerable scrutiny, especially from outside the school. Administrators need to have good access to data such as retention, attrition, graduation rates, and test scores, all of which can be used extensively in data-driven decision-making activities. Student enrollment data are also usually critical for state and local funding formulas, and accurate data on students in attendance are an absolute necessity.

Curriculum database applications are vital to internal academic operations. Curriculum meetings and discussions are the centerpieces of academic planning in many schools. Data on student performance related to curriculum and course enrollment become critical for such planning. A good curriculum and course database are also necessary for developing a student scheduling application, the most time-consuming activity when done manually.

Personnel and financial database applications are frequently the first to be implemented. In public schools, they may tie into other local government agencies for applications such as payroll, accounting, and purchasing, controlled at the municipal or county levels. For any administrator, the management of a budget is a critical responsibility. Access to up-to-date and accurate information on budgets and finances is a necessity and affects all of a school's operations. Personnel files are important complements to the financial data files for purposes of managing a budget, because the major costs in school operations involve personnel items such as salaries and fringe benefits.

Facilities are generally the last of the database applications to be implemented. Facilities data are not as critical or volatile as other data and do not need to be as tightly integrated. Nevertheless, applications such as space utilization, equipment inventory, and supplies inventory should not be ignored, because they contribute to overall effectiveness and efficiency. Many school districts, especially those with increasing enrollments or influxes of immigrant families, are struggling in over-crowded schools and classrooms. Information systems that integrate student demographics with instructional space and facilities can be most helpful in planning appropriate academic programs to meet the enrollment needs.

As Figure 2-2 shows, the information system integrates all of the school district's applications. The figure assumes that a sophisticated database management software system or management information system is common to all of the applications and serves as the integration mechanism. By developing such a system, school districts greatly enhance administrative cohesiveness, as schools and offices become more dependent on one another by virtue of sharing common data files. A single system also significantly improves the consistency of information and eliminates issues involving the accuracy of one school's or office's data versus another's. Data warehousing, mentioned in Chapter 1, and the creation of longitudinal data become much easier when a single database system is integrating all of a school's or district's data resources.

In developing an overall plan for a database management system, school district administrators should assess their ability to collect and maintain data in the five major application areas identified in Figure 2-2. More resources may have to be provided in areas where data collection has been poor or nonexistent. In addition, all database applications, even the most established, need regular modifications and upgrades. In many cases, the ongoing costs for modifying and upgrading an existing database system may equal the original implementation, particularly when staff time is considered. The ability to bring order and easy access to information resources is well worth the price.

DATABASE MANAGEMENT SYSTEMS

In the past 40 years, **database management systems** have grown in complexity and sophistication, particularly those of large organizations. The more data to be collected, verified, updated, and reported, the more complex and expensive becomes the task of establishing and maintaining an accurate database. However, the alternative is unthinkable. Not having access to data eventually becomes a serious problem that leaves the administration of an organization vulnerable. Collecting data manually as needed can also be expensive and is prone to problems of inaccuracy and inconsistency. All school districts, regardless of their level of operation, should make the development, improvement, or upgrading of their database management systems a priority in overall planning.

The terminology used for describing a database has been inconsistent, so certain terms may mean different things to different people. The primary definition of a **database** is a collection of files in which data can be created, updated, and accessed. However, a more modern definition requires that **data files** be interrelated, or integrated, so that data can be accessed easily across all files and redundancy of the data can be kept to a minimum. (Readers not familiar with database management systems can refer to the Technical Support D section of this book.)

Within a database management system, **data elements** are organized through and documented in a **data element dictionary**, which includes tables used to identify the content and coding schemes of the database. These tables are stored in a computer file to be used by the database management system software, and they are included in documentation materials for reference by staff and teachers who need to maintain or access this file.

As databases grow and become more complex, the task of documenting and maintaining a data element dictionary also becomes more complicated. Large- and medium-sized school systems that operate a dedicated information services, **data processing**, or computer center, frequently have full-time staff functioning as database administrators who are assigned these responsibilities. All school districts, regardless of their size, should have someone performing these tasks. Failure to do so will render a database useless in time, because staff will forget how to update or access the files.

When reviewing and evaluating information about database management software, administrators will see references to the **data structure**, or data organization, used. Data structure is the method by which one data element relates to other data elements. Many books and articles explore and compare the benefits of different data structures and approaches taken by software developers. Among the more popular structures is the **relational database**. Although a simple structure, a relational database views all data as being stored as tables or matrices, with each data element having access to the other data elements. Figure 2-3 is an illustration of how a student file and a course file might relate to one another in such a structure. In this illustration, the course codes serve to "relate," or link, student **data records** to course data records.

One feature of database software that is especially important for data-driven decision making is the ability to generate reports and subsets of data files. Generally, a **query language** is provided that enables users to access data in many different ways. These languages are powerful for creating customized reports and temporary data files. Designed for nontechnical staff, the languages give users excellent access to data without waiting for computer or data processing personnel to perform the task

Figure 2-3 Sample relational database structure for student and course files.

Student Records

NAME	ID	YEAR	COURSE CODE
SMITH, JAN	31122	10	A1, E1, S2, F2
FOX, ANNE	21667	11	E1, S2, L3, M2
FELD, LOIS	11233	9	E1, F1, L1, M1

Course Records

COURSE CODE	SUBJECT	CREDITS	ROOM
A1	ART 1	1.0	H100
E1	ENG 1	1.0	H101
E2	ENG 2	1.0	H102
E3	ENG 3	1.0	H103
F1	FRE 1	1.0	L100
F2	FRE 2	1.0	L101
L1	LAT 1	1.0	L110
M1	MATH 1	1.0	H120
S2	HIS 2	1.0	L105

for them. Through this type of access, the real benefit of a database can be realized: Essentially, information resources are available and shared among stakeholders for improving schools; they are not simply a data depository. As part of a case study, Craig (2004) tells the story of a principal of an urban high school who wants to improve his school based on the most current school reform thinking and research but who is also torn by the need to improve and raise student test scores as mandated by the state's accountability system. The principal commented:

> One part of the conflict is that we are going to have to deal with the school's test scores. The other part of the conflict is that we have some reforms we want to do, and they involve the *application of knowledge* rather than the *accumulation of knowledge . . ."* (p. 1244)

LONG-TERM AND SHORT-TERM DATA RESOURCES

As indicated in the previous section, development of information resources within a school district is a long-term undertaking. Administrators in school districts where information resources are not in place might assume that they have to put their decision-making plans on hold. This is not the case. Although the most desirable approach is the development of a comprehensive information system, many districts are able to begin making data-driven decisions without such a system. Most school districts collect and maintain some data, and it is possible to cull these data to support decision-making activities.

A number of short-term data collection activities may help start data-driven decision making. The five major database applications (student, curriculum, finance,

FIGURE 2-4 Sample page from student data handbook.

Data Element Outline and Definition

The following entries outline the organization of the section titles, categories, and data elements (with the data element numbers), as well as their definitions, included in this handbook.

A. PERSONAL INFORMATION

Section A, Personal Information, includes information about a student's personal, family, and demographic status. **Entity uses:** Student, Parent/Guardian, Employer, Sibling(s) or Other School-Age Children Living in Student's Household, Responsible Adult of Student's Household, Other Adult Living in Student's Household, Sponsor, Emergency Contact

Name—A word or series of words by which a subject is known and distinguishable.

0010	First Name
0020	Middle Name
0030	Last/Surname
0040	Generation Code/Suffix
0050	Personal Title/Prefix
0060	Alias
0070	Former Legal Name
0080	Last/Surname at Birth
0090	Nickname
0100	Tribal or Clan Name
0110	Name of Individual
0120	Name of Institution

Background Information—Personal information about (and particular to) an individual, organization, or institution.

0130	Identification Number
0140	Identification System
0149	Hispanic or Latino Ethnicity
0150	Race
0160	National/Ethnic Origin Subgroup
0170	Sex
0180	Birthdate
0190	Birthdate Verification
0200	City of Birth
0210	Country of Birth
0220	State of Birth
0230	Country of Birth Code
0231	Name of Country of Birth
0232	Born Outside the U.S.
0240	First Entry Date (into the United States)
0250	Citizenship Status
0260	Country of Citizenship

Source: From National Center for Education Statistics, 2000. Washington, DC: U.S. Department of Education. Retrieved June 2, 2003, from http://nces.ed.gov/pubs2000/studenthb/

personnel, and facilities) are the long-term goal, but development should be prioritized. The school district might start with development of the student and curriculum databases. Because of the emphasis on student performance during the past few years, many government agencies are providing support to school districts for developing their information resources. For example, the U.S. Department of Education maintains a Web site to assist educators in developing a student information system. Figure 2-4 is a sample page of a recommended file layout for developing a student database system. (The entire file layout can be found in the Technical Support D section of this book.)

State education agencies are also providing support to school districts by standardizing reporting requirements for critical data elements related to student performance, attendance, and budgeting. In many cases, these reporting requirements are in the form of data files that can be uploaded to state agencies and downloaded back to schools as needed for data-driven decision-making activities. Professional organizations such as the American Association of School Administrators also provide Web sites to assist school districts in implementing data-driven decision making. Private companies such as the Center for Resource Management, Incorporated, and the Grow Network provide services to help school districts jump-start their

FIGURE 2-5   Web site addresses (URLs): Resources for data-driven decision making.

http://www.aasa.org/cas/resources_and_tools.htm
http://www.aasa.org/cas/
   American Association of School Administrators

http://www.crminc.com/socrates/Page2.htm
   Center for Resource Management, Inc. – Socrates Data System
   Commercial School Database Software

http://www.ncrel.org/policy/pubs/html/pivol6/nov2000.htm
   North Central Regional Policy Laboratory

http://www.nsdc.org/library/data.html
   National Staff Development Council

http://www.grownetwork.com/
   Grow Network

http://nces.ed.gov/pubs2000/building/
http://nces.ed.gov/pubsearch/pubsinfo.asp?pubid=97531
http://nces.ed.gov/pubs2000/studenthb/
   U.S. Department of Education, National Center for Educational Statistics (NCES), *Student Data Handbook*

http://www.edsmartinc.com
   EDsmart Incorporated

http://www.aecf.org/kidscount/
   Annie E. Casey Foundation

efforts in building information systems. All of these resources should be evaluated and considered if a school district does not have a well-developed information system from which accurate and timely data can be collected. Figure 2-5 is a list of Web site addresses (URLs) of agencies that can suggest ideas for developing information resources for data-driven decision making.

If it is necessary to take a short-term approach to developing information resources, school districts should not abandon thinking about the long term. For instance, if a district decides to use data files provided by a state education agency to monitor student performance on standardized tests, these data files should be collected and maintained over time, not just for the current year. The real power of data-driven decision making is not found in one-time or one-semester activity but in looking at student progress over a period of time (i.e., longitudinally).

SUMMARY

In a school organization, the school district should provide the leadership for assessing and developing information systems. A model that defines overall information needs in a school organization includes five major database components: student, curriculum, personnel, financial, and facilities. Each database contributes uniquely to the information resources of a school. Student database applications are the most complex.

All school districts should make development, improvement, or upgrading of their database management systems a priority in overall planning. Regardless of their size, all school districts should have someone assigned to database administration. Some districts will need full-time staff functioning as database administrators.

Although development of the five major database applications is the long-term goal, initially, short-term approaches may be necessary. A school district might start by developing the student and curriculum databases. Government agencies, state education agencies, professional organizations, and private companies provide development support through their Web sites.

Case Study

Center City School District

Center City is an urban school district in the midwestern United States with a student population of 85,000. A central board of education governs 175 primary, middle, and secondary schools. Overall, the district does well on standardized tests administered by the state. Some schools, however, do better than others. About 16 schools continually have had more than a third of their students fail one or more competency tests. Of these, 6 schools have had more than half of their students fail one or more tests.

The central board of education, through the superintendent's office, provides a number of information resources, including full database systems for financial and personnel record keeping. A new student database system has been planned to replace a system developed in 1984. To support instructional activities, hard copy (paper) reports are provided by the state to the principal of each school. These reports list each student who took a state-mandated test and indicate scores and subscores as well as basic demographic data such as age, gender, special education status, and bilingual education status. Principals use these reports as best as they can to help develop instructional programs, especially for those failing one or more tests.

Last year, Dr. Evelyn Richards was appointed as the new superintendent for the Center City School District. Dr. Richards' goals for the coming year are to begin the implementation of the new student information system and to begin a process whereby data are used throughout the district to make more informed decisions about instruction and instructional strategies. Assume you are Dr. Richards. How would you begin to develop a plan to achieve the two goals? Whom would you involve in the planning? Will you have a short-term as well as a long-term plan?

References

Craig, C. (2004). The dragon in school backyards: The influence of mandated testing on school contexts and educators' narrative knowing. *Teachers College Record, 106*(6), 1229–1257.

Drucker, P. F. (1993). *Post-capitalist society.* New York: HarperCollins.

Duderstadt, J. J. (1997). The future of the university in an age of knowledge. *Journal of Asynchronous Learning Networks, 1*(1), 78–88. Retrieved on May 7, 2005, from http://www.aln.org/publications/jaln/v1n2/v1n2_duderstadt.asp

Skinner, R. A., & Staresina, L.N. (2004). State of the states. *Education Week, 23*(17), 97–153.

Chapter 3

Hardware, Software, and People

In 1997 North Dakota began a Teaching with Technology (TWT) initiative that involved a number of school districts throughout the state. The purpose of this initiative was to assist schools in integrating technology into instruction in pedagogically meaningful ways. TWT was a three-phase project, with Phases I and II concentrated on self-study, planning, and staff development activities. Phase III, which coined the phrase *No Teacher Left Behind,* represented the fruits of 5 years of labor and involved the entire school staff in integrating educational technology. Indeed, without the full involvement of teachers and other school-based staff, the TWT initiative had little hope for success. Improving schools through data-driven decision making requires that teachers, administrative staff, and others be full partners in developing and implementing solutions. In this chapter, the three major components (**hardware, software**, and **people**) of data-driven decision making are examined from the perspective of the major stakeholders in schools, namely, principals, teachers, students, and parents.

A BRIEF LOOK AT INFRASTRUCTURE

Webster's Third New International Dictionary defines the term *infrastructure* as the underlying foundation or basic framework of an organization or system. The term can be applied to a host of entities (e.g., energy, water, and communications) that undergird an organization—state, city, corporation, medical center, or school district—and its operations. Conceptually (see Figure 3-1), an organization's infrastructure might include a hub, or central point (e.g., energy power station, water supply, communications center), that distributes resources through a series of nodes. The flow is a two-way, back-and-forth movement between the hub and the nodes.

In the case of information technology and the distribution of data throughout an organization, the emergence of **digital** communications and the Internet and World Wide Web has changed the conceptual framework of infrastructure. Central hubs for communications and data processing activities might still exist. However, an appropriate diagram (see Figure 3-2) of an organization's technology infrastructure would show a network in which resources are shared across all nodes rather than moving only back and forth between the hub, or central point, and the nodes within the organization. This model is particularly important when developing the information infrastructure for data-driven decision making in a school district. Everyone is involved and able to share activities, strategies, and data. Although guidance, support, and perhaps databases may be provided centrally at the district level, ultimately the success of the data-driven decision making process rests with the ability of individuals in schools to share in the process of effecting changes in classrooms, offices, and support areas. It is highly desirable, if not critical, for administrators and teachers in the schools to share their knowledge, expertise, and experiences with others across the district. This network-based framework for sharing information resources across the school district is the foundation that will

Figure 3-1 Hub-based infrastructure.

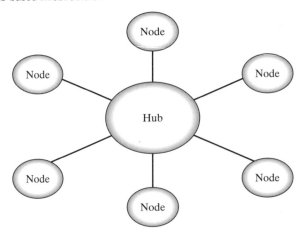

Figure 3-2 Network-based infrastructure.

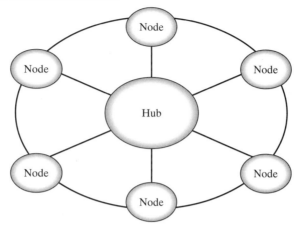

empower shareholders and enable them to realize the potential of data-driven decision making activities in their schools.

HARDWARE FOR EFFECTIVE DATA MANAGEMENT AND ACCESS

During the past several decades, educators have seen data communications systems and **networks** develop in size, sophistication, and the ability to communicate over distances. In the late 1970s and 1980s, schools began to install their first **local area networks** (LANs; see Figure 3-3). The use of LANs in computer laboratories,

Figure 3-3 Simple local area network.

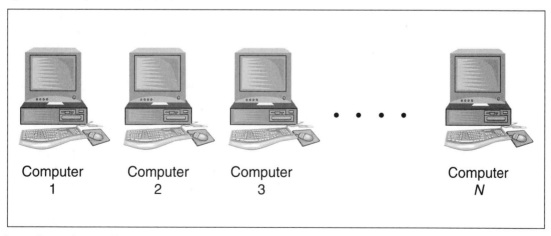

Source: From *Educational leadership and planning for technology (4th ed.),* by A. G. Picciano, 2005. Upper Saddle River, NJ: Pearson Education.

Figure 3-4 Multiple networks; example of a wide-area network.

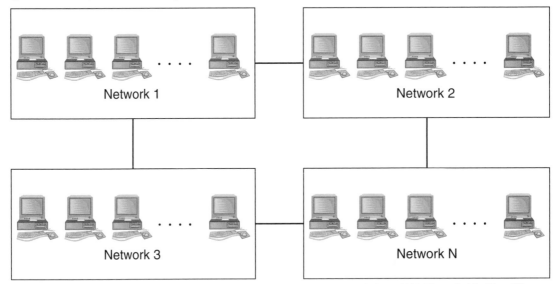

Source: From *Educational leadership and planning for technology (4th ed.),* by A. G. Picciano, 2005. Upper Saddle River, NJ: Pearson Education.

libraries, and administrative offices has become commonplace. By the mid-1990s, more than 90% of the 15,000 plus school districts in the country had established one or more LANs (Quality Education Data, 1995). In larger school districts, **wide area networks** (WANs) are in evidence as well, connecting computers and LANs that are dispersed throughout the district, sometimes miles apart (see Figure 3-4).

In a WAN configuration, a large computer network integrates the activities of smaller computer networks. Using a district-wide WAN, a student in one school can determine whether a library in another school has a particular book, an assistant principal can examine the transcript of a student who has just transferred from another school, or a district business manager can monitor the daily expenditures of several schools.

The data communications technology (e.g., telephone lines or satellite transmission) that enables a computer in one school to communicate with a computer in another school is essentially the same whether the schools are many miles apart or in close proximity. Once a WAN has been established, the distance between sites is immaterial. In the late 1980s, this concept was taken a step further as computers in school districts began to communicate with computers on networks outside the school district. A student looking for a particular book might use a computer in a school's library to locate the book at a local public library or a local college library. A superintendent using a computer in a school district office was able to transfer data on student demographics to a computer located in a state education office.

Data communications technologies have advanced to the point where a computer on one network can easily communicate with a computer on another network thousands of miles away. The grants officer in a local school district office in Juneau, Alaska, can examine a database of funded programs on a computer network maintained by the U.S. Department of Education in Washington, DC. A state education department administrator in Albany, New York, can e-mail a new curriculum proposal to all 800 school district superintendents on a statewide education network. A social studies teacher in Tulsa, Oklahoma, developing a module in cultural studies can access a database of curricular materials maintained by the National Geographic Society.

With the expansion of data communications' capabilities over the past several decades, networks have expanded to cover greater distances and to link with many other networks. Increasingly, this data traffic, which occurs on thousands of networks throughout the country and the world, is passing over a common universal network called the **Internet**. As of 2003, 97% of all schools in the United States were connected to the Internet (Park & Staresina, 2004). To support data-driven decision making, the fundamental hardware configuration consists of computer workstations distributed throughout the district on a high-speed digital network that is fully compatible with the Internet. Each node in the school district's network may be a school or office with its own mininetwork capable of intercommunication with any other node in the district, as well as with networks outside of the district. For more detailed descriptions of network configurations, see Baran (1964) and Barabasi (2002). The Baran reference is particularly interesting because Baran worked at the Rand Corporation and was involved with designing the ARPANET system, which was the precursor to today's Internet. Barabasi links networking principles to a number of social as well as technological systems.

CLIENT-SERVER ARCHITECTURE

To understand the nature of the Internet and its underlying software system, the **World Wide Web**, a discussion of the term *protocol* as used in data communications is necessary. **Protocol** is a general term for a set of rules, procedures, or standards used in exchanging data in a data communications system. Here are three examples of protocols: (1) a code or signal indicating the beginning of a message; (2) a code or signal indicating the end of a message; and (3) a code or signal indicating that a device is busy. Computer and communications equipment manufacturers established different protocols for the exchange of data, which complicated the ability of one manufacturer's computer to communicate with another manufacturer's computer. This incompatibility problem was resolved to some degree by the development of protocol conversion software that enabled computers to translate and convert the data messages of other computer protocols. The Internet established a standard protocol for all its activity called **transmission**

control protocol/Internet protocol (TCP/IP). All computers using the Internet had to exchange data using TCP/IP. The World Wide Web's data transfer method or protocol, called **hypertext transfer protocol** (http), was designed to run "over" or in conjunction with the TCP/IP. Many other protocols have also been designed to run in conjunction with TCP/IP on the Internet; however, because of its hypertext and multimedia capabilities, the Web has become the most popular.

The Web's hypertext facilities makes it an excellent software system to run on a client-server data communications system, which is how the Internet functions. The standard network model in the early days of data communications was a central computer that controlled all of the activity and functioned as the central depository for data files and programs. The client-server data communications model does not require a central depository or controlling computer. To the contrary, the basis of the Internet is broadly distributed or shared control among the networked computers.

In a **client-server system**, computers essentially perform two major functions. The client, or end-user, function makes a request or query for data to a server. The server function, performed by one of many computers sharing network control, processes the request and returns the results to the client. Many computers can function as servers. Furthermore, servers can forward requests to other servers and create a chain reaction to process the original client's data request. In designing or expanding a network to support information sharing activities such as data-driven decision making, a school district will likely use client-server architecture to bring resources to clients (administrators, teachers, and other staff throughout the district).

Once the network is in place, the next question asks where the computer workstations should be located. The answer is everywhere. The Internet was established as an ubiquitous resource; users are able to connect to it from anyplace. Administrators have computer workstations in their offices, teachers in their classrooms, parents and students in their homes. As early as 1989, the National Education Association recommended that a computer be installed on the desk of every teacher (National Education Association, 1989). The emergence of portable electronic devices and laptop computers allows connectivity to the network from anyplace where there is a telephone connection or a clear satellite signal. All school districts have not yet provided computers to all their teachers and staff, but this is the direction in which Internet-based technology is heading. The long-range plan in developing data-driven decision making calls for providing access to information resources to just about everybody in a school. Principals, teachers, and administrative staff should have ready access to information about students, budgets, and personnel.

Increasingly, schools are also providing more information electronically to parents. Harold Levy, former chancellor of the New York City public schools, wrote an op-ed piece to the *The New York Times* two days after he left office titled "What a Chancellor Needs Most." In this piece Levy identified several accomplishments of his administration that helped improve the school system. Among them was the creation of a new Board of Education Web site that provided "information and analysis about everything from student performance to teacher certification" (p. A17). He specifically praised the benefits of this technology beyond the classroom. Parents can benefit greatly from well-planned, informative school Web sites that celebrate student work, provide important information about the school, or make available electronic forums for discussing community issues. As a result, Levy recommended that parents be involved with all aspects of schooling, including the development of information resources.

The implementation of an extensive data communications system to support the development of information resources needed for data-driven decision making may appear daunting. Nevertheless, most school districts have begun to make this investment. If we consider other enterprises where access to information is critical, we can easily understand the need for this investment in our schools. If we go into a bank, we expect to see tellers accessing information about our accounts via computer workstations. We make deposits and expect ready access to our funds at ATMs from almost anywhere. What would we think if the teller at our local bank accepted our funds and wrote the transaction in a notebook rather than entering it into the bank's computer system? Or suppose we could only have access to the deposited funds at the branch where we made the deposit. Our children are more important than our bank accounts; therefore, the most efficient methods must be used for monitoring their "educational transactions."

SOFTWARE FOR DATA ANALYSIS

In Chapter 2, database management was discussed as the underlying software system for developing and supporting a school district's information resources and data communications. The Internet and World Wide Web were described as the major software vehicles for providing access to the information resources. A third type of software critical to data-driven decision making provides the tools needed to conduct data analysis.

One of the most commonly used tools for analyzing data is an **electronic spreadsheet** program such as Excel, Lotus 1-2-3, and Quattro Pro. Electronic spreadsheet software is essentially an electronic grid or matrix of rows and columns used for applications that require frequent analysis and manipulation of numbers, such as budgeting, accounting, enrollment projections, and test scores. The electronic spreadsheet replaces the accounting tablet as a tool for organizing numbers into appropriate boxes or cells, and it performs automatically the arithmetic operations that formerly were performed manually or with calculators. It also provides graphics capabilities for producing bar graphs, pie charts, and line graphs, which are very effective in longitudinal and trend analyses.

Figure 3-5 is an example of an electronic spreadsheet for a school district's yearly budget summary and proposal. This figure shows a grid of rows numbered 1, 2, 3, 4,

Figure 3-5   Sample electronic spreadsheet.

	A	B	C	D	E	F	G
1							
2			North Central School District No .1				
3			Proposed Budget 2002/2003				
4							
5			2001-02	2001-02	2002-03	Approved vs.	
6			Estimated	Approved	Proposed	Proposed Budget	
7	Category		Expend. ($	Budget ($)	Budget ($)	Change ($)	
8							
9	General support		3,888,500	4,222,500	4,100,000	-122,500	
10	Instruction		38,250,500	39,000,000	42,000,000	3,000,000	
11	Transportation		3,555,000	3,550,000	3,600,000	50,000	
12	Plant operations		5,150,500	5,200,000	5,300,000	100,000	
13	Employee benefits		7,250,000	7,200,000	7,500,000	300,000	
14	Community service		3,050,000	3,150,000	3,100,000	-50,000	
15	Interfund transfer		800,000	800,000	800,000	0	
16	Debt service		7,200,000	7,200,000	7,000,000	-200,000	
17							
18		Totals	69,144,500	70,322,500	73,400,000	3,077,500	

and so forth, and columns lettered A, B, C, D, and so on. Entries are made into the spreadsheet by pointing or moving a cursor to the appropriate cell as identified by grid coordinates (e.g., A1, A2, B4, C6). Each cell can also contain a formula or arithmetic operation that uses data existing in any of the other cells. The major benefit of spreadsheet software is that these arithmetic operations can be performed automatically so that a change in any one cell will almost instantaneously change all other cells that may be affected. This provides a very rapid "what if?" facility. For example, consider preparation of a school's budget projections. To know the effect of a percentage reduction on all the various cost centers or departments, the entry in only one cell needs to be changed. This calculation can easily be performed over and over again by entering different percentages. Financial staff who regularly perform spreadsheet-type applications manually can learn to use an electronic spreadsheet in a matter of hours and become proficient after doing a few applications. Once proficiency has been achieved, electronic spreadsheets can replace all similar applications that had been performed manually.

Optimum management of information resources requires that all data files and applications be integrated where appropriate. Therefore, the source data for electronic spreadsheet applications should come from the district's database files whenever possible. The process used for obtaining data from the database for use by other computer applications is referred to as **downloading**. It can be done electronically by creating aggregate data files to be accessed by the electronic spreadsheet software. Of course, if a database does not exist or if the particular data needed are not available, then the data must be gathered from other sources.

Electronic spreadsheet software is effective in manipulating any aggregate data that are typically presented in tabular form. The number of reports that can use student data in this fashion is endless. Enrollment projections at various levels, test score analyses, and grade evaluations are common applications. Personnel costs account for the major portion of the budget, so salary projections are invaluable during budget planning and collective bargaining negotiations. Staffing and salary projections related to enrollment and course offerings can be done routinely. Entire budget-planning processes are conducted with school board members, superintendents, and others using the printed output from spreadsheets as the basis for discussion. This activity can also be conducted using a projector to view a "live" spreadsheet, which can be changed easily as the discussion progresses and decisions are made. Complex facilities management applications such as space utilization, space needs projections, and equipment and supplies inventory analyses are more easily done on spreadsheets. Project management timetables, cost projections, and cash flow analysis for capital construction can also be done effectively.

A complementary and a more powerful tool for data-driven decision making is a statistical software package such as the **Statistical Package for the Social Sciences** (SPSS) or the **Statistical Analysis System** (SAS). These packages can perform most of the routines that Excel and other spreadsheet programs do; in addition, they can perform statistical routines such as **contingency tables** (cross tabulations), analysis of variance, and correlations. Spreadsheet software is a good starting point for doing simple data analysis, but statistical packages can take the analysis much further. The latest version of SPSS has been converted to a spreadsheet-like format so that users familiar with software like Lotus, Excel, or Quattro Pro can easily learn SPSS. In this book, Excel and SPSS will be used as the main demonstration software tools for doing data analysis.

Data analysis software tools are critical in analyzing, manipulating, and presenting data, and they are most effective when integrated with database management systems. The benefits of these tools are best realized if they have good data sources from which the aggregate data are drawn.

DEVELOPING PEOPLE RESOURCES

In considering resources for data-driven decision-making activities, emphasis is usually placed on the hardware and software needed for developing the requisite information systems. However, just as critical is the development of the people resources. Decision making is a people-intensive activity that relies extensively on insight, experience, and expertise. Hardware and software are the vehicles for delivering accurate and timely information, but decisions cannot be made without trained and informed people. Most of these school-based people will be administrators who know their schools and constituents; teachers who know their students and curricula; and staff who know their operations and services. All of them need to be trained in the use of the information resources that will help them make informed decisions.

First, a successful training program must include hardware and software that is reliable and as easy to use as possible. Although it is true that the development of extensive information resources using current technology is complex, the complexity of the design should not be passed to the end users. On the contrary, modern design emphasizes the importance of providing user-friendly interfaces to information resources. Information systems that require many levels of inquiry to download basic information, World Wide Web interfaces that are overly cluttered, or database software that lacks a friendly query language are indicative of systems that will be difficult for end users.

Second, training workshops and classes must be readily available in person or online. The nature of these sessions will depend on the level of technological expertise that exists within the staff. If technology and sophisticated information systems are new to a school district, then staff training and development will be extensive. Technology is constantly evolving, so even experienced users of technology will need to refresh and update their knowledge and skills on a regular basis. Learning to use an information system and its resources for data-driven decision making will require specialized staff development activities that are not limited to the use of technology. Training in other areas such as curricula, standards, testing, and the fundamentals of quantitative analysis might be necessary.

Third, every good staff development training program is ongoing; one-time workshops are only modestly successful. If data-driven decision making is to be integrated into the administrative fabric of a school or district, then ongoing training will be needed to keep skills honed and to initiate new teachers and staff. Furthermore, much educational activity is influenced and guided by multiple levels of government, so decision making must regularly adjust to the newest regulation, standard, or directive. Participants in decision-making activities need to be up-to-date if they are to be effective.

Fourth, data-driven decision making requires enhanced leadership skills on the part of district supervisors, principals, and other administrative staff. Data-driven decision making incorporates teachers and staff as well as information into the process. Fullan (2001), in *Leading in a Culture of Change,* comments that knowledge is "people" and information becomes knowledge only when it takes on "a social life" (p. 78). School leaders must be capable of establishing a climate that allows for a "we" process rather than a "me" process. Teachers and staff need to feel comfortable that they are not the objects of data-driven exercises wherein their skills and abilities are constantly questioned. Because of the emphasis on accountability and standards, teachers have become a focus of attention when asking why children are succeeding or failing. Teachers and other staff are, indeed, critical to the educational enterprise; they should be treated, assigned, and developed with skill and competence on the part of school leaders. Price (2004), in an article titled, "New Age Principals," expressed this concern: "Both current principals, and those entering the principalship for the first time, find that they are ill-prepared to manage an infrastructure that supports instruction and has as its constant focus the technical core of teaching and learning" (p. 36). He recommended that all principals, new and old, develop four key skills to create and manage the type of infrastructure needed to support instructional improvement:

1. Ability to manage information
2. Ability to analyze and use data to determine areas in need of improvement
3. Ability to align and monitor curriculum to meet needs
4. Ability to build a professional community of learners (stakeholders) committed to instructional improvement

Although all four of these skills are important, the last is the most critical and undergirds the others.

THE DATA ANALYST

As school districts invest in data-driven decision processes, the need for someone with technical expertise in data analysis becomes more apparent. The data analyst who is familiar with information systems and fundamental statistical analysis serves as an important resource person for others (administrators, teachers, and parents) in using data effectively. The data analyst also performs a coordinating function by providing data in a timely manner to coincide with a district's or school's planning activities. Minimally, districts have one person performing this function on a full-time basis; large districts employ more data analysts. In addition, individual schools have someone performing this function, perhaps on a part-time basis. Large schools, especially middle and high schools, will likely have a full-time person.

The need for a data analyst has grown considerably, as data are used more frequently in shaping instructional activities. In other areas where data are critical for decision making, such as budget and finance, most likely staff have had some formal training in information systems management and business statistics or quantitative analysis. In addition, generally a small cadre of business personnel work with data files on a daily basis and are comfortable mining these files to support decision-making activities. Instruction, however, requires sharing data on students, testing, and other performance indicators with teachers and parents who are less familiar with data analysis. The data analyst can design standard reports that are produced on a cyclical basis and that serve as common resources in the discussion and planning of instructional activities. After receiving some training and assistance, teachers can use the standard report to further mine the data as group and individual judgments about instruction evolve. The support of a data analyst with expertise in information processing and quantitative methods will facilitate their analysis and judgments.

Another way in which a data analyst can be most helpful is in monitoring the external environment. Although much of data-driven decision making is internal to a district or school, scanning the external environment for resources or keeping abreast of data-related mandates and compliance issues can be helpful if not critical. Front-line administrators have difficulty finding the time to do this effectively, but a data analyst may be able to do this quite well.

Data-driven decision making for instruction also assumes that the community, especially parents, will be invited to become more involved in the process. To be effective, reports on students must be easily understood by the broader population. Having a knowledgeable data analyst design, explain, and answer questions about these reports will contribute to the success of such reporting activity.

SUMMARY

Critical to the development of effective data-driven decision making in a school organization is careful planning and implementation of the technological support infrastructure. Fundamental to this infrastructure is the distributed information system that is made available and accessible to all stakeholders in the school. The key components of the technological infrastructure are: hardware, software, and people.

Digital networks are considered the basic hardware needed for effective data management and analysis. Local and wide area networks, which continue to evolve and expand, create the electronic paths for moving data throughout the school organization.

Database management systems, which have grown considerably in sophistication, provide the main information depository from which data-driven decision-making activities emanate. Database management systems also provide the software tools for maintaining, storing, and manipulating data in a timely and efficient way.

As in any new technological endeavor, the people resources and staff development needed for using data effectively in decision-making activities are most important. Too often in the past, emphasis was placed strictly on hardware and software components, with the assumption that the people involved would learn when needed. This approach did not work well in the past and surely will not work well now. Initial as well as ongoing training of all staff members who are expected to maintain and use the data systems is necessary. Larger school systems will need to hire specialists such as data analysts to assist administrators and teachers in using data and information effectively.

Case Study

Hamilton Middle School, Center City

Hamilton Middle School is a middle school (sixth through eighth grades) located in Center City. It has an enrollment of 600 students and its principal, Joanna Pequot, is generally recognized as one of the more effective school leaders in Center City. Almost 90% of the students regularly pass the state-mandated competency tests. Ms. Pequot credits the success of Hamilton mostly to a dedicated teacher corps and an involved community, especially the parents.

About 5 years ago Ms. Pequot and one of her assistant principals (Patrick Guiterrez) took a workshop offered by a local college titled "Using Data to Guide Instruction." Both were impressed with the concepts and decided to try to implement some of them at Hamilton. The biggest obstacle was the absence of a user-friendly database system in the school and district. They were required to maintain basic student information on an old database system at the district office, and accessing the data was slow and cumbersome. Nevertheless, working with data provided by the state education department and with several reports generated by the district, Ms. Pequot and Mr. Guiterrez were able to establish a small but effective database that contained some basic student demographic information as well as performance data on mandated tests. Mr. Guiterrez was especially attentive in keeping the data accurate.

After about a year, Ms. Pequot and Mr. Guiterrez introduced the concepts of data-driven decision making to the teaching staff. Teachers were generally willing to try it, and a data-driven decision making process was implemented with sixth-grade teachers. Teachers meet and discuss student performances class by class. Performance goals and strategies for each class are subsequently established for the following year, and particular attention is paid to individual students who did not pass the state competency tests. Teachers were responsive to the approach and the process was extended to the other grades the next year.

Mr. Guiterrez performs all of the responsibilities of a data analyst and coordinator for Hamilton. He has had to invest many hours to collect and provide the data on a timely basis. He is having some difficulty meeting his other responsibilities and has discussed the situation with Ms. Pequot. She recognizes that he is spending much more time on this than she originally anticipated and she is concerned.

Recently Ms. Pequot received a telephone call from the district superintendent, Dr. Evelyn Richards, who asked her to serve on a districtwide committee to guide the development of a new student information system. Dr. Richards indicated that she chose Ms. Pequot for this assignment because Hamilton Middle School is one of the few schools in the district that has managed to collect student information capable of supporting a data-driven decision making process for instruction. In preparation for the first meeting of the committee, Dr. Richards has asked Ms. Pequot to write a position paper on her experiences with data-driven decision making at Hamilton and, more importantly, to provide her views and recommendations on how the district should proceed. Assume you are Ms. Pequot. What are your recommendations for the district? Be sure to consider whether what has been accomplished in one middle school can easily be adapted to the entire district.

References

Baran, P. (1964, August). *Memorandum RM 3420-PR on distributed communications: Introduction to distributed communications networks*. New York: The Rand Corporation. Retrieved on January 3, 2005, from http://www.rand.org/publications/RM/RM3420/

Barabasi, A. L. (2002). *Linked: The new science of networks*. Cambridge, MA: Perseus Publishing.

Gove, P. B. (Ed.). (1986). *Webster's third new international dictionary of the English language*. Unabridged. Springfield, MA: Merriam-Webster.

Fullan, M. (2001). *Leading in a culture of change*. San Francisco, CA: Jossey-Bass.

Levy, H. (2002, August 21). What a chancellor needs most. *The New York Times,* p. A17.

National Education Association. (1989, July). Report of the NEA special committee on educational technology. *Paper presented at the 127th Annual Meeting of the National Education Association*, Washington, DC.

Park, J., & Staresina, L. (2004, May 6). Tracking U.S. trends. *Education Week,* pp. 64–97.

Price, W. J. (2004, January 7). New age principals. *Education Week, 23*(16), 36–37.

Quality Education Data. (1995). *Education market guide*. Denver, CO: Quality Education Data.

Chapter 4

Educational Research Methods and Tools

In Chapter 3, the major components (hardware, software, and people) of data-driven decision making were examined from the perspective of the major stakeholders in schools, namely, principals, teachers, students, and parents. Just as important to the planning and implementation of successful data-driven decision making processes is a conceptual understanding of educational research methods and tools. Educational research is the seeking or searching for knowledge within the field of education. The word *research* is derived from the French word *rechercher,* meaning to travel through. The formal definition of educational research is a careful, systematic investigation of, or "traveling through," any aspect of education.

Successful school leaders are always seeking to increase their knowledge and improve their understanding of their field. The search for knowledge, which can be formal or informal, includes observation, gathering and analysis of performance data, individual case studies, and tightly controlled experiments. In this chapter, educational research methods and tools are presented to provide a conceptual understanding of some of the research techniques used in data-driven decision making. This chapter is not meant to be a total review of the educational research field; it concentrates on aspects important to data-driven decision making.

THE SCIENTIFIC METHOD AND EDUCATIONAL RESEARCH

Educational research and data-driven decision making are based on the **scientific method**. Figure 4-1 compares the essential steps in the scientific method, the educational research process, and data-driven decision making. The scientific method consists of four steps:

1. Defining a problem
2. Stating a main question or hypothesis
3. Collecting relevant data
4. Analyzing the data to answer the question or test the hypothesis

Paralleling the scientific method, the educational research process consists of the following steps:

1. **Identifying a problem.** The researcher selects a topic in which she or he is genuinely interested, then tries to establish why the problem is important and worthy of research.
2. **Clarifying the problem.** The researcher reviews the research literature to determine what is known and what still needs to be known about the problem.

Figure 4-1 Comparison of the scientific method, the educational research process, and data-driven decision making.

Scientific method	Educational research process	Data-driven decision making
Defining a problem	Identifying a problem Clarifying the problem	Identifying a problem, issue, or alternative courses of action
Stating a hypothesis or main question	Formulating a hypothesis or research question	Stating a question
Collecting relevant data	Developing a methodology	Collecting relevant data
Analyzing the data to the answer the question or to test the hypothesis	Reporting the findings	Analyzing the data to answer the question and to select the course(s) of action
	Drawing conclusions	

3. **Formulating a hypothesis or research question.** The researcher refines and states the problem in the form of a hypothesis(es) or research question(s).
4. **Developing a methodology.** The researcher selects an appropriate research methodology and implements procedures for collecting, summarizing, and analyzing data.
5. **Reporting the findings.** Based on data analysis, the researcher presents a clear statement of the findings.
6. **Drawing conclusions.** Using the hypotheses or research questions as the guide, the researcher forms conclusions based on the findings.

In data-driven decision making, the process is as follows:

1. **Identifying a problem, issue, or alternative courses of action.** Educators (administrators, teachers) select a topic or issue that is important for the functioning or improvement of a school or district. The topic frequently involves alternative courses of action.
2. **Stating a question.** The educators refine and state the problem in the form of a research question(s). Hypotheses generally are not used.
3. **Collecting relevant data.** The educators determine what data are readily available from existing school resources and what additional data have to be collected.
4. **Analyzing the data to answer the question and to select the course(s) of action.** The educators analyze the data to answer the research question and make a decision about a course of action.

Fundamental to all three approaches are the collection and analysis of data. The tools and methods used to collect data are comparable for all three.

EDUCATIONAL RESEARCH METHODS

Although the scientific method is a well-defined concept, educational research can take several different forms. An important distinction in educational research is between nomothetic and idiographic approaches. **Nomothetic research** involves the study of large groups, often on one occasion. Nomothetic researchers search for and believe that their research results apply to larger populations. **Idiographic research**, on the other hand, involves the study of one or a few subjects, often over a long period of time. Results may or may not apply to larger populations. Nomothetic research is oriented to the production and testing of theories, that is, generalizations based on comparisons. Idiographic research takes the form of narratives about individual or unique situations, for example biography, history, and case studies. These two approaches need not be entirely exclusive; indeed, they can complement one another.

One of the major debates in educational research centers on the appropriateness of qualitative versus quantitative research approaches. On March 29, 1989, N. L. Gage gave an address on the occasion of his receipt of the American Educational Research Association's Award for Distinguished Contributions to Educational Research. During his address, he referred to educational research as a great battlefield upon which "paradigm" wars were being fought. He specifically made note of the antagonism between educational researchers who espoused a qualitative approach and those in favor of a quantitative approach (Gage, 1989).

If we accept the definition of data-driven decision making used in Chapter 1, that is, using data analysis to inform educators in determining courses of action involving policy and procedures, then it is obvious that data in any form is appropriate for *informing* decision makers. It is a fallacy to assume that data-driven decision making depends exclusively on quantitative approaches. On the contrary, some of the most important decisions that school leaders make (e.g., teacher evaluation, student disciplinary decisions, or the design of a new facility) might be based more on qualitative approaches such as observation, interviews, or visits to other sites.

Quality refers to the essence (what, why, when, and how) of things, whereas quantity refers to the amounts of things. Qualitative research relies on meanings, concepts, context, descriptions, and settings, and quantitative research relies on measurements and counts (Berg, 2004). Both approaches stress the importance of objectivity in observations and data collection, although qualitative research by its nature is more dependent on a researcher's subjective interpretation. Qualitative research requires seeing, hearing, and experiencing activities in natural environments. Quantitative research requires distancing from the object of study; also, the sorting, counting, and analysis of numeric data must be done, away from their sources. As indicated earlier, a grand debate has existed on the virtues of one approach over the other. Rather than enter this debate, this book recognizes that both approaches are highly respected, and when done well, add equally to knowledge. Where possible, educators should consider using the techniques of both approaches to collect and analyze data, thereby validating results through more than one perspective. Figure 4-2 provides a brief comparison of the two approaches.

Figure 4-3 provides descriptions of seven of the most popular forms of educational research methods. The specific method used depends on the nature of the problem to be studied. For example, in conducting an ethnographic study of classroom behavior and interaction among students, the assumption is that the problem or phenomenon requires careful observation in its natural setting. The researcher blends into the environment, minimally disturbs it in any way, and carefully collects field notes that are rich in textual descriptions for subsequent analysis and reporting. The researcher records student-to-student and student-to-teacher interactions. The subtlety of the turn of a phrase or a facial expression can be as important as direct conversation among the subjects. What is critical is that the researcher minimizes any changes to what is occurring naturally. In contrast, while conducting an experiment on two teaching methods, the researcher might conduct an experiment

Figure 4-2 Qualitative versus quantitative methods.

	Qualitative	Quantitative
Data collection tools	Direct observation Structured interviews Document analysis	Surveys Testing
Data analysis tools	Review of field notes Discussions among team members	Statistical analysis
Reporting format	Rich textual descriptions	Interpretations of results Frequency distributions Contingency tables Statistical charts and displays
Research methods	Ethnography Historiography Case study Descriptive research Action research	Correlation Causal Comparative Experimental Descriptive Action research

and manipulate classes so that one group of students (**experimental group**) is assigned to one class and another group (**control group**) of students assigned to another class. Teachers might be specifically trained to teach one way or another to the two groups. The researcher might require specific pretests and posttests to determine the effects of the two teaching methods. Quantitative data from the test results would be carefully analyzed and reported using statistical analysis such as a **t test**, **analysis of variance**, or **analysis of covariance**. The two methodologies (ethnographic and experimental) are different in their approaches, yet each is appropriate for what the researcher wanted to study.

In data-driven decision making, the techniques used depend as well on the problem or issue to be studied or resolved. For example, if the issue relates to whether teachers are using technology effectively in their classes, observations of actual lessons (not unlike an ethnographic approach) might be appropriate. On the other hand, if the issue relates to the effectiveness of a new reading program, student test results can be analyzed before and after the new program is implemented. In some cases, several techniques can be used, more than one of which might yield data for further action. To determine if teachers are using technology effectively in their classes, a survey of teachers and/or students could be followed by observations or structured interviews. The use of multiple data sources is highly desirable in any data collection activity so that one source can validate the findings of another source.

In examining Figure 4-3, a legitimate question might be asked: Which of these methods is more or less appropriate for data-driven decision making processes? The answer depends on the topic or issue being addressed. However, a brief review

Figure 4-3   Types of educational research methodologies.

Research methodology	Description
Ethnographic	Attempts to describe group behavior and interactions in social settings. It relies on qualitative techniques, especially observation and careful recording of events and social interactions.
Historical	Attempts to describe and explain conditions of the past. It generally relies on qualitative data such as written documents and oral histories.
Descriptive	Attempts to describe and explain conditions of the present. It can be qualitative, such as in a case study, or quantitative, using descriptive statistics such as frequency distributions, contingency tables, and means. Descriptive research can rely on data gathered from a broad range of sources such as written documents, personal interviews, test results, and surveys.
Correlational	Attempts to explore relationships or make predictions. It relies on quantitative data such as test scores, grade point averages, and results of attitudinal instruments, which can be correlated to show that a relationship may exist between or among variables.
Causal comparative (also referred to as ex post facto research)	Attempts to explore cause and effect relationships where causes already exist and cannot be manipulated. It relies mostly on quantitative data sources such as written documents, interviews, and test scores.
Experimental	Attempts to explore cause and effect relationships where causes can be manipulated to produce different kinds of effects. It relies on quantitative data such as test scores and measures of performance.
Action research	Attempts to determine the value of a program, procedure, or product in a particular setting (e.g., school) with the goal of improving the same. Action research does not attempt to generalize results for a broader population.

of each of these methods and their relationship to data-driven decision making yields helpful insights.

Ethnographic Research

Ethnography stems from the Greek *ethnos* for people, tribes, or nations and *graphy* for writing. Ethnographic research is the writing about people in their natural or social setting. It is a form of descriptive research and is also referred to as observational research and naturalistic inquiry. As a part of the social sciences, it has been especially popular in cultural anthropology research because of the work of Margaret Mead and other noted anthropologists. Ethnography is well suited for research in education as well, because so much of what is done in education is based on human interaction in natural and social settings such as schools, classrooms, and playgrounds. A major benefit of ethnographic research is that it provides rich descriptions of human behavior in natural settings, not in artificially constructed, experimental settings.

The observation of a phenomenon in its natural or social setting may appear on the surface to be straightforward. In this regard, Yvonna Lincoln, an expert in the use of qualitative research approaches, refers to the work of Alfred Schultz who formulated a theory of multiple realities. This theory essentially proposes that what we see is shaped by our own value systems and that the same phenomenon might be "seen" and interpreted differently depending on our background, experiences, and values. In terms of naturalistic research, "participants . . . create realities . . . that are based on multiple and often conflicting value systems. Evaluators must take each construction into account and recognize that no single reality exists . . ." (Lincoln, 1986, p. 1). If this is so, ethnographic researchers need to understand the lens through which they see the world and provide for other interpretations.

In data-driven decision making, ethnographic research techniques can be used in any data collection situation where observation of an activity is important. Examples include teacher observation and evaluation, instructional and social student activities, classroom management, and facilities design and development. Ethnographic data collection is largely qualitatively based and complements quantitative approaches.

Historical Research

Historical research, also referred to as historiography, is a form of descriptive research. It involves describing and interpreting events, conditions, or situations that have occurred in the past to understand the present, and perhaps to plan for the future. A common characteristic of historical research is in-depth analysis of source documents (e.g., student transcripts, policy statements, memorandums) and oral histories, if individuals or recordings are available from the period. In terms of number of studies conducted on an annual basis, it is possibly the least popular form of educational research, because foundations, government agencies, and other funding organizations tend to favor current issues and conditions. Furthermore, historical research can be difficult if the period being studied is remote to the extent that records are not readily available and individuals associated with the period or event are no longer alive.

Nevertheless, historical research can be a most interesting activity as the researcher attempts to recreate or uncover a "story" from the past. Its value increases significantly if a connection can be made to a present issue or situation. For example, Linda Darling-Hammond (2004) commented on New York City's policy to retain (leave back) students. She specifically questioned the lack of any "institutional memory" that a retention program established in the early 1980s, rescinded in 1988, was reinstated in 1999 and rescinded again a year later. In 2004, as one of its major new school reform efforts, retention of students was reinstated in New York City.

In relation to data-driven decision making, historical research probably has the least application potential as a research method. However, some of its techniques, especially document analysis, can be helpful when school policies are being considered or reconsidered.

Descriptive Research

The purpose of descriptive research is to describe and explain conditions of the present. It can be qualitative, such as in a case study, or quantitative, using descriptive statistics such as **frequency distributions**, contingency tables, and **means**. Descriptive research can rely on data gathered from a broad range of sources such as written documents, personal interviews, test results, and surveys. Of all the research methods, it is perhaps the most popular in terms of the number of studies conducted each year.

A descriptive study can be especially effective when comparing subpopulations such as students, schools, or school districts. Comparative descriptive studies are popular among many educational researchers and especially government funding agencies. Critical to the design of a descriptive study that compares subpopulations is the careful identification of the **variables** that will be used in the analysis. Once the data have been collected, it is difficult to collect additional data. Students move, educational policies change, or new teachers are assigned, all of which can affect data reporting. Even though most descriptive research is limited to local populations, it does have the potential for generalization. If a **random sample** of a larger population has been selected, a researcher can appropriately suggest that the findings be extended to the larger population.

The data collection techniques used in descriptive research are extensive and draw from all of the tools available to both qualitative and quantitative researchers. For this reason, its applicability to data-driven decision making is most important. The desirability of using multiple data resources is fundamental to data-driven decision making; likewise, multiple data resources are commonly used in descriptive research. The observation of a classroom teacher combined with an analysis of student test performance data can support decisions involving curriculum, teacher assignments, and academic program development.

Correlational Research

Correlational research uses numeric data to explore the relationship between two or more variables. The exploration of the relationship between the variables provides insight into the nature of the variables themselves as well as an understanding of their relationships. Furthermore, if the relationships are substantial and consistent, they enable the researcher to make predictions about the variables. The purpose of correlational research, therefore, is to describe relationships and to predict future events based on these relationships. A correlational study may be designed to meet one or both of these purposes.

The fundamental statistical measure (see **statistics** in Glossary) used in correlation is a **correlation coefficient**, which varies between −1.00 and +1.00. Different methods and formulas for calculating this coefficient can be used, depending on the type of data being analyzed. One of the more commonly used is the Pearson product–moment correlation, which requires two sets of values that represent continuous interval data, such as standardized test scores and grade point averages. A negative coefficient (less than 0.00) indicates an inverse correlation; that is, as one variable changes (increases or decreases), the other changes in the opposite direction. A positive coefficient (greater than 0.00) indicates that as one variable changes, the other changes in the same direction. A coefficient of 0.00 indicates that there is no relationship between the variables.

In doing correlational studies, remember that a relationship does not necessarily indicate causality. There can be substantive correlations between two variables without one variable causing the other. For example, a researcher might find a high correlation between student participation in extracurricular activities and student performance, but participation in extracurricular activities does not *cause* high performance. Perhaps other variables related to participation in extracurricular activities such as self-esteem and a positive attitude toward school might cause highly participative students to work harder and therefore to perform well.

In a correlational study designed to predict events related to two variables, one variable is identified as the **predictor variable** or **independent variable**, and the other variable is identified as the **criterion variable** or **dependent variable**. The value of the predictor, or independent, variable is used to predict the value of the criterion, or dependent, variable.

In data-driven decision making, correlational research methods are used extensively to examine relationships between a host of activities, especially those related to student test scores. Teacher attitude assessments, student attitude assessments, grade point averages, and the results of local testing instruments are frequently correlated with standardized test scores to identify relationships or lack thereof.

Causal Comparative Research

One limitation of correlational research is that a relationship between two variables does not indicate causality. Establishing a **cause–effect relationship** requires careful and rigorous research methods. Causal comparative research, also known as ex post facto research, is one of the more common nonexperimental methods that address cause and effect. It attempts to establish cause-effect relationships between two variables where a causal, or independent, variable cannot be changed or manipulated. For example, certain personal characteristics such as race and ethnicity, which cannot be changed, may effect an educational outcome such as student achievement. Generally, the independent variable refers to events or conditions that have already occurred. Suppose a research project involves stress or burnout (effect variable) of regular education and special education teachers in a particular school setting. The researcher cannot manipulate the licenses and assignments of teachers (causal variable), so that he or she might survey or interview a sample of regular and special education teachers to determine their level of stress or burnout.

To establish a cause–effect relationship in causal comparative research, it is necessary to build a persuasive, logical argument that the independent variable is affecting the dependent variable. The researcher must establish that other, uncontrolled, extraneous variables have not had an effect on the dependent variable. To this end, the researcher must be scrupulous in drawing a sample that minimizes the effects of other extraneous variables. The researcher is free to use a number of research tools and methods, including qualitative research techniques, to collect data. Surveys, questionnaires, test data, school databases, and interviews are all appropriate. For data analysis, descriptive statistics, correlations, and differences of means, standard deviations, and variances can be used.

In data-driven decision making, causal comparative techniques provide a rigorous method for seeking reasons why situations have occurred in a school. The effect of socioeconomics, for example, on student achievement has been well documented as far back as the major national studies conducted by Coleman et al. (1966) and Jencks et al. (1972). Well-developed school databases can provide a plethora of information on students; such databases are ideal for data mining and searching for clues as to why certain students or groups of students are performing or not.

Experimental Research

The purpose of experimental research is to study cause (independent variable) and effect (dependent variable) relationships between two or more variables where the causal variable can be manipulated. Consider this classic example of a true experiment in education. Two randomly selected groups of students are similar in key characteristics. One group (experimental) is taught for a period of time using a new technique or treatment. A second group (control or placebo) is taught using a traditional technique. At the conclusion of the experiment, the two groups are tested to determine if there is a difference in their achievement. The teaching technique represents the causal, or independent, variable, and student achievement is the effect, or dependent, variable. In this example the causal variable has been manipulated by assigning students to two groups in which different teaching methods are used. If student achievement was greater in the experimental group, then the researcher can claim that the new teaching technique (treatment) was the cause. This type of experiment represents a basic experimental research model that has been used many times. Although the technique appears to be relatively simple, most researchers will encounter a number of issues that might make it difficult for them to conduct the experiment. For instance, one question might be, do we really want to experiment with the achievement of children?

The difficulty of conducting true experiments has been well documented, and educators need to be careful when designing or approving them in their schools. Cook (2002) in an article titled, "Randomized Experiments in Educational Policy Research: A Critical Examination of the Reasons the Educational Evaluation Community Has Offered for Not Doing Them," reviewed the literature and identified a number of practical and ethical issues associated with conducting true experimental research studies in schools. For data-driven decision making, experimental research methods can be very powerful, but they need to be used carefully and with a good deal of expertise. Educators would be wise to seek assistance from experienced individuals or research organizations when considering conducting an experiment, even on a small scale. Regardless of the associated data collection and analysis techniques, experimental research should be part of a school's data-driven decision-making repertoire.

Action Research

Of the various research methodologies, action research relates most directly to data-driven decision making in many of its forms and approaches. Action research (see Figure 4-4) focuses on the development, implementation, and testing of a program, product, or procedure. It almost always occurs in school settings and is frequently conducted by or with the assistance of teachers, administrators, and other practitioners. A number of school reform models (e.g., teacher as researcher, principal as researcher) incorporate action research as an activity to infuse vibrancy, reflective practice, and collaborative relationships in education (Mills, 2000; Stewart, 2000; MacLean & Mohr, 1999).

Action research projects can vary significantly and frequently do not follow the standard format (purpose, hypothesis, methodology, findings) that usually characterize other research studies. Any research methodology (qualitative or quantitative) can be adopted, statistical procedures may be used or not, and methodologies may be mixed and matched to meet goals. Because action research is associated with the need to improve school functions related to teaching, learning, counseling, and administration, this methodology is closely akin to data-driven decision making. Much of the literature on action research is relevant and can provide important insights into data-driven decision-making activities. For further information on educators as researchers, see the McDowell Foundation resources Web site: http://www.mcdowell foundation.ca/main_mcdowell/current/resources_for_teacher_researchers.htm. Action research will be discussed in greater detail in Chapter 5.

Figure 4-4   Characteristics of action research.

Characteristic	Explanation
Purpose	The purpose of action research is to improve performance and to solve problems in the local school setting.
Hypotheses/research questions	Research questions are almost always used instead of hypotheses. They are stated broadly and usually early on as part of the research planning process.
Data collection/sources	Qualitative and quantitative data can be collected. School records, surveys, and questionnaires are popular.
Data analysis	Qualitative data can be analyzed using any tools appropriate to the data collection method. Likewise, quantitative data can be analyzed using a computer software program such as SPSS, usually to conduct simple descriptive analysis (e.g., frequency distributions, means, standard deviations).
Reporting results	Relatively brief reports are prepared that are shared within a school community. The format of these reports is frequently informal; that is, the format is not that of a rigid research report. Sometimes action researchers wish to share their work with a larger professional community and publish reports of their findings in journals. In these cases, the reports should be organized more formally. Action research concentrates on an activity in a specific school, so the researcher should not infer that findings can be generalized to larger populations.

DATA COLLECTION TOOLS

The data collection tools available for educational research are appropriate for data-driven decision making as well. Among the popular qualitative tools are direct observation, structured interviews, and document analysis. Surveys and testing are the primary tools used for quantitative approaches. As mentioned earlier in this chapter, the use of multiple data sources is highly desirable in any data collection activity.

Triangulation is a technique used in several types of research. Triangulation takes many forms, but essentially it is a multipronged approach to data collection. Two or more data collection techniques (e.g., surveys and interviews; observations and testing; documents, observations, and interviews) are used to collect data on the same item of analysis. For instance, in collecting data on school spirit, a researcher might look at documents such as school newspapers; examine student records to determine participation in extracurricular activities; observe behaviors of teachers in social settings such as the teachers' lounge; or survey students. Where there is convergence or consistency among the different data collection techniques, the researcher can be secure in pursuing or reporting a particular finding. If there is no convergence or consistency, the researcher can either develop further data collection techniques to seek corroboration or abandon a particular finding or interpretation. The same concept can be used in data-driven decision-making processes. For some issues it might be desirable to collect data from several sources to corroborate the course(s) of action.

Direct Observation

Some methods such as ethnography and forms of descriptive study require observation of activities in a school or other natural setting. The observation may be conducted in person or by videotaping, each of which has its drawbacks and benefits.

In-person observations allow an activity to be scanned extensively for relevant behaviors and context. Observers are trained to take careful notes as they look and listen for subtle comments, clues, and nuances such as facial expressions or inflection and tone of voice. However, many times even the best trained observers might miss something important. Also, other researchers not present must rely entirely on the descriptions and notes provided by the observer to re-create the details of the observation in their own minds.

Videotaping requires that a camera and other equipment be set up to record an activity. One benefit of videotaping is that the tape can be observed over and over again. A videotape can also be shared with experts who were not present during the original taping to obtain their comments and advice. Videotaping, however, usually allows for a limited number of camera angles, and some behaviors might happen outside or in the far reaches of the viewing field. In addition, although videotaping avoids the presence of a stranger or outsider in the setting, the visibility of a camera or other equipment might lead some individuals "to play to the camera" instead of acting as they normally do.

When conducting in-person observations, the observer may or may not be an active participant in an activity. If the purpose of the observation is to record behaviors as objectively and completely as possible with little or no interaction, then the observer must be trained to keep his or her presence to a minimum. On the other hand, if the observer is to participate and assume a role in an activity, the observer must be trained to act the role. For example, if an observer is assuming the role of a team-teacher in a class, he or she must be trained to be a teacher for the duration of the observation.

Observations, whenever possible, should be conducted over a period of time. One-time observations have questionable value, because people act and respond differently depending on circumstances and situations. Accurate depictions require the observer to see, to hear, and to record activities over time. It is not unusual for observations, particularly those involving an educational activity, to go on for a semester, a year, or more.

Structured Interviews

Structured interviews are carefully scripted tools for collecting data. The structured interview should be well organized. All questions should be developed in advance and written as part of a script that the interviewer follows. The interview script should contain identification of who is being interviewed and where the interview is being conducted, short-answer questions (either fill in the blank or multiple choice), and open-ended questions that allow the responder to explain how or why something exists or occurs. Open-ended questions also allow the interviewer to pursue a line of questioning and to follow up with additional questions when the interviewee has mentioned something interesting or provocative. A good technique for designing a structured interview is to start with broad, general questions and move on to more direct, specific questions depending on the responses.

Structured interviews are effective data collection tools when the interviewer is adept at questioning, can make an interviewee feel comfortable, and is able to prompt honest responses. By the same token, structured interviews can be problematic if the interviewer is not adept or objective. One major concern is prompting an interviewee to respond in a particular way. This is especially pertinent when interviewing children. Whether the subjects are children or adults, questions should be worded carefully to minimize leading the interviewee. For example, an interview of students concerning school safety might start with one of the following questions:

- How do you feel about the safety in your school?
- Do you feel this is a safe school?
- Do you feel more secure inside or outside your school?

Questions designed to provoke, such as the following, should be minimized:

- Have you heard any students talking about guns or knives in this school? or
- Do you know of anyone who has had money or other things stolen in this school?

Structured interviews take time to conduct properly; therefore, they are conducted with a limited number of interviewees. Unless there is substantial time and funding, a small **sample** of interviewees is usually selected; members of the sample may or may not represent a larger population. If a larger sample is selected and more than one interviewer is used, then the interviewers need to be trained to be consistent in their line of questioning. A good technique in designing a structured interview is to field-test it several times with a very small group of representative interviewees. This technique will determine if there are any problems with the wording of questions or any other aspect of the interview. Structured interviews should also be designed to repeat key or important questions in slightly different forms to determine if the interviewees are consistent in their responses. If the interviewees allow it, making an audiotape of each interview provides a simple mechanism for reviewing notes and responses.

Document Analysis

Document analysis refers to the review of documents that might be of importance to a project or decision. These can be official policy statements, memorandums and other types of correspondence, government regulations, and written operating procedures, as well as individual personnel and student files. Frequently, document analysis is used for gathering background information on an issue. It also helps establish insights for further data collection activities.

Document analysis is particularly important in research and data-driven decision making activities involving individual cases. A student file that contains teacher commentary, prescriptions, or evaluation plans can provide valuable insight into instructional issues relevant to student performance.

Surveys

Although observations and structured interviews are appropriate data collection tools for small populations, financially and logistically it is difficult, if not impossible, to use them for a large number of subjects. Surveys, on the other hand, are one of the most popular tools for collecting data on large samples. The literature on survey research techniques is extensive and what follows is but a brief introduction and review.

The art of conducting a survey includes the following steps:

- Design the instrument.
- Conduct a pilot test.
- Select a sample.
- Distribute the survey.
- Follow up.
- Record the data.
- Analyze the results.

Designing a survey instrument relates directly to the problem or topic at hand and the target survey population. The design of the survey instrument requires in-depth knowledge of the issue, so that the questions formulated are accurate in content and easily understandable by the survey respondents. Consideration must be given to the reading levels of target populations, especially those of children whose literacy skills are still developing.

Simplicity of format is also an important aspect of survey design. **Likert scales**, which ask respondents to select a response from three to seven options presented in a consistent format, are popular in surveys. Depending on the questions, options might be worded as follows:

- Strongly Disagree—Disagree—No Opinion—Agree—Strongly Agree
- Never—Rarely—Sometimes—Most of the Time—Always
- Strongly Disagree—Somewhat Disagree—Disagree—No opinion—Agree—Somewhat Agree—Strongly Agree

The following suggestions can help in wording survey questions appropriately:

- Keep questions short and direct.
- Include only one idea or concept per question.
- Avoid complex terms and difficult language.
- Make sure that the content is accurate.
- Make sure that the grammar is correct.
- Avoid leading the respondent to certain conclusions.

These suggestions should be considered carefully, because many potential respondents will not answer a survey if it looks overly complex or time-consuming, or if it contains questions that are intimidating or confusing. Consistency in question format significantly helps respondents to understand and to respond to a survey.

Once a survey instrument has been developed, a pilot test or field test should be conducted on a small group of representative respondents. The pilot test should be designed to determine if any questions are difficult or confusing. A time study should also be conducted to determine how long it takes to complete the survey, as the longer the survey takes, the lower the response rate will be. If the pilot test indicates a need for minor or modest changes to the instrument, these changes should be made immediately and preparations should be made to distribute the survey to a larger population. If major changes are required, the instrument should be pilot-tested a second time after the changes are made.

Selecting a sample depends on the type of survey to be conducted. In any case, the survey population will be much smaller than the larger population that is the focus of the study. The art of selecting a random sample can be complex, but essentially it requires that all the subjects in a population have an equal chance of being selected for the sample. Here is one popular way to select a random sample: (1) assign each potential subject a number; (2) have a computer sort the numbers randomly; then (3) have the computer select every number at a certain interval (e.g., every fifth, tenth, or hundredth) depending on the desired size of the survey sample.

A **stratified sample** is a type of random sample that attempts to include representative proportions of certain characteristics (e.g., gender, ethnicity, income levels) of the larger population. Sometimes in generating a random sample, a disproportionate percentage of subjects with a particular characteristic are selected (e.g., too many females, too many high-income families). The stratified sample corrects for any disproportion.

A third type of sample popular in education is a **cluster sample** in which the entire population is divided into groups, or clusters, and a random sample of these clusters is selected. All subjects in the selected clusters are included in the sample. In education, clusters might consist of school districts, schools, or classes. For example, suppose the U.S. Department of Education wants to do a study that requires interviewing teachers in urban high schools. Rather than obtaining a random sample of all teachers in all urban high schools in the country, it might be much easier to take a random sample of urban high schools and interview all teachers in the schools selected.

In considering how to select a sample, the researcher must decide whether the survey will be administered once or several times. In a cross-sectional study, stratified random sampling techniques are used if the survey is conducted once. In a longitudinal study, several surveys of a population are conducted over time. A new random sample may be used for each administration of the survey or the original sample may be followed up over time. In the latter case, the random sample selected for the first administration of the survey is used for each successive administration. When selecting this option, the researcher should make a determination of the sample's mobility and whether subjects are likely to remain reachable during the period of study.

Surveys are distributed in several ways. Mailings are the most popular. The costs for mailing are modest, postal services are reliable, and respondents have a chance to peruse the instrument and determine if they wish to participate. If a survey is short and the sample is relatively small, the telephone can be used to contact potential respondents. This will likely be more costly than mailings, and several attempts may be required to contact respondents who are away from their phones. To assist in conducting telephone interviews, new computer software called CATI (computer-assisted telephone interviewing) is available. With this software, telephone interviews are conducted entirely by a computer. The major benefits of CATI are that, because answers are entered directly into the computer, data entry is eliminated; and data analysis can start immediately. In recent years, survey designers have also been using Internet Web sites to conduct surveys. This type of survey is relatively inexpensive, but its greatest benefit may be that results are collected in electronic form and are available for immediate analysis. The major drawback is that not everyone is connected to the Internet.

Researchers face a major question in conducting a survey: What is an acceptable response rate? This question is difficult to answer, and the answer depends on the nature of the survey. In surveys of stable populations, questions that are not considered overly sensitive should yield high (e.g., in excess of 50%) response rates. However, if the survey touches on sensitive issues (e.g., sexual practices or drug use) or if the population is highly mobile (e.g., student dropouts), then lower response rates are to be expected. If there is any question about the response rate, a second or third follow-up distribution of the survey is appropriate.

If survey data have been collected using print media or the telephone, results need to be recorded and stored in an electronic (computer) form. Depending on the size of the sample, this can be a time-consuming task, and it can be an error-prone task if not done properly. To minimize errors, survey designers should consider how the results will be recorded, so that coding schemes can be simple and straightforward.

A coding scheme refers to the final, valid possibilities that can occur for an item on a survey. For instance, gender might appear on the survey as check-off boxes that indicate female or male. When the response to this question is recorded electronically, it may appear as a code such as 1 or 2, or F or M. The coding of a survey may not be done by someone intimately familiar with the study, so the simpler the code, the fewer the errors. For most statistical analyses, a coding scheme that converts item responses into numbers rather than letters of the alphabet is highly recommended.

Once the data are converted into electronic form, they are ready to be analyzed. The nature of survey analysis requires that a computer software program be used to sort and perform the appropriate statistical routines on the data.

Test Instruments

Test instruments are common for collecting data on many education-related issues and problems. For instance, student achievement is an area of study that frequently requires testing. Over the past 40 years, many excellent test instruments on a wide variety of topics have been developed. Test instruments are available from commercial vendors, colleges and universities, and test organizations. *Tests in Print* is probably the best source for locating an appropriate test instrument. This multivolume reference, which is published by the Buros Institute of Mental Measurements and is updated every 3 or 4 years, contains reviews of thousands of test instruments. The Buros Institute also maintains a database of reviews of test instruments at http://buros.unl.edu/buros/jsp/search.jsp. Another popular source is the Educational Testing Service (ETS) Test Locator Web site which is available at http://www.ets.org/testcoll/index.html. This database contains thousands of descriptions of test instruments and publishers. It is updated regularly by ETS. The source material for this Web site is the *ETS Collection of Tests*, which is available in multivolume print form as well as on microfiche.

In reviewing the appropriateness of a test instrument, particular attention must be paid to the information provided on **reliability** and **validity**. Correlation coefficients are used extensively to measure the reliability (consistency of results) and validity (measures what it is supposed to measure) of standardized tests. To establish the reliability and validity of standardized tests, very high correlations are expected.

Determining reliability usually involves giving the same test to the same sample of subjects two or more times. Results are compared using correlations, which one would expect to be very high. In another approach, the same sample of subjects answers a different set of questions of the same test at two different times, and results are compared using correlation coefficients. For example, the sample may take the odd-numbered questions on a Monday, then take the even-numbered questions on a Thursday. A correlational analysis is then performed on the results of the two days of testing. In establishing the reliability of a standardized test, very high correlations (+0.80) are expected.

Validity tests are sometimes performed by correlating the results of one test with a similar measure that has already established its validity. For example, validity tests for making predictions such as the use of Scholastic Aptitude Test (SAT) scores to predict college grade point average might use correlation coefficients of the two measures (SAT scores and grade point averages) of a sample population to establish the predictive validity of the SAT. Sometimes an appropriate measure to compare results of a test is not available. In such cases validity tests for content of subject matter have to be done by a panel of experts who attest to the validity of the test.

This chapter is a review of some of the critical elements of educational research that have applicability for data-driven decision making. Surely the material in one chapter does not do justice to an entire field. For further information, consult some of the excellent books on this topic: Charles & Mertler (2002 or latest), Gay (1992 or latest), McMillan (2004 or latest), Picciano (2004), and Wiersma (2000 or latest). Technical Support A of this book also reviews the statistical analysis tools referred to in this chapter.

SUMMARY

Educational research techniques play an essential role in data-driven decision making. The scientific method is the root process for both educational research and data-driven decision making.

In educational research the distinction between the nomothetic and idiographic approaches is important. Nomothetic research involves the study of large groups, often on one occasion. Nomothetic researchers believe that their research results apply to larger populations. Idiographic research, on the other hand, involves the study of one or a few subjects, often over a long period of time. Results may or may not apply to larger populations. Nomothetic research is oriented to the production and testing of theories, and generalizations based on comparisons; idiographic research takes the form of narratives about individual or unique situations, biography, history, and case studies. These two approaches need not be entirely exclusive; indeed, they can complement one another.

Related to the nomothetic and idiographic discussion is the issue of qualitative versus quantitative research. Quality refers to the essence (what, why, when, and how) of things, whereas quantity refers to amounts of things. Qualitative research relies on meanings, concepts, context, descriptions, and settings; quantitative research relies on measurements and counts. Educators should consider using the techniques of both approaches to collect and analyze data, thereby validating results through more than one perspective.

Seven major research methodologies are presented in this chapter. The appropriate method to be used depends on the issue or topic to be researched.

The chapter concludes with a review of major data collection tools such as direct observation, structured interviews, surveys, and test instruments that are commonly used in educational research. Multiple data collection techniques (e.g., triangulation) are encouraged, because they help researchers corroborate findings and determine courses of action.

Case Study

Thurgood Marshall High School

Thurgood Marshall High School has an enrollment of 3,500 students and is one of six comprehensive high schools in Franklin City. Although it offers a comprehensive curriculum, Marshall High is especially known for its business and technology programs. The school has established relationships with major local businesses and corporations, and it has a great deal of support from the Franklin City Board of Education.

In 2004, the principal, Janet Konniff, completed a major new technology initiative to integrate technology into the entire curriculum. The communications infrastructure was improved to provide high-speed access to the Internet; every classroom was equipped with computer workstations; teachers were provided extensive development opportunities; and two full-time technicians were hired to maintain hardware and software. The total cost for this initiative was approximately $2 million; half of the money was provided by local businesses. The Franklin City Board of Education sees Marshall High as a model of school-community collaboration. At its June meeting, the president of the board asked the superintendent, Elaine Patterson, if the Marshall High technology initiative could be duplicated in other high schools in Franklin City. Ms. Patterson indicated that she would discuss the question with Ms. Konniff.

At the subsequent meeting between the two administrators, Ms. Koniff commented that although the technology initiative has been beneficial to Marshall High, it has not been completely effective in all academic programs and subject areas. The teachers in business, art, and the sciences appear to be using the technology well, but Ms. Koniff is not sure the same can be said for the other subject areas. She recommends an action research study this summer on the effectiveness of the technology initiative. The Board of Education will not meet again on this issue until the fall, so Ms. Patterson approved Ms. Konniff's recommendation.

Assume you are Ms. Konniff, what is your plan of action? Specifically, whom will you involve in the design of the study? What data do you think you need to collect? What sources and tools will you use for data collection?

References

Berg, B. L. (2004), *Qualitative research methods* (5th ed.). Boston: Pearson Education.

Charles, C. M. & Mertler, C. A. (2002). *Introduction to educational research* (*4th ed.*). New York: Allyn & Bacon.

Coleman, J. S., Campbell, E., Mood, A., Weinfeld, E., Hobson, D., York, R., et al. (1966). *Equality of educational opportunity*. Washington, DC: Government Printing Office.

Cook, T. D. (2002). Randomized experiments in educational policy research: A critical examination of the reasons the educational evaluation community has offered for not doing them. *Educational Evaluation & Policy Analysis, 24*(3), 175–199.

Darling-Hammond, L. (2004). Standards, accountability, and school reform. *Teachers College Record, 106*(6), 1047–1085.

Gage, N. L. (1989). The paradigm wars and their aftermath: A "historical" sketch on research on teaching since 1989. *Teachers College Record, 91*(2), 133–150.

Gay, L. R., Mills, G. E., & Airsasian, P. W. (2006), *Educational research: Competencies for analysis and application* (*8th ed.*). Cols OH: Merrill Education.

Jencks, C., Smith, M., Bane, M. J., Cohen, D. Gintis, H., Heyns, B., et al. (1972). *Inequality: A reassessment of the effects of family and schooling in America*. New York: Basic Books.

Lincoln, Y. S. (1986). Negotiating politics in organizational cultures: Some considerations for effective program evaluation. *Paper presented at the annual meeting of the Association for the Study of Higher Education*, Kansas City, MO. ERIC Document No. ED268893.

MacLean, M. S., & Mohr, M. M. (1999). *Teacher-researchers at work*. Berkeley, CA: The National Writing Project.

McMillan, J. H. (2004), *Educational research: Fundamentals for the consumer* (*4th ed.*). Boston, MA: Pearson Education, Allyn & Bacon.

Mills, G. E. (2000). *Action research: A guide for the teacher researcher*. Upper Saddle River, NJ: Prentice Hall.

Picciano, A. G. (2004). *Educational research primer*. London: Continuum.

Stewart, D. (2000). *Tomorrow's principals today*. Massey University: Kanuka Grove Press.

Wiersma, W. (2000), *Research methods in education* (*7th ed.*). Boston, MA: Allyn & Bacon.

Chapter 5

Teachers and Administrators as Researchers

Chapter 4 addressed the benefits of establishing processes wherein teachers and administrators pursue issues as researchers. Some school reform models incorporate *action research* as an activity to infuse vibrancy, reflective practice, and collaborative relationships into education. Richard Sagor (2000) has written an excellent book titled *Guiding School Improvement with Action Research,* in which he refers to the work of Deborah Meier, Ted Sizer, Carl Glickman and others who incorporate elements of action research into their school improvement models. Sagor sees action research as critical for reprofessionalizing teaching. Joe Kincheloe (2003), in *Teachers as Researchers,* also speaks of the importance of this approach: "A vibrant professional culture depends on a group of practitioners who have the freedom to continuously reinvent themselves via their research and knowledge production" (p. 19). Note the phrase "group of practitioners." To be most effective, action research to improve/ reinvent/advance schools and schooling is not an individual activity but a group or community activity.

LEARNING COMMUNITIES

Peter Senge's (1990) seminal work, *The Fifth Discipline: The Art and Practice of the Learning Organization*, describes five concepts or disciplines critical to developing effective learning organizations:

* Systems thinking
* Team learning
* Personal mastery
* Mental models
* Building a shared vision

For Senge, systems thinking is the "fifth discipline" (p. 12) — the discipline that integrates the other four disciplines. The systems approach, as described in Chapter 1 of this book, has been established as the overall framework for examining how effective data-driven decision making requires planning, developing efficient and reliable data resources, and knowledge sharing among all stakeholders in our schools. However, the other four disciplines are important, especially within the context of collaborative action research.

Others such as Etienne Wenger (1999, 2002; communities of practice) and Richard Sagor (2000; culture of inquiry) likewise suggest that organizations study their processes, procedures, inputs, and outputs in order to understand themselves and to grow. In a sense, organizations are transformed into organic entities that learn and advance; advance and learn. Sergiovanni and Starratt (1998) redefined education administration as relying on "organic management" (p. 320) that makes the promotion of the community the centerpiece of supervision. Senge, Wenger, Sagor, and Sergiovanni and Starratt are promoting concepts that raise schools above the bureaucratic, top-down, do-it-this-way style of administration to another level of collaborative, we-are-in-this-together communities. This chapter suggests that collaborative action research can assist in building these kinds of learning communities.

ACTION RESEARCH IN ACTION

Action research (see Figure 4-4) focuses on the development, implementation, and testing of a program, product, or procedure. It is a flexible research approach designed to yield valuable information that can provide guidance about issues in the local school setting. At the core of action research is the scientific method, which provides a process for problem solving. Identifying problems, collecting data, and analyzing results to inform action can be applied to a plethora of education-related situations. In this chapter, action research is examined as an aid to decision making with regard to the improvement of teaching and learning. In the following three examples of action research, emphasis is placed specifically on the *design* of the project, not on actual data collection or analysis. Note the overall plan for the project, group activities, and use of multiple (quantitative and qualitative) data collection techniques.

TRIAL TESTING A PEER TUTORING PROGRAM

Adams Middle School is a sixth- through ninth-grade program in San Claren, a growing township just outside a large metropolitan area in the southwestern part of the United States. The principal, Jan Delgado, would like to establish a peer tutoring program to assist students in language arts and mathematics. After discussion with the teachers, a decision was made to begin a trial program in January 2006 to assist students who are having difficulty in language arts or mathematics. Peer tutors will be eighth- or ninth-grade students who scored in Level 4 (exceeded the standard) on the state's standardized tests or who achieved a grade of 90% or higher in their classwork at Adams. Tutors will be supervised at all times by a full-time member of the teaching staff. Two teachers (one language arts and one mathematics) agreed to administer the after-school program and work with the tutors as well as with teachers in the school who recommend students for tutoring. Participation by students recommended by their teachers will be voluntary. The program may be extended beyond the trial period (January 2006 through June 2007) depending on feedback and results.

The two teachers who will supervise the trial program suggested an action research project to assess the program's effectiveness and designed a plan. First, they will maintain a record-keeping system of all students (tutees) who come for tutoring. A master record for each tutee will include the student ID number, name, class assigned, teacher making the recommendation, and subject(s) in which assistance is needed. For each tutoring session, a record will be kept of the tutor assigned, the subject area, and the number of hours of tutoring received. Second, they will need access to student demographic, grade, and test score data to review past and current performance on standardized tests. Third, they will set up a process to keep track of students recommended for peer tutoring. This will be a simple referral form which the recommending teacher completes and forwards to them.

Evaluation of the program will be based on the following four data sources:

1. Final grades for the year for all students recommended for tutoring
2. Scale scores and performance levels on state standardized language arts and mathematics tests for all students recommended for tutoring (Tests are given in April and results are made available in late May or early June.)
3. An open-ended survey asking for feedback sent to the teachers of all students recommended for tutoring and who attended at least 6 hours of tutoring
4. A discussion with the peer tutors about the administration, benefits, and any problems or issues they encountered in working in the program

The first two items should be readily available in the Adams Middle School student information system. All that is necessary is to receive permission from the principal for access.

Data analysis will be done in June 2006 and again in June 2007. A data analysis record (see Figure 5-1) will be created for every student recommended for tutoring (whether they attend or not) and will include the following:

- Student ID
- Student name
- Basic student demographic data
- Number of hours of tutoring received for the year
- Final grade in subject area as assigned by teacher
- Scale score on state standardized test
- Performance level on state standardized test

Figure 5-1   Data analysis record layout for a peer tutoring program study at Adams Middle School.

Data field	Source	Field length	Coding scheme
Student ID	SIS*	6	
Student last name	SIS	20	
Gender	SIS	1	1 = female, 2 = male
Grade level	SIS	1	1 = freshman, 2 = sophomore 3 = junior, 4 = senior
Hispanic/Latino	SIS	1	1 = yes, 2 = no
Race	SIS	1	U.S. Department of Education code
Qualify for free lunch	SIS	1	1 = yes, 2 = no
English language learner	SIS	1	1 = yes, 2 = no
Special education	SIS	1	1 = yes, 2 = no
Subject area for tutoring	PTPF**	1	1 = language arts, 2 = mathematics
Hours of tutoring	PTPF	3	
Final grade in subject area	SIS	2	
Scale score on state standardized test	SIS	3	
Performance level on state standardized test	SIS	1	Level 4: Students exceed the learning standards. Level 3: Students meet the learning standards. Level 2: Students show partial achievement of the learning standards. Level 1: Students do not meet the learning standards.

* = student information system. ** = Peer tutoring program files.

Data will be entered for each student for each subject area into a spreadsheet or a SPSS file. Then data will be analyzed to compare the final grades, scale scores, and performance levels of all students recommended for tutoring, "controlling for" (see following paragraph) the number of hours they attended tutoring sessions on a three-level category variable as follows:

1. Students recommended but not attending any or a minimal number of hours of tutoring
2. Students recommended and attending a modest number of hours of tutoring
3. Students recommended and attending a significant number of hours of tutoring

Minimal, modest, and significant number of hours of tutoring can be determined by establishing each student's number of hours of attendance, ranking them, then establishing a lower third category (minimal), middle third (modest), and upper third (significant). A basic statistical comparison of final grades and performance levels by the tutoring category variable can be done as a simple contingency (cross tabulation in SPSS) table. A one-way analysis of variance will show statistically significant differences in the means of the final grades and scale scores of the three categories. All of the analyses could also be conducted controlling for various student demographic data codes (e.g., special education, English language learner, qualifies for free lunch).

The term *controlling for* applies to the statistical procedures used. Frequently, statistics and measures of association such as cross tabulations are computed for two-way tables of rows and columns. However, it is also possible to specify a third, or control, variable. For example, if gender is a control variable for a table of grades and hours of tutoring, the results for a two-way table for the females are computed separately from those for the males.

Quantitative analysis will be followed up by a review of the qualitative data collected from the surveys of teachers who recommended students for the tutoring program. If necessary, several small-group meetings with these teachers will be conducted to gain insights into the program. Meetings with the peer tutors may also yield critical information on how well the program accomplished its goals and objectives. In the long run, the quantitative data analysis might yield the most important information on the broad impact of the peer tutoring program. Nevertheless, the survey and face-to-face meetings with teachers and peer tutors might yield the most important insights for improvement.

An interim report (summer 2006) integrating the information from all of the activities will be shared with administrators, teachers, and peer tutors. Depending on the results, the peer tutoring program will be adjusted or modified. After a year of operation, a second round of data collection and analysis will be undertaken and a final decision will be made on the benefits of the program and whether it should be continued, modified, or discontinued.

MULTIPLE INTELLIGENCES IN A FOREIGN LANGUAGE PROGRAM

Beth Whitfield is the recently appointed assistant principal at Roosevelt High School, a large, comprehensive high school in a major city in the northeastern United States. Before coming to Roosevelt, Ms. Whitfield taught foreign languages (Spanish and French) for 8 years at another public high school, the Columbus Street School for the Performing Arts, a selective theme school. Students applied to Columbus Street from anywhere in the city, and admission was based on a qualifying assessment of basic intelligence as well as talent in the performing arts. Throughout much of her career at the Columbus Street School, Ms. Whitfield used Howard Gardner's theory of multiple intelligences to guide her pedagogical approach (see Gardner, 1983, 1993, 2000). In addition to the standard approaches to teaching grammar and vocabulary, she incorporated video, cultural exploration, group activities, and small skits and performances. She also used student portfolios extensively, which fit well with the school's performing arts theme. Students did well on the state achievement tests in foreign languages as well as in most other subject areas.

At Roosevelt High School, students are admitted from a wide attendance area. The school offers a comprehensive academic program and has developed a reputation as a "good" high school in the community. About 75% of the students pass state-administered achievement tests. In foreign languages, about 68% of the students pass state tests. When she was appointed assistant principal at Roosevelt, Ms. Whitfield was given the charge of reinvigorating the foreign language program. The principal, who was particularly impressed with Ms. Whitfield's creative approaches to teaching foreign languages, wanted to see improvement in the passing rates on state tests.

Ms. Whitfield decided to introduce the concept of multiple intelligences to the six foreign languages teachers at Roosevelt, but she was not sure that the approach would result in improvement on state tests. A basic tenet of multiple intelligences theory is that a variety of techniques and approaches (linguistic, logical-mathematical, kinesthetic, social interaction, etc.) can be used to teach as well as to assess student achievement. On the other hand, the state achievement tests in foreign languages rely entirely on written responses and expression. The teachers were enthusiastic about trying new approaches to teaching and were willing to experiment with multiple intelligences. Ms. Whitfield proposed that they conduct an action research project with the third-year and fourth-year foreign language classes.

Ms. Whitfield and her staff have designed a plan for implementing the project. First, they plan to spend the summer becoming more familiar with multiple intelligences, including taking a workshop, and to begin developing new curriculum material. The curriculum development work will continue into the fall semester. Second, they plan to establish enrollments in the 12 third-year and fourth-year foreign language classes by distributing students as evenly as possible across the classes in terms of student ability and demographic characteristics. All 12 classes will be taught with the traditional curriculum in the fall semester. In the spring semester, 6 of the classes will switch to a multiple intelligences curriculum. Third, at the end of the spring semester, data will be collected to compare student performance in the 6 multiple intelligences classes with the 6 traditional classes.

Ms. Whitfield shared the action research plan with the principal who endorsed it and has agreed to provide assistance, especially with data collection and funding for the summer workshop and curriculum development work.

Data collection to compare the 12 courses will consist of the following three items:

1. Final grades in the foreign language for the year for all students in the 12 classes
2. Scores on the state foreign language achievement tests for all students in the 12 classes
3. Teachers' journals of activities, progress, and problems, encountered in all 12 classes

The first two items will be readily available at the end of June from Roosevelt's student information system. During the summer, the journals will be summarized by each teacher and shared with colleagues.

Data analysis will be done in July. A data analysis record (see Figure 5-2) will be created for every student who was enrolled in one of the 12 foreign language classes. The record will include these items:

- Student ID
- Student name
- Basic student demographic data
- Class assigned
- Final grade
- Score on state foreign language achievement test

The student data will be entered into a spreadsheet or SPSS file and analyzed to compare the final grades and state achievement scores, controlling for the classes (traditional or multiple intelligences). A one-way analysis of variance will show statistically significant differences in the means of the final grades and achievement scores of the students in the traditional and multiple intelligences classes. The analyses will also be conducted controlling for various student demographic data codes (e.g., special education, English language learner, qualifies for free lunch).

After the quantitative data analysis, a series of meetings of the teachers in the foreign language program will be held. The summaries of their journals will form the bases of these meetings. In all likelihood, insights into pedagogical techniques (what worked well, what needs improvement, etc.) will emerge during these meetings and provide direction for modifying and adjusting the curriculum for the coming year.

Figure 5-2   Data analysis record layout for foreign language/multiple intelligences study at Roosevelt High School.

Data field	Source	Field length	Coding scheme
Student ID	SIS*	6	
Student last name	SIS	20	
Gender	SIS	1	1 = female, 2 = male
Grade level	SIS	1	3 = junior, 4 = senior
Hispanic/Latino	SIS	1	1 = yes, 2 = no
Race	SIS	1	U.S. Department of Education Code
Qualify for free lunch	SIS	1	1 = yes, 2 = no
English language learner	SIS	1	1 = yes, 2 = no
Special education	SIS	1	1 = yes, 2 = no
Class assigned	SIS	1	
Class assignment code	BW**	3	
Final grade in subject area	SIS	2	
Score on state achievement test in foreign language	SIS	3	
Pass/fail indicator on state achievement test	SIS	1	1 = pass, 2 = failed

* = Student Information System. ** = Will be assigned by Beth Whitfield.

A report will be written in the summer that represents the views of all participating teachers and will be forwarded to the principal. Depending on the results, the multiple intelligences curriculum will be modified as needed and tested again in the subsequent year.

ADVANCING TO AN INCLUSION PROGRAM

Edward Arkin is the principal of the Redwich Primary School in a large suburban school district in New England. Originally he was a primary school teacher but he switched to special education. Mr. Arkin has been a school administrator at Redwich for 7 years and became principal 2 years ago. Among his goals for Redwich is a more inclusive teaching environment for all students. The Individuals with Disabilities Act (IDEA) of 1997 requires that the general education setting be considered first as the *least restrictive environment* for all students. However, the legislation allows for a number of circumstances where full inclusion of students with special needs in general education classes are not required. Nevertheless, many school districts have been moving to full inclusion, depending on local circumstances and individual student needs. Mr. Arkin is well aware of the philosophy and practice of inclusion and has guided Redwich to a phased-in approach. Now he thinks that Redwich is ready to move to a fully inclusive environment.

In the spring semester, Mr. Arkin shared his thoughts with a group of fourth- and fifth-grade teachers. He indicated that in these two grades he would like Redwich to move to a full inclusion model for the following year. He asked the teachers for suggestions and they focused on the need for training, team teaching, and reduction of class size.

Mr. Arkin hopes that Redwich might serve as a model for the entire district; therefore, a plan was developed that includes an implementation and research component. First, a comprehensive training program will be provided during the summer for eight teachers. The program will include (1) training in developing Individualized Education Plan components; (2) coteaching and collaboration; and (3) establishing peer tutoring systems in classroom environments. Second, two fourth-grade and two fifth-grade classes will be established in the fall as inclusion classes. They will be team taught by a general education teacher and a special education teacher. Class enrollment will be 17 students, 8 less than the district limit of 25 students for fourth and fifth grades. Third, if Redwich is to serve as a model for the school district, data will be collected and analyzed as part of an action research project as follows:

1. Final grade point average for the year will be obtained for all students enrolled in the inclusion classes.
2. Scale scores and performance levels on state standardized language arts and mathematics tests will be determined for all students enrolled in the inclusion classes. Tests are given in early spring and results are made available in late May or early June.
3. A simple sociometric survey will be administered to all students in the inclusion classes to determine their attitudes toward their classmates.
4. The eight teachers teaching in the inclusion classes will keep a journal of activities, progress, and problems encountered in the four classes.

Data for the first two items will be readily available from the Redwich student information system. The sociometric survey will be administered at the beginning and at the end of the school year to all students enrolled in the inclusion classes. In the summer, journals will be summarized by each teacher and shared with colleagues. Data analysis will be done in July. A data analysis record (see Figure 5-3) will be created for every student enrolled in the inclusion classes. The record will include these items:

- Student ID
- Student name
- Basic student demographic data
- Class assigned
- Final grade point average

Figure 5-3 Data analysis record layout for inclusion program at Redwich Primary School.

Data field	Source	Field length	Coding scheme
Student ID	SIS*	6	
Student last name	SIS	20	
Gender	SIS	1	1 = female, 2 = male
Grade level	SIS	3	4 = fourth grade; 5 = fifth grade
Hispanic/Latino	SIS	1	1 = yes, 2 = no
Race	SIS	1	U.S. Department of Education Code
Qualify for free lunch	SIS	1	1 = yes, 2 = no
English language learner	SIS	1	1 = yes, 2 = no
Special education	SIS	1	1 = yes, 2 = no
Year grade point average	SIS	1	
Scale score on state standardized test in language arts	SIS	3	
Performance level on state standardized test in language arts	SIS	1	Level 4: Students exceed the learning standards.
			Level 3: Students meet the learning standards.
			Level 2: Students show partial achievement of the learning standards.
			Level 1: Students do not meet the learning standards.
Scale score on state standardized test in mathematics	SIS	3	
Performance level on state standardized test in mathematics	SIS	1	Level 4: Students exceed the learning standards.
			Level 3: Students meet the learning standards.
			Level 2: Students show partial achievement of the learning standards.
			Level 1: Students do not meet the learning standards.

* = Student Information System.

- Scale score on state standardized test
- Performance level on state standardized test

Data for each student will be entered into a spreadsheet or SPSS file. Data will then be summarized for final grade point average, scale score, and performance level, controlling for the student special education code (general education or special education). To determine if there are any differences in student performance because of the inclusion program, the results of the analysis will be compared with the present and past noninclusion fourth- and fifth-grade classes at Redwich.

Results from the student sociometric survey will be tabulated during the summer to determine if there were any differences in the attitudes of students toward one another, especially between general education and special education students. It will be important to determine if attitudes changed from the beginning to the end of the school year.

Teachers will meet in summer to summarize and to share their journal entries. These meetings will provide the basis for modifying and improving the program for next year.

A report describing the results of all of the data analyses will be completed by the end of summer and shared with the Redwich school community in the fall at a staff development day.

SUMMARY

Action research is an important technique for building communities in schools. It is a flexible research approach designed to yield valuable information that can provide guidance about issues in the local school setting. By its nature, action research encourages collaboration among teachers and administrators, which in turn helps to build learning communities.

Action research is especially helpful as an aid in decision making to improve teaching and learning. Three examples show how action research can be used in different school environments. In these examples emphasis is placed on the importance of planning, group activities, and use of multiple (quantitative and qualitative) data resources.

Activities

1. Do a brief literature review of one or more of the three pedagogical approaches described in this chapter: peer tutoring, multiple intelligences and standardized testing, or inclusion programs. Try to locate research studies, preferably action research. Consider especially whether there is consistency in the research results or findings.
2. Identify a project in a school that might be appropriate for action research. Develop a plan for carrying out the project. Include who would be involved, data collection techniques and sources, and a time frame for completing the project.

References

Gardner, H. (1983). *Frames of mind: The theory of multiple intelligences*. New York: Basic Books.

Gardner, H. (1993). *Multiple intelligences: The theory in practice*. New York: Basic Books.

Gardner, H. (2000). *Intelligence reframed: Multiple intelligences for the 21st century*. New York: Basic Books.

Kincheloe, J. (2003). *Teachers as researchers: Qualitative inquiry as a path to empowerment* (*2nd ed.*). London: Routledge-Falmer.

Sagor, R. (2000). *Guiding school improvement with action research*. Alexandria, VA: Association for Supervision and Curriculum Development.

Senge, P. M. (1990). *The fifth discipline: The art and practice of the learning organization*. New York: Doubleday Currency.

Sergiovanni, T. J., & Starratt, R.J. (1998). *Supervision: A redefinition* (*6th ed.*). Boston, MA: McGraw-Hill.

Wenger, E. (1999). *Communities of practice: Learning, meaning, and identity*. Cambridge, MA: Cambridge University Press.

Wenger, E., McDermott, R., & Snyder, W. (2002). *Cultivating communities of practice*. Boston, MA: Harvard Business School Press.

Section II
Basic Applications

Each chapter in this section provides examples in which data-driven decision-making concepts and applications are used to assist in resolving school or district-based issues. You are encouraged to work through the examples using an electronic spreadsheet such as Microsoft Excel or a statistical software package such as SPSS.

Chapter 6

Student Data, Demographics, and Enrollments

Chapter 2 explained how the school district needs to provide the leadership for developing and implementing data-driven decision-making processes. This is especially true with respect to large, overall issues and questions. Brubacker (1997) cautioned about the volatility of enrollment projections and their impact on school facilities and emphasized the importance of these projections in the design of school facilities. For example, how many students are in attendance or will be attending the schools in the district? Do they have any special needs? Will the staff and budget be adequate? Although these questions are important at any level of the education organization, they are critical to districtwide planning and decision making. In this chapter, several data-driven applications address major, districtwide decision-making issues.

STUDENT DATA

A logical starting point for developing data-driven decision-making processes at the school district level centers on knowledge of the potential student population. Primary data need to be collected through a census or other means to assist school administrators in planning their programs. This activity cannot wait for the first day of school; on the contrary, good leadership is a continual process that looks to the future and plans accordingly. Liu (1998) commented on the need for careful enrollment projections by administrators, if school districts are to allocate space, financial, and personnel resources effectively. Kennedy (1999) described how some school districts have been experiencing "explosive" enrollment growth and how they are coping with providing the necessary facilities. Seminole County in central Florida, for instance, had an average increase of 1,500 students per year for the previous 20 years. Keeping up with facilities planning tested the wherewithal of the district administration. In addition to building new schools, Seminole County experimented with year-round schooling and purchased portable classrooms.

Enrollment projections constitute an important data-driven decision-making application that can be used at the district or school level. Decisions regarding staffing, class size, and transportation are based on such projections. In the following pages, a case study illustrates how enrollment projections are developed and used.

ENROLLMENT PROJECTIONS AT THE DISTRICT LEVEL

Several reliable sources (e.g., a census, a county building department) may collect data pertinent to enrollment from the community. Even in the best of circumstances, however, such data may be less than a hundred percent accurate. A few percentage points can have serious ramifications on a school district's operations. Therefore, the school district leadership needs to develop models that provide an accurate picture of enrollments for the next 2 or 3 years. Every district office should employ individuals who are familiar with community characteristics such as population growth and economic factors, and who can provide insights into trends and developments in the district that might affect enrollments. In addition, accurate data from the past are critical to every enrollment projection.

The Haldane School District is a medium-sized district with approximately 16,000 students spread over a significant geographic area in the southwestern United States. The district operates 16 primary schools (average enrollment = 490), 6 middle schools (average enrollment = 700), and 2 high schools (average enrollment = 2,000) located in six attendance zones.

Figure 6-1 Basic enrollment projections using averages from previous years. Base year is 2000.

Haldane School District Enrollment Data and Projections

| | Actual | | | | | Projected | | |
	Year 2000	Year 2001	Year 2002	Year 2003	Year 2004	Year 2005	Year 2006	Year 2007
Enrollment	15400	15550	15700	15750	16100	16275	16456	16645
Change		150	150	50	350	175	181	189
% Change		0.010	0.010	0.003	0.022	0.011	0.012	0.012

 For the actual data set for Figure 6-1, go to the Companion Website at
www.//prenhall.com/picciano

Figure 6-1 is a spreadsheet for a simple enrollment projection for the Haldane School District. Previous enrollment data for 5 years serve as the basis for projecting the enrollments for the next 3 years. This is a common technique used by many school districts. In this example, an Excel spreadsheet was used to develop the model, which uses data from Year 2000 as the base, then averages (calculates a mean) the actual enrollment increases of the previous 4 years (2001–2004) to project enrollments for the next 3 years (2005–2007). The formula used is as follows:

Sum each actual year's enrollment increase and divide by N years:

$$(150 + 150 + 50 + 350)/4 = 175$$

$$16{,}100 + 175 = 16{,}275 \text{ for Year 2005}$$

In this projection, the percentage change from year to year (shown in last row of the spreadsheet and expressed as a decimal) is fairly stable, except for a little move upward for Year 2004 when the enrollment in the district increased by 350 students, or 2.2%. The method used to make the projection (yearly average increase) is simple and direct, especially when enrollments are fairly stable and do not change significantly from one year to another.

Figure 6-2 also uses enrollment data for 5 previous years as the basis for projecting enrollments for the next 3 years. However, it does not compute simple averages of the enrollment increases of each of the previous years. Instead, weighted averages are computed, which give more "weight" to the immediate past year and less weight to the more distant past year. The formula used is as follows:

Each year's enrollment increase is assigned a weight in increments of one:

Year 2001 increase × 1   Year 2003 increase × 3

Year 2002 increase × 2   Year 2004 increase × 4

Figure 6-2   Basic enrollment projections using weighted averages from previous years. Base year is 2000.

Haldane School District Enrollment Data and Projections

	Actual			Projected			
	Year 2000	Year 2001	Year 2002	Year 2003	Year 2004	Year 2005	Year 2006	Year 2007
Enrollment	15400	15550	15700	15750	16100	16300	16510	16729
Change		150	150	50	350	200	210	219
% Change		0.010	0.010	0.003	0.022	0.013	0.013	0.014

For the actual data set for Figure 6-2, go to the Companion Website at
www.//prenhall.com/picciano

Sum the weighted increases and divide by the sum of the weights as follows:

$$\text{Year 2001 increase } (150 \times 1) = 150$$
$$\text{Year 2002 increase } (150 \times 2) = 300$$
$$\text{Year 2003 increase } (50 \times 3) = 150$$
$$\text{Year 2004 increase } (350 \times 4) = 1{,}400$$
$$\text{Sum} = 2{,}000/10 = 200$$
$$16{,}100 + 200 = 16{,}300 \text{ for Year 2005}$$

Use of weighted averages gives an increase of 200 students, compared with 175 students when nonweighted averages were used. This change reflects the additional weight given to the increase (350 students) in the most recent year (2004) compared with the earlier years.

Graphics provide a visual representation of the trend data that some people find helpful. Figure 6-3 is a simple line chart that represents the enrollment projections provided in Figure 6-2.

ATTENDANCE ZONES AND INDIVIDUAL SCHOOLS

Assume that it is the summer of 2004. In addition to the projections for 2005–2007, the school district has decided to conduct an analysis for the school year beginning in fall 2004. The student census data has just been collected and it would be good to know in more detail what effect the 350 new students will have on the school district. An examination of the enrollment projections provided in Figures 6-2 and 6-3 shows that the district enjoys a relatively stable environment with modest yearly growth. If the 350 new students are evenly distributed among the six

Figure 6-3 Line chart of the enrollment projections presented in Figure 6-2.

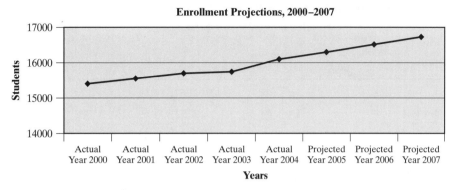

attendance zones and schools in the Haldane School District, then the impact on staffing, class size, and so forth, should be easily managed. Nevertheless, further comparison of Year 2003 and Year 2004 data by attendance zone would be helpful.

Figure 6-4 presents data on Year 2003 and Year 2004 enrollments by attendance zone. The increase (350) of students in the Haldane School District is not evenly distributed throughout the six attendance zones but is concentrated in one zone, Attendance Zone 5. An increase concentrated in one zone is a common occurrence, frequently when a new housing development is completed and populated. Provision

Figure 6-4 Enrollment data for Year 2003 and Year 2004 by attendance zone.

Haldane School District Enrollment Data by Attendance Zone

Attendance Zone No.	Year 2003 Enrollment	Year 2004 Enrollment	Change	% Change
1	2420	2435	15	0.0061983
2	2610	2640	30	0.0114943
3	2650	2645	−5	−0.0018868
4	2905	2910	5	0.0017212
5	2700	2990	290	0.1074074
6	2465	2480	15	0.0060852
	15750	16100	350	0.0222222

For the actual data set for Figure 6-4, go to the Companion Website at
www.//prenhall.com/picciano

Figure 6-5 Carlson primary school class enrollments for Year 2003 and Year 2004. ELL = English language learner.

Carlson Primary School Enrollment by Class (2003–2004)

	Year 2003						Year 2004					
	General Educ.	Special Educ.	ELL Educ.	Totals	Classes	Class Average	General Educ.	Special Educ.	ELL Educ.	Totals	Classes	Class Average
Pre-K	58	2	5	65	3	21.67	69	4	7	80	4	20.00
Kindergarten	59	4	4	67	3	22.33	69	5	7	81	4	20.25
1st	58	3	5	66	3	22.00	69	4	7	80	4	20.00
2nd	63	5	6	74	3	24.67	65	7	7	79	4	19.75
3rd	61	6	5	72	3	24.00	67	7	7	81	4	20.25
4th	68	6	5	79	3	26.33	72	6	5	83	4	20.75
5th	63	4	5	72	3	24.00	71	6	4	81	4	20.25
	430	30	35	495	21	23.57	482	39	44	565	28	20.18

For the actual data set for Figure 6-5, go to the Companion Website at
www.//prenhall.com/picciano

of increased resources for the 290 new students in Attendance Zone 5 will require significant planning on the part of the school district administration.

Three schools (two primary and one middle) in Attendance Zone 5 will each experience an increase of approximately 70 new students. Eighty of the new students in Attendance Zone 5 will be attending one of the two high schools in Haldane. For the two primary schools (Pre-K through grade 5) and the one middle school (grades 6 through 8), the increase will probably mean adding at least one new class for each grade in the fall of 2004. Haldane has a policy that limits class size in the primary schools to 25 students. Haldane also is an inclusive school district where students with special needs (e.g., special education, English language learners) are enrolled into general education classrooms as much as possible. Figure 6-5 projects the impact of the increase in enrollment on classes and class size for one of the primary schools (Carlson Primary School) based on the information collected in the census.

TAKING A CENSUS

School districts should establish procedures to collect census data on a regular basis, preferably yearly. The purpose of the census is to identify new students in the school district, not to collect an extensive amount of data on district residents. Most school districts use a simple form (see Figure 6-6) to gather this information. The name of the person responsible for the child or children, address, and

Figure 6-6 Sample school district census form.

Haldane School Census
June 2004

Parent, guardian, or other person completing this census:

Last Name: _____ First Name: _____ M.I.:____

Street Address: _____

City:_____ State:_____ Zip code: _____

List the name and date of birth for all person(s) in the family who will have reached their fourth (4th) birthday, and who will not have reached their twentieth (20th) birthday on December 31, 2004.

| Name | Date of Birth |
| (Last Name/First Name/M.I.) | (Month/Day/Year) |

Name
(Last Name/First Name/M.I.)

Date of Birth
(Month/Day/Year)

_____   _____

_____   _____

_____   _____

_____   _____

_____   _____

_____   _____

If you have any questions or concerns, please contact Sandy Jones or Carla Johnson at (443) 296-5777 or by e-mail at: sandyjones@haldane.edu or carlajohnson@haldane.edu.
Please return by June 30, 2004.

Thank you very much for your time and cooperation.

---

names and date of birth of the child or children will suffice. Some school districts also attempt to collect information about special needs of the children. This should be done carefully, as it may cause concerns for parents. An in-person interview is recommended to assess special needs once a new child has been identified. Figure 6-7 lists procedures for conducting a census. Many school districts also use electronic means (e.g., Internet) for contacting parents and guardians to complete census forms.

Figure 6-7   Conducting a census.

Procedures for Conducting a Census

1. Paid census takers should be used to go door to door; this is the most efficient means of conducting a census.
2. Paid census takers should be used rather than volunteers; this results in considerably higher accuracy overall.
3. A door-to-door census could be conducted by

   a. service groups,
   b. Parent Teacher Association or Parent Teacher Organization,
   c. professional employees of the district, or
   d. senior citizens, including retired teachers.

4. A public awareness thrust should be made before the census to inform the public that the census will be taken. If the question regarding the existence of children with disabilities will be included, alert the public before the census.
5. Census takers should wear some means of identification such as badges or buttons.
6. The responsibilities and duties of census takers should be well defined in advance. A training session is important. A handbook could be provided for each census taker.
7. The importance of confidentiality of information should be emphasized with census takers.
8. A statement may be added to the census form that recommends that the parent contacts the local school district if a concern arises during census taking.

SPECIAL STUDENT POPULATIONS

The census should be used to identify students in the school district. Once identified, a major effort has to be made to collect as much data a possible about the students themselves. Part D in Section III (Technical Support) of this book provides the scope of data that eventually should be collected for each student. Initially, it is important to identify and assess students who need special services and who qualify for special programs. This is best accomplished through face-to-face interviews with parents or guardians.

New students, whether just starting their education or transferring from another school district, should be thoroughly evaluated for the following needs:

- Academic programs (e.g., special education, bilingual or English language learner education, accelerated programs)
- Participation in entitlement programs such as Title I
- Health requirements

The types of assessments that can be undertaken are extensive. Figure 6-8 (purposes of assessments) and Figure 6-9 (types of assessments) are parts of the coding schemes provided by the U.S. Department of Education, National Center for Education Statistics, for its recommended student data element outline (see Technical Support Part D).

Note in Figure 6-5 that the Carlson Primary School students are categorized according to general education, special education, and English language learners

Figure 6-8 Codes/options for data element 1880, purpose (under section on assessment).

01 *Admission*—An examination used in the admission procedure for an educational program. It may be used as a part of a selective admission process for an educational institution or as a device for predicting the success of a student in an education program.

02 *Assessment of student's progress*—An examination used to measure the progress of a student in a particular content area.

03 *Development of an individualized educational program (IEP)*—An assessment used to determine whether a student is in need of special education and, if so, what types of special education services would most benefit the student. This information is often incorporated into a student's individualized educational program (IEP).

04 *Development of an individualized family service program (IFSP)*—An assessment used to determine whether a child is in need of early intervention services mandated by the Individuals with Disabilities Education Act (IDEA). This information often contributes to the development of an individualized family service program (IFSP).

05 *Diagnosis*—An assessment (other than for the development of an IEP or IFSP) used to examine in-depth information about specific strengths and weaknesses in a student's skill development.

06 *Graduation requirement*—An assessment given to students on the basis of which an appropriate state authority may certify that an individual has met state requirements for high school completion or graduation.

07 *Instructional decision*—An assessment used to determine whether the instructional path of a student should be maintained or altered.

08 *Program eligibility*—An assessment (other than for the development of an IEP or IFSP) used to determine whether a student is eligible to participate in a specific program.

09 *Program evaluation*—An assessment given to a student as part of an effort to evaluate a program's effectiveness. Results of the assessment may or may not be reported at an individual student level.

10 *Program placement*—An assessment used to determine the most appropriate instructional program for a student.

11 *School performance evaluation*—An assessment of a student to determine the effectiveness of a school or an educational institution. Results of the assessment may or may not be reported at the individual student level.

12 *Screening*—An examination used to determine the need for or suitability of additional tests in any of a variety of disciplines or for a specific reason (e.g., a home language survey to identify language minority students who may need assistance).

13 *Promotion to or retention in a grade or program*—An assessment of a student to determine whether he/she is eligible for promotion to a higher grade level or to a more advanced program.

14 *Course credit*—An assessment of a student to determine whether he/she should be awarded the credit(s) for completing the course requirements.

Source: From Student Data Handbook, National Center for Education Statistics, 2000. Washington, DC: U.S. Department of Education. Retrieved July 3, 2003, from http://nces.ed.gov/pubs2000/2000343.pdf.

Figure 6-9   Codes/options for data element 1890, assessment type (under section on assessment).

01   *Achievement test*—An assessment to measure a student's present level of knowledge, skill, or competence in a specific area or subject.

02   *Advanced placement test*—An assessment to measure the achievement of a student in a subject matter area, taught during high school, which may qualify him or her to bypass the usual initial college class in this area and begin his or her college work in the area at a more advanced level and possibly with college credit.

03   *Alternative assessment*—An assessment provided to children with disabilities who cannot participate in a State or district-wide assessment program, even with appropriate accommodations.

04   *Aptitude test*—An assessment to measure a student's potential ability to acquire specific knowledge or master a specific skill.

05   *Attitudinal test*—An assessment to measure the mental and emotional set or pattern of likes and dislikes or opinions held by a student or a group of students. This is often used in relation to considerations such as controversial issues or personal adjustments.

06   *Cognitive and perceptual skills test*—An assessment to measure components of a student's mental ability such as visual memory, figure-ground differentiation, auditory memory, reasoning ability, and sequential processing.

07   *Developmental observation*—An assessment to measure a child's development based on observation. This is most frequently associated with early childhood education and care. Areas of observation and/or evaluation may include, but are not limited to, a child's cognitive and language development, social and emotional development, hygiene, nutrition, and self-help skills, as well as gross and fine motor skills.

08   *Interest inventory*—An assessment used to measure the extent to which a student's pattern of likes and dislikes corresponds to those of individuals who are known to be successfully engaged in a given vocation, subject area, program of studies, or other activity.

09   *Language proficiency test*—An assessment used to measure a student's level of proficiency (i.e., speaking, writing, reading, and listening) in either a native language or an acquired language.

10   *Manual dexterity test*—An assessment to measure a student's ability to move his or her hands easily and skillfully. This test may be used in the identification of aptitudes for certain occupations.

11   *Mental ability (intelligence) test*—An assessment to measure a student's general ability to successfully and rapidly adapt to new situations and to learn from experience.

12   *Performance assessment*—An assessment to measure a student's knowledge or skill by requiring him or her to produce an answer or product that is not necessarily in a standardized format. Examples of performance assessment include writing short answers, solving complex mathematical problems, writing an extended essay, conducting an experiment, presenting an oral argument, or assembling a portfolio of representative work.

13   *Personality test*—An assessment to measure a student's affective or nonintellectual aspects of behavior such as emotional adjustment, interpersonal relations, motivation, interests, and attitudes.

14   *Portfolio assessment*—An assessment to measure the quality of a collection of student work or a series of student performances as interpreted by the student, a teacher, or an independent evaluator.

15   *Psychological test*—An assessment to measure a sample of behavior in an objective and standardized way.

16   *Psychomotor test*—An assessment to measure the motor effects of a student's mental or cerebral processes.

17   *Reading readiness test*—An assessment to measure interrelated factors contributing to a student's readiness to learn to read (e.g., linguistic maturity, experiential background, perceptual maturity, and responsiveness to books and storytelling).

Source: From Student Data Handbook, National Center for Education Statistics, 2000. Washington, DC: U.S. Department of Education. Retrieved July 3, 2003, from http://goal/ ncrel.org/winss/sampques.asp?intCategoryID=1006.

(ELL). These are important distinctions, because the needs of these children will have significant ramifications on the educational program provided. Even as American education continues to move toward more inclusive classrooms, many of these students will need special education services regardless of the mainstream classroom environment. The same is true for ELL students.

The information gathered in the census and displayed in Figure 6-5 will assist the school district in providing services for these students through careful budgeting. Fortunately, additional funding is available from the U.S. federal government for special education and ELL student populations. Every school district needs to have administrators who can use data and are completely aware of all special funding sources (e.g., federal government, state government, localities) that might be available for special student populations. The Elementary and Secondary Education Act (ESEA) and Individuals with Disabilities Education Act (IDEA) are the major federal programs for funding poor, ELL, and special education students in American schools.

SUMMARY

An application involving student enrollment projections at the school district level serves as an example of how data-driven decisions can be used in planning. School district leadership needs to develop models that project enrollments for the entire district, for attendance zones, and for individual schools, so that data can be analyzed at different levels to assist in planning. Census and other information-gathering techniques are critical in establishing accurate and timely student data. Identification of students with special needs is important because the school district provides services for these students that require budgeting and use of targeted funding sources.

Activities

1. Visit a district office or school and meet with an administrator (e.g., superintendent, assistant superintendent, principal). Determine how enrollment projections are done for the district or school. Specifically ask how data are collected (e.g., forms, schedule, methods) and who is responsible for developing projections.

2. Curtis Primary School is a new school that opened in 2003 to relieve overcrowding in 12 other primary schools in the district. Assume you are the principal of Curtis and you have been informed by the superintendent of your school district that Curtis can anticipate a 3%, 4%, and 5% increase in your

(continued)

school's population in each of the next three years (School Years 2006, 2007, and 2008). Develop an enrollment projection for Curtis using the base data shown in the accompanying table.

Enrollment (school year 2005)

Grade	General education	Special education	ELL education
Pre-K	42	3	2
Kindergarten	39	3	3
1st	44	4	2
2nd	41	3	4
3rd	40	4	2
4th	41	3	3
5th	43	3	4
Totals	290	23	20

Assume that the district has a policy limiting class size to 24 students. Currently each grade has two classes; most are within the 24-student limit. Also assume that the district is an inclusive district where special education and ELL students are enrolled in general education classes for a substantial part of the day.

References

Brubacker, C. W. (1997). *Planning and designing schools.* New York: McGraw-Hill.

Kennedy, M. (1999). Bursting through: How schools are meeting the enrollment explosion. *American School and University, 71*(9), 18–20.

Liu, R. (1998). Short-term enrollment projection: An example at the state level. *Education, 118*(4), 597–601.

Chapter 7

School and the Community

Brown and Dugard (2000), in their seminal work *The Social Life of Information*, commented: "For all information's independence and extent, it is people in their communities, organizations, and institutions who ultimately decide what it all means and why it matters" (p. 18).

Don Hooper, president of the American Association of School Administrators, in an article titled "School/Community Relationships: A Vital Lifeline" (Hooper, 2001), called on school leaders to actively engage their communities in support of their schools. He recommended that every school leader ask the following questions:

- Who are our community stakeholders? Who is connected to our schools and who needs to be?
- How are we communicating with our stakeholders? Are we using effective methods to interact with our stakeholders to provide them with important and useful information and to gain their feedback?
- What do our stakeholders know and think about our schools? Are we giving them the information they want and need to fully understand our educational programs?

Hooper further recommended in this article that

> the best way to find out what people know and want to know is to ask them—and then to listen to what they have to say . . . Surveying your public is one of the most effective ways to collect useful information. (http://www.aasa.org/publications/sa/2001_08/prezcorner.htm)

In this chapter, the school-community relationship is examined with regard to data-driven decision making. Particular attention is paid to data collection techniques such as surveys and questionnaires for finding out about community opinions and involving the community in school decisions. The importance of schools building relationships with their communities cannot be overstated. For more information on this topic, refer to Gallagher, Bagin, and Kindred (2004).

PARTNERING WITH THE COMMUNITY: BROAD-BASED SURVEYS

The Wisconsin Department of Public Instruction (2003) undertook a project titled "Characteristics of Successful Schools". After a period of study and review by experts in education, seven critical characteristics of the successful school were identified:

- Vision
- Leadership
- High academic standards
- Standards of the heart
- Family, school, and community partnerships
- Professional development
- Evidence of success

With the assistance of the North Central Regional Educational Laboratory, a series of surveys was designed to help schools assess these characteristics. Figure 7-1 is an excerpt from the survey designed for assessing family, school, and community relations and serves as a good model for gathering broad-based data in a school community. In all, 29 questions in the survey seek information on parental involvement, information dissemination, communication, and family support services. The survey is well designed, with all questions presented in the same manner. Responses are gathered through an easy-to-understand, 5-point Likert scale. The survey is also available in a Web-based format, which is more convenient for some participants.

The simplicity of the survey design makes converting the responses for subsequent data analysis straightforward, with minimal data errors. If the survey is completed online, data are automatically converted into a file for processing by an electronic spreadsheet or statistical software program. This type of survey can easily be administered on a yearly basis to a random sample of the school community population. If the survey is administered over several years, the school or district administrators will have ready access to trend data that could track any changes in parent or community attitudes. The results of such a survey can be distributed as a formal report in print form or on the Internet, or informally as a discussion item at a school board or meeting.

Figure 7-1   Excerpt from a survey designed for assessing family, school, and community relations.

	Strongly Agree	Agree	Neutral	Disagree	Strongly Disagree
1. A committee of parents and staff members makes the decisions about ways to involve all families in children's learning.	○	○	○	○	○
2. District policy promotes family involvement in school.	○	○	○	○	○
3. The school communicates its family involvement policy to parents.	○	○	○	○	○
4. Parents know when and where school committees meet.	○	○	○	○	○
5. Parents feel welcome to make comments at school meetings.	○	○	○	○	○
-----					
28. Volunteers feel appreciated and recognized by the school.	○	○	○	○	○
29. The school distributes information about community programs for families.	○	○	○	○	○

Source: From characteristics of successful schools—survey questions for family-school-community partnerships, North Central Regional Educational Laboratory. Retrieved August 1, 2003, from http://goal/ncrel.org/winss/sampques.asp?intCategoryID=1006

ANATOMY OF A SURVEY

In a book titled *The Psychology of Survey Response*, Tourangeau, Basinski, and Rips (2000) have a chapter called "The Anatomy of a Survey." This is the most appropriate description of how one or more individuals might approach the design of a survey. A survey, like the structural makeup of an organism, has several parts that need to work together in order to function properly.

The broad-based survey described in the previous section is relatively easy to administer and is readily available. In contrast, the design of a survey to collect community opinions about such things as starting or eliminating an academic program, expanding or reducing an after-school activity, student access to technology, or the quality of counseling services, requires customization and careful analysis of both content and format. The following case study illustrates how a survey might be developed and used.

Richter Park High School is an urban school located in the northeastern part of the United States; the school has approximately 2,300 students. In 2004, Richter Park considered a plan to infuse technology into its programs and operations. A committee, which included members from the school district office, had been discussing this initiative for about 8 months. Although Richter Park was the focus of the discussions, the district superintendent saw the need for a broader initiative for the entire district.

Several of the academic programs at Richter Park make significant use of technology through computer workstations located in computer laboratories, the library, and classrooms. The plan under consideration would make greater use of the Internet to connect the school to students, parents, and the community. For example, teachers and tutors could be available to students through e-mail; parents would be notified of any concerns or questions regarding their children through e-mail. To help defray some of the costs, a major private foundation had been approached. The foundation indicated interest in providing initial start-up funds to purchase and upgrade equipment in the school; however, ongoing costs would have to be absorbed by the school district. At one point, the school board considered implementing a laptop-for-every-student program, but the board found that the ongoing costs for support and upgrades would be prohibitive. The argument of the staff was that many students had access to the Internet in their homes. There was concern, however about a "digital divide" within the school's population; that is, many children from poor and immigrant families might not have Internet access except at school. During one committee meeting, a decision was made to survey the community.

In designing any survey, two key questions must be answered:

* Who will participate in the survey?
* What data are to be collected?

Who Will Participate in the Survey?

The committee decided that both parents and students would participate in the survey in some way. Students would be given the survey at school to take home; responses would be completed for the household and signed off by a parent or guardian. A stratified random sample of the students and their families at Richter Park was selected to participate in the survey. The total Richter Park school population was stratified by gender, income, and English language learner (ELL) status (see Figure 7-2). The committee decided not to ask for income data, because some parents might consider this sensitive information. The superintendent indicated that income data could be obtained from the district's student information system.

In any survey design, a major decision is the size of the sample. An appropriate sample size is 10% to 20% as long as controls (e.g., stratified sample) have been put into place to ensure that the sample represents the larger population. The committee decided that 10% of the students and their families would be sufficiently representative of the total Richter Park High School population. The fact that the survey was being given to students by name maximized the probability of a good return.

When the question of anonymity arose, the committee decided that because technology information is not particularly sensitive, parents or guardians would not have

Figure 7-2 Stratified random sample for Richter Park High School. ELL = English language learner.

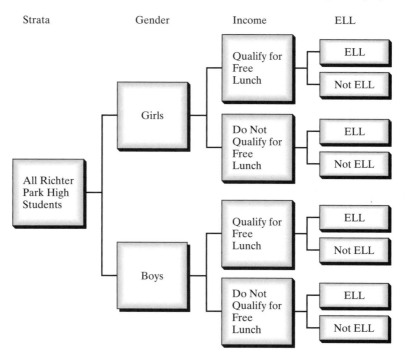

a problem with being identified when answering the survey. Identification of the participants also made it easier to collect reliable data (e.g., income level, ethnicity) from the school district's student information system and to conduct a meaningful follow-up survey at a later date, if needed.

What Data Will Be Collected?

The data to be collected focused on the following aspects of technology:

* Access or lack of access to the Internet in the home
* Speed of access
* Type of equipment
* Typical uses of the Internet by children
* Future plans to acquire or improve access to the Internet

After several meetings that included the members from the district office, the committee agreed on the format and content of the survey (see Figure 7-3). The superintendent secured approval from the board of education to conduct this survey. The committee decided to include a covering letter from the principal, Sandra Patterson. This letter would briefly describe the purpose of the survey to allay any concerns from the students or parents.

Figure 7-3   Richter Park High School access to technology survey.

Richter Park High School
Technology Survey

Dear <Student First Name>:

You and your family have been selected to participate in a survey about technology use in your home. This survey will only be used to help our high school plan for the future technology needs of all of our students. Please have your parent or guardian complete the questions in this survey as best he or she can. If you or your parent or guardian have any questions, feel free to contact either Ms. Laura Kelly or Ms. Yvonne Vasquez in the school office at: 212 772-4666.

Thank you for your help in this important project.

Sandra Patterson
Principal
_____

Student name: _____

Name of the person completing this survey: _____

Relationship to the student of the person completing this survey:

Father: _____ Mother: _____ Guardian: _____

1. Does the student named above have access to a computer outside of Richter Park High School?

   Yes: _____ No: _____

   If no, please go to Question 8. If yes, continue on to Question 2.

2. Where does the student have access to a computer?

   At home: _____   At the public library: _____   At a community center: _____

   Other (Please Specify): _____

   If the student does not have access to a computer at home, please go to Question 8; otherwise, go to Question 3.

3. What manufacturer/brand of computer do you have in your home? Check all that apply if you have more than one computer.

   Dell: _____   IBM: _____   Compaq: _____   Apple: _____   Gateway: _____

   Other (Please Specify): _____

4. How old is the computer (or main computer if you have more than one) that you have in your home?

   Less than 1 year: _____   1–3 years: _____   More than 3 years: _____

5. Do you have Internet access for the computer (or main computer if you have more than one) in your home?

   Yes: _____ No: _____

Figure 7-3 *(continued)*

If yes, what type of Internet access do you have?

Dial-Up: _____   DSL: _____   Cable Modem: _____   Wireless: _____   Other: _____

6. How often does the student named above use a computer in your home?

Several times a day: _____ Once a day: _____ Once a week: _____

Other (please specify): _____

7. Does the student use a computer mainly for:

School work: _____   Social activities: _____   Games: _____   Other: _____

Please go to Question 10.

8. If you do not have a computer in your home now, do you have any plans to purchase one in the immediate future?

Yes: _____ No: _____

9. Would you like any assistance or help in selecting a computer?

Yes: _____ No: _____

10. Do you have any suggestions for how Richter Park High School can use technology in its academic programs or to communicate with you? (Use the reverse side if you need more space.)

_____

_____

_____

_____

_____

11. Would you like to be invited to a meeting to discuss further how Richter Park High School can use technology in its programs or to communicate with you?

Yes: _____ No: _____

Thank you again for participating in this survey. Please mail the completed survey in the envelope enclosed. Again, if you have any questions or wish to speak to anyone about this survey, please contact Ms. Kelly or Ms. Vasquez in the school office at: 212 772-4666.

During the committee's discussions, one of the high school counselors asked whether the survey could be used to provide guidance to parents regarding appropriate uses of the Internet by children. The committee decided to keep the survey simple and suggested that the counselor's idea might be the subject of a pamphlet sent home with all students at a later date. Before administering the full survey, a pilot test was conducted with 20 students and their parents. All of these surveys were returned promptly, and several small changes were made to the questions. For example, the possible answers to Question 2 were expanded to include a community center.

DATA ANALYSIS

For purposes of data analysis, a file layout and coding scheme were designed (see Figure 7-4). The data file layout contained data fields from two sources: the school

Figure 7-4 Technology use survey data file layout and coding scheme. SIS = student information system.

Data field	Source	Coding scheme
Student ID	SIS	
Student last name	SIS	
Gender	SIS	1=female, 2=male
Grade level	SIS	1=freshman, 2=sophomore 3=junior, 4=senior
Hispanic/Latino ethnicity	SIS	1=yes, 2=no
Race	SIS	U.S. Department of Education code
Qualify for free lunch	SIS	1=yes, 2=no
English language learner	SIS	1=yes, 2=no
Special education indicator	SIS	1=yes, 2=no
Name of person completing survey	Survey	
Relationship of person completing survey	Survey	1=father, 2=mother, 3=guardian
Q1—Student Access	Survey	1=yes, 2=no
Q2—Where student has access	Survey	1=home, 2=public library, 3=community center, 4=other
Q3—Brand of computer	Survey	1=Dell, 2=IBM, 3=Compaq, 4=Apple, 5=Gateway, 6=Other
Q4—Age of computer	Survey	1=less than 1 year, 2=1–3 years, 3=more than 3 years
Q5A—Internet access	Survey	1=yes, 2=no
Q5B—Level of access	Survey	1=dial-Up, 2=DSL, 3=cable modem, 4=wireless, 5=other
Q6—Frequency of use	Survey	1=several times per day; 2=once a day; 3=once a week
Q7—Purpose of student use	Survey	1=school work, 2=social activities, 3=games, 4=other
Q8—Future purchase plans	Survey	1=yes, 2=no
Q9—Assistance	Survey	1=yes, 2=no
Q10—Attend a meeting	Survey	1=yes, 2=no

district's student information system and the survey. The school district's coding schemes-were used where appropriate. Data collected from the survey were coded using simple numeric codes. The data file was then constructed by downloading the data from the school district's information system and appending the survey results through individual data entry.

To perform the data analyses, the Statistical Package for the Social Sciences (SPSS) was used. A spreadsheet such as Excel could have been used, but SPSS has greater facility in dealing with certain statistical procedures that are helpful for data disaggregation (e.g., contingency tables or crosstabulations).

Figure 7-5 is the SPSS file layout (Variable View) used for data analysis of the survey. SPSS uses the term *variable* to refer to a data field. The SPSS layout corresponds exactly to the data file layout defined in Figure 7-4. Figure 7-6 shows a portion of the SPSS actual file (Data View) containing the survey data used in the data analysis.

Is the Sample Representative of the High School Population?

The first stage of data analysis determines if the returned surveys are representative of the total population. Of the 230 surveys (10% of the total Richter Park High School population) distributed, 212 surveys (92%) were returned—a very good response rate. To make sure that the responses were representative of the total high school population, several simple statistical procedures were conducted. Proportions of three variables in the total population were compared with the survey sample population.

School and school district records indicated the following proportions in the total Richter Park High School population:

* Females = 53%; males = 47%.
* Students qualifying for free lunch = 35%; students not qualifying = 65%.
* ELL students = 31%; non-ELL students = 69%.

For the survey responses, frequency distributions were generated by the SPSS program for three variables: gender, qualify for free lunch, and ELL. The data in Figure 7-7 indicate those proportions:

* Females = 52.4%; males = 47.6%.
* Students qualifying for free lunch = 32.5%; students not qualifying = 67.5%.
* ELL students = 28.3%; non-ELL students = 71.7%.

A comparison of the percentage distribution of the three variables in the survey responses with the distribution in the total population indicates that the sample population was representative. If there were any doubts, additional comparisons could be conducted based on other variables such as race or grade level. In addition, a statistical procedure called the chi-square test could be

Figure 7-5   SPSS data file layout for the Richter Park High School survey.

	Name	Type	Width	Decimals	Label
1	id	Numeric	8	0	
2	name	String	10	0	
3	gender	Numeric	1	0	Gender
4	grade	Numeric	1	0	Grade
5	ethnic	Numeric	2	0	Ethnicity
6	race	Numeric	1	0	Race
7	lunch	Numeric	1	0	Free Lunch
8	ell	Numeric	1	0	ELL
9	speceduc	Numeric	1	0	Special Ed
10	person	String	10	0	
11	complete	Numeric	1	0	Person Completing Survey
12	access	Numeric	1	0	Student Access
13	location	Numeric	1	0	Location
14	brand	Numeric	1	0	Computer Brand
15	age	Numeric	1	0	Age of Computer
16	internet	Numeric	1	0	Internet Access
17	level	Numeric	1	0	Level of Internet Access
18	frequenc	Numeric	1	0	Frequency of Use
19	activity	Numeric	1	0	Type of Activity
20	future	Numeric	1	0	Future Plans
21	assist	Numeric	1	0	Need Assistance
22	meeting	Numeric	1	0	Attend a Meeting

For the actual data set for Figure 7-5, go to the Companion Website at
www.//prenhall.com/picciano

conducted in SPSS to determine if the differences between the sample and total population were statistically significant. For example, say the percentage distribution of the gender variable indicated that females equaled 57% of the survey population and males equaled 43%. The chi-square statistical procedure could be conducted to determine if this distribution was statistically different

Figure 7-6 Sample data records for the Richter Park High School survey.

	id	name	gender	grade	ethnic	race	lunch	ell	speceduc
1	66367366		1	1	2	5	2	2	2
2	36664765		1	2	2	2	2	2	2
3	33222211		2	1	2	5	2	2	2
4	23234444		2	3	2	2	2	2	2
5	33245643		1	4	2	3	2	2	2
6	12212556		2	4	2	3	1	2	2
7	43335678		2	2	1	5	1	1	2
8	23234444		1	3	2	2	2	2	2
9	33245643		1	4	2	3	2	2	2
10	12212556		2	4	2	3	2	2	2
11	93335678		1	2	1	5	1	1	2
12	23234444		2	3	2	5	2	2	2
13	44443323		1	4	2	3	2	2	2
14	12232786		1	4	2	3	1	2	2
15	10038837		1	2	1	5	1	1	1
16	74477321		1	1	1	5	1	2	2
17	28846579		2	3	1	5	2	1	1
18	87336478		1	1	1	5	1	1	2
19	34409876		1	1	1	5	2	2	2
20	12234677		2	2	2	5	2	2	2
21	13342345		1	1	2	5	2	2	2
22	66367366		2	1	2	5	2	2	2

from the total population where females equaled 52.4% and males equaled 47.6%. If the procedure indicated that there was a statistically significant difference, the results of the survey would have to be questioned as perhaps not being representative of the larger population.

Do Students Have Access to the Internet?

A major purpose for conducting this survey was to determine if the students at Richter Park High School and their parents had access to the Internet in their homes. Figure 7-8 is a frequency distribution for the variable Student Access (Question 1 of the survey). Results indicate 71.7% of the students have access outside of Richter Park and 28.3% do not have access. The percentage of students who do not have access was substantial, so further analysis was done to learn more about the sample population.

Figure 7-7 Frequency distribution of gender, qualify for free lunch, and English language learner (ELL).

Gender

		Frequency	Percent	Valid Percent	Cumulative Percent
Valid	Female	111	52.4	52.4	52.4
	Male	101	47.6	47.6	100.0
	Total	212	100.0	100.0	

Free Lunch

		Frequency	Percent	Valid Percent	Cumulative Percent
Valid	Yes	69	32.5	32.5	32.5
	No	143	67.5	67.5	100.0
	Total	212	100.0	100.0	

ELL

		Frequency	Percent	Valid Percent	Cumulative Percent
Valid	Yes	60	28.3	28.3	28.3
	No	152	71.7	71.7	100.0
	Total	212	100.0	100.0	

Figure 7-8 Frequency distribution of student access to technology.

Student Access

		Frequency	Percent	Valid Percent	Cumulative Percent
Valid	Yes	152	71.7	71.7	71.7
	No	60	28.3	28.3	100.0
	Total	212	100.0	100.0	

Figure 7-9 is a crosstabulation of the variables Student Access and qualify for free lunch. Students who qualify for the U.S. federal government's free lunch program are considered to be members of low-income families. This is a standard measure maintained by all school districts. The data in Figure 7-9 indicate that 40.6% of the students who qualify for free lunch have access to computer technology outside of Richter Park High School, whereas 86.7% of the students who do not qualify for free lunch have access.

Figure 7-10 is a crosstabulation of the variables Student Access and ELL. Students who are designated as ELL come from families where the home language is not English and receive additional services to learn English. Typically, students designated as ELL include large percentages of recent immigrants. The data in Figure 7-10 indicate that 51.7% of ELL students have access to computer technology outside of Richter Park High School, whereas 79.6% of the non-ELL students have access.

Figure 7-9 Crosstabulation of student access by qualify for free lunch.

Student Access * Free Lunch Crosstabulation					
			Free Lunch		
			Yes	No	Total
Student Access Yes		Count	28	124	152
		% within Student Access	18.4%	81.6%	100.0%
		% within Free Lunch	40.6%	86.7%	71.7%
		% of Total	13.2%	58.5%	71.7%
	No	Count	41	19	60
		% within Student Access	68.3%	31.7%	100.0%
		% within Free Lunch	59.4%	13.3%	28.3%
		% of Total	19.3%	9.0%	28.3%
Total		Count	69	143	212
		% within Student Access	32.5%	67.5%	100.0%
		% within Free Lunch	100.0%	100.0%	100.0%
		% of Total	32.5%	67.5%	100.0%

Figure 7-10 Crosstabulation of student access by English language learner (ELL).

Student Access * ELL Crosstabulation					
			ELL		
			Yes	No	Total
Student Access Yes		Count	31	121	152
		% within Student Access	20.4%	79.6%	100.0%
		% within ELL	51.7%	79.6%	71.7%
		% of Total	14.6%	57.1%	71.7%
	No	Count	29	31	60
		% within Student Access	48.3%	51.7%	100.0%
		% within ELL	48.3%	20.4%	28.3%
		% of Total	13.7%	14.6%	28.3%
Total		Count	60	152	212
		% within Student Access	28.3%	71.7%	100.0%
		% within ELL	100.0%	100.0%	100.0%
		% of Total	28.3%	71.7%	100.0%

Figure 7-11 is a crosstabulation of the variables Student Access and ethnicity (Hispanic/Latino). Because Hispanic/Latino students compose the largest ethnic group in Richter Park, the data file was constructed to include an identification variable for this group. The data in Figure 7-11 indicate that 38.9% of Hispanic/Latino students have access to computer technology outside of Richter Park High School, whereas 88.6% of the non-Hispanic/Latino students have access.

Figure 7-11 Crosstabulation of student access by ethnicity.

Student Access * Ethnicity Crosstabulation			Ethnicity		
			Hispanic/ Latino	Non-Hispanic/ Latino	Total
Student Access Yes		Count	28	124	152
		% within Student Access	18.4%	81.6%	100.0%
		% within Ethnicity	38.9%	88.6%	71.7%
		% of Total	13.2%	58.5%	71.7%
	No	Count	44	16	60
		% within Student Access	73.3%	26.7%	100.0%
		% within Ethnicity	61.1%	11.4%	28.3%
		% of Total	20.8%	7.5%	28.3%
Total		Count	72	140	212
		% within Student Access	34.0%	66.0%	100.0%
		% within Ethnicity	100.0%	100.0%	100.0%
		% of Total	34.0%	66.0%	100.0%

The overlap among students who are designated ELL, who qualify for free lunch, and are of Hispanic/Latino ethnic background (91.7%) can be seen in Figure 7-12. Data from the survey indicate that a substantial percentage of students who do not have access to technology are poor, of Hispanic/Latino ethnicity, and designated as ELL. Indeed, a digital divide does exist within the population at Richter Park High School.

THE COMMITTEE'S NEXT STEPS

The committee continued to analyze and review additional data from the survey in order to develop a recommendation for infusing technology into the programs at Richter Park High School. The committee was able to determine that a number of students who did have access to computers did not have access in their homes. Figure 7-13 illustrates that small percentages of students without home access had access at a public library (7.9%) or a local community center (5.3%). Of the total survey population, 132 students (62%) had access to computers in their homes. Of these, all had access to the Internet, 95% used their computers several times each day, and 72.7% indicated that they used their computers primarily for school work. One committee member suggested that a grade point average comparison be done between students who had access to computers in their homes and those who did not. The principal, Ms. Patterson, noted that other factors, such as the large number

Figure 7-12 Crosstabulation of qualify for free lunch by ethnicity, controlling for English language learner (ELL).

				Ethnicity		
				Hispanic/ Latino	Non-Hispanic/ Latino	Total
ELL						
Yes	Free Lunch	Yes	Count	44	4	48
			% within Free Lunch	91.7%	8.3%	100.0%
			% within Ethnicity	83.0%	57.1%	80.0%
			% of Total	73.3%	6.7%	80.0%
		No	Count	9	3	12
			% within Free Lunch	75.0%	25.0%	100.0%
			% within Ethnicity	17.0%	42.9%	20.0%
			% of Total	15.0%	5.0%	20.0%
	Total		Count	53	7	60
			% within Free Lunch	88.3%	11.7%	100.0%
			% within Ethnicity	100.0%	100.0%	100.0%
			% of Total	88.3%	11.7%	100.0%
No	Free Lunch	Yes	Count	9	12	21
			% within Free Lunch	42.9%	57.1%	100.0%
			% within Ethnicity	47.4%	9.0%	13.8%
			% of Total	5.9%	7.9%	13.8%
		No	Count	10	121	131
			% within Free Lunch	7.6%	92.4%	100.0%
			% within Ethnicity	52.6%	91.0%	86.2%
			% of Total	6.6%	79.6%	86.2%
	Total		Count	19	133	152
			% within Free Lunch	12.5%	87.5%	100.0%
			% within Ethnicity	100.0%	100.0%	100.0%
			% of Total	12.5%	87.5%	100.0%

*Table title: Free Lunch * Ethnicity * ELL Crosstabulation*

Figure 7-13 Location of computers for students with access.

		Frequency	Percent	Valid Percent	Cumulative Percent
Valid	Home	132	86.8	86.8	86.8
	Public library	12	7.9	7.9	94.7
	Community center	8	5.3	5.3	100.0
	Total	152	100.0	100.0	

Table title: Location

of ELL students who did not have access to technology, would skew the results. In continuing its deliberations, the committee also met with parents in the community. Specifically, the committee invited the small group of parents who had indicated on the survey (Question 11) that they would be willing to attend such meetings.

The committee finally issued a report in which it laid out a plan for infusing technology into Richter Park High School, including extended connections to the students' homes. The committee also made these recommendations:

1. The library, which houses a large computer center, should remain open until 7:00 p.m. each evening to allow students greater access to its computer equipment and other facilities. In addition, weekend hours should be considered.

2. Data about student access to technology should be added to the district's student information system and be collected and updated on a regular basis along with other student demographic data.

3. Parents of students without access to technology should continue to be contacted by telephone or other means. Additional tutoring support should be provided to ELL students and students who qualify for free lunch.

4. The district office should provide advice and assistance to parents who wish to purchase computers for their homes. A pamphlet describing appropriate equipment and desirable use of technology in the home will be developed and distributed to all students.

5. A group student-discount policy with a major local computer retailer should be explored, in addition to the group discounts that already exist with two computer manufacturers.

When the report was issued, the committee held an open meeting with the community to discuss its recommendations. More than 300 parents attended the meeting; more than attended any other open meeting held that year.

SUMMARY

Survey research is one way to involve the community in decision making in a school district. The case study of Richter Park High School illustrated how to design, develop, and conduct a survey. A committee, which included members of the school district office, wanted to determine if students and their families have access to computer technology. The committee decided to survey the school community, and a stratified random sample was drawn from the total Richter Park High School population. After several meetings, the committee agreed on the format and content of the survey. Students and parents participated in the survey.

The Statistical Package for the Social Sciences was used to perform data analysis, which determined that the survey sample was representative of the total student population. Survey results indicated that although a majority of the students had access to technology at home, a disproportionate number of low-income, Hispanic/Latino, and ELL students did not have access. On the basis of survey results, the committee charged with making recommendations for infusing technology into the curriculum recommended greater access to Richter Park's computer facilities and more tutoring services for low-income, Hispanic/Latino, and ELL populations.

Activities

1. Visit a district office or school and meet with an administrator (e.g., superintendent, assistant superintendent, principal). Ask if they have ever used survey research to gather data from the community. Specifically ask who designed the survey and who interpreted and reported the results. Also ask how decisions were affected by the findings.
2. Assume you are a principal of a high school and you are considering implementing a new extended-day program. Because of overcrowding, your school is faced with the possibility of expanding the school day from 8:30 a.m.–3:00 p.m. to 8:00 a.m.–5:00 p.m. You have been chairing a committee that is reviewing this issue and a suggestion has been made to conduct a survey of the various stakeholders. You are favorably disposed to the idea. Develop a proposal to conduct a survey; be sure to include (1) who will participate in the survey, (2) what data will be collected, and (3) a sample of the survey. Describe in some detail the process you would use and the issues that might arise in developing the survey.

References

Brown, J. S., & Dugard, F. (2000). *The social life of information*. Boston, MA: Harvard Business School Press.

Gallagher, D. R., Bagin, D., & Kindred, L. W. (2004). *School and community relations* (8th ed.). Boston, MA: Allyn & Bacon.

Hooper, C. (2001, August). School community relationships: A vital lifeline. In *The School Administrator* Web Edition. Retrieved August 1, 2003, http://www.aasa.org/publications/sa/2001_08/prezcorner.htm

Tourangeau, R., Basinski, K., & Rips, L. (2000). *The psychology of survey response*. New York, NY: Cambridge University Press.

Wisconsin Department of Public Instruction. (2003). *Characteristics of Successful Schools*. Retrieved August 6, 2003, from http://www.dpi.stato.wi.us/dpi/dlsea/sit/cssindey.html

Chapter 8

Financial Management and Budgeting

In the previous chapter's case study of Richter Park High School, the school board rejected a laptop-for-every-student program because the ongoing costs for support and upgrades were deemed to be unaffordable. In a November 2003 issue of *Education Week,* Trotter (2003) reported that a number of school districts throughout the country were having second thoughts about participating in similar laptop initiatives. School districts in Maine, Michigan, Washington, and South Carolina had decided not to participate in state-sponsored programs or to withdraw from programs they had already started. Too often, policymakers invest significant resources on initial funding without considering future costs. For many technology programs, ongoing costs for staff support, training, repairs, and upgrades frequently equal if not exceed the start-up costs. This scenario provides an appropriate introduction to this chapter, which examines data-driven decision making in school budgeting.

BASIC TERMINOLOGY

The purpose of this section is not to provide an in-depth tutorial on school finance but to present several key definitions and terms that will make it easier to understand the chapter material. For a more in-depth review of the basics of school finance, refer to Ray, Candoli, and Hack (2004), Droms (2003), or Brimley and Garfield (2002). School finance and budgeting have a language of their own. Although the basic concepts are not difficult to learn, terms such as *GASB, encumbrance accounting,* and *OTPS* have little meaning in everyday life. Yet, when one assumes responsibility for leading a school organization, familiarity with such terms is imperative. Budgeting is integrally tied to sound educational planning. Goals and objectives must relate to spending and vice versa. Furthermore, without an understanding of the available financial resources, an educational leader will have difficulty moving the school or district forward.

The best, simple definition of a budget is a financial plan. Brimley and Garfield (2002) formally define a budget as

> a financial plan that involves four elements:
>
> 1. planning
> 2. receiving funds
> 3. spending funds
> 4. evaluating results
>
> all performed within the limits of a predetermined time. (p. 294)

A budget based on this definition becomes a plan for using one's resources wisely and effectively. School districts and states are free to develop their own approaches to budget administration, but standards do exist, most notably, those of the Government Accounting Standards Board (GASB) and the Financial Accounting for Local and State School Systems. Most school districts follow one of these two standards and vary them slightly to fit their own situations.

A most important concept in school and public finance is encumbrance accounting. All monies that are to be expended must first be encumbered. An **encumbrance** is a commitment or contract to pay for goods or services. An encumbrance may take the form of a written purchase order for goods or a contract with a vendor or employee to perform a service. Upon receipt of the goods or services, an expenditure is authorized for paying the vendor or employee. Most important to the concept of encumbrance accounting is the commitment. Once a commitment has been made, monies must be set aside in anticipation of the delivery of the goods or services and may not be used for other purposes.

In this chapter, different accounting categories or descriptions will be presented. The two most important categories are **personnel services** (PS) and **other than personnel services** (OTPS). Personnel services refer to expenditures for full-time or part-time employees. OTPS refers to things such as supplies, textbooks, equipment, and contracts to repair or to replace facilities.

Funds for schools come from several sources. The federal government, the states, and local school districts are the most important funding groups. In addition, gifts and grants are common sources of funding. In most cases, strict rules are observed with regard to the administration of these funds. Generally, there is not to be any commingling of **tax-levy funds** (from taxes levied on citizens) and **non-tax-levy funds** (from private individuals, corporations, or special-purpose government programs).

SCHOOL DISTRICT BUDGET

Each year the 15,000 school districts in the United States navigate a budget process during which school administrators, locally elected officials, and school board members develop and approve an operating budget for the subsequent year. This process is critical to every school's operation and generally involves many hours of meetings and discussions with stakeholders. Proposals and initiatives are evaluated, revenues are adjusted, and decisions are made about what will be funded.

Typically, a working draft of a budget (see Figure 8-1) is developed, then adjusted during the budget process. Figure 8-1 is in electronic spreadsheet format and

Figure 8-1   Working draft of Glenn Fall Central School District budget.

	A	B	C	D	E	F
1		Glenn Fall Central School District No. 1				
2		Proposed School District Budget				
3		2005-2006			3-Feb-05	
4						
5		2004-2005	2004-2005	2005-2006	Approved vs.	
6		Estimated	Approved	Proposed	Proposed Budget	
7	Category	Expend. ($)	Budget ($)	Budget ($)	Change ($)	
8	Personnel - Salaries	$43,056,986	$44,220,000	$45,100,000	$880,000	
9	Personnel Fringe Benefits	12,301,242	12,450,000	12,950,000	500,000	
10	Non-Personnel (OTPS)	11,256,432	10,500,000	11,500,000	1,000,000	
11	Debt Service	7,100,000	7,200,000	7,000,000	-200,000	
12	Totals	$73,714,660	$74,370,000	$76,550,000	$2,180,000	
13						
14						
15		Revenue Projection				
16		2005-2006				
17		2004-2005	2004-2005	2005-2006	Approved vs.	
18		Estimated	Approved	Anticipated	Anticipated Revenue	
19	Category	Revenue ($)	Revenue ($)	Revenue ($)	Change ($)	
20	Local Taxes	$45,956,788	$45,950,000	$47,900,000	$1,950,000	
21	State Aid	26,667,990	26,950,000	27,200,000	250,000	
22	Miscellaneous	645,500	620,000	650,000	30,000	
23	Fund Balance	550,000	550,000	500,000	-50,000	
24	Debt Service Transfers	300,000	300,000	300,000	0	
25	Totals	$74,120,278	$74,370,000	$76,550,000	$2,180,000	

For the actual data set for Figure 8-1, go to the Companion Website at
www.//prenhall.com/picciano

represents the basic information needed to start the budget development process. The four columns show (1) estimated current (2004–2005) expenditures and revenues, (2) current approved budget and revenues, (3) proposed (2005–2006) budget and revenues, and (4) the dollar change between what was approved and what is being proposed. Why the need for the first column showing *estimated* expenditures and revenues? The budget development process generally starts 5 to 6 months earlier than the beginning of the budget year, so the current year expenditures and revenues are still evolving. In this case, the budget year starts on July 1, 2005, and the working draft was developed on February 3, 2005, hence 5 months of activity remain in the current year. As a result, end-year expenditures and revenues need to be estimated.

The early part of the budget development cycle focuses decision making on the revenue projections. As indicated earlier in this chapter, funding for the school district can come from a number of different sources (state, local, and federal governments). Each of these sources may be going through a similar budget development process in which ongoing decisions are being made that will effect the funding provided to school districts. Most school districts can control and therefore project with fair accuracy funding from local tax sources. In contrast, projecting funding from outside the district, especially the state, is more difficult. Also, many of the funds provided by the federal government are generally distributed first to the states for subsequent distribution to school districts. For many school districts, the state contribution drives key elements of the budget decision making process. Therefore, school districts must adjust up or down as state governing bodies make their decisions.

Because of these uncertainties during the early phase of the budget development process, school district administrators frequently ask what-if questions. Use of an electronic spreadsheet allows for testing what-if possibilities over and over as the process continues and projections become more refined. One helpful technique is to establish early on the outside limits for the part of the budget that is most difficult to project. Figure 8-2 depicts the working draft presented in Figure 8-1 with two columns added to provide low-end and high-end projections for the state aid portion of the budget. Inclusion of the two projections provides decision makers with a constant reminder of the parameters of the budget. As the state portion of the budget becomes clearer, these projections can be adjusted depending on local circumstances. School district administrators must ensure that the data are carefully collected and monitored over a period of time and that decisions are made accordingly.

In the budget draft shown in Figure 8-2, the difference in state aid between the best-case and worst-case scenarios does not effect the budget bottom line. Why not? In this example, a projected change in local taxes makes up for any differences in state aid. This may or may not be a palatable option, depending on local circumstances. It is a direction many school district administrators would consider, however, given that most local school districts in the United States raise revenues through

Figure 8-2 Working draft with two revenue projections for Glenn Fall Central School District budget.

	A	B	C	D	E	F	G	H
1		Glenn Fall Central School District No. 1						
2		Proposed School District Budget						
3			2005-2006				3-Feb-05	
4					State Aid Increase $1.25M	No Increase in State Aid		
5								
6		2004-2005	2004-2005	2005-2006	Approved vs.	2005-2006	Approved vs.	
7		Estimated	Approved	Proposed	Proposed Budget	Proposed	Proposed Budget	
8	Category	Expend. ($)	Budget ($)	Budget ($)	Change ($)	Budget ($)	Change ($)	
9	Personnel Salaries	$43,056,986	$44,220,000	$45,100,000	$880,000	$46,100,000	$1,880,000	
10	Personnel Fringe Benefits	12,301,242	12,450,000	12,950,000	500,000	12,950,000	$500,000	
11	Non-Personnel (OTPS)	11,256,432	10,500,000	11,500,000	1,000,000	10,500,000	$0	
12	Debt Service	7,100,000	7,200,000	7,000,000	-200,000	7,000,000	-$200,000	
13	Totals	$73,714,660	$74,370,000	$76,550,000	$2,180,000	$76,550,000	$2,180,000	
14								
15								
16		Revenue Projection						
17		2005-2006						
18		2004-2005	2004-2005	2005-2006	Approved vs.	2005-2006	Approved vs.	
19		Estimated	Approved	Anticipated	Anticipated Revenue	Anticipated	Anticipated Revenue	
20	Category	Revenue ($)	Revenue($)	Revenue ($)	Change ($)	Revenue ($)	Change ($)	
21	Local Taxes	$45,956,788	$45,950,000	$46,900,000	$950,000	$48,150,000	$2,200,000	
22	State Aid	26,667,990	26,950,000	28,200,000	1,250,000	26,950,000	$0	
23	Miscellaneous	645,500	620,000	650,000	30,000	650,000	$30,000	
24	Fund Balance	550,000	550,000	500,000	-50,000	500,000	-$50,000	
25	Debt Service Transfers	300,000	300,000	300,000	0	300,000	$0	
26	Totals	$74,120,278	$74,370,000	$76,550,000	$2,180,000	$76,550,000	$2,180,000	
27								

For the actual data set for Figure 8-2, go to the Companion Website at
www.//prenhall.com/picciano

property taxes. The bottom line might also represent a budget ceiling or floor that cannot be exceeded or reduced.

During the budget development cycle, most school districts hold public meetings where parents, residents, and other stakeholders can provide input into decisions. At such meetings, attendees need as much information as possible. The data provided in Figure 8-2 are a good staring point. A simple pie chart (see Figure 8-3) is also useful for conveying budget data.

Figure 8-3 Pie chart of the proposed budget for the Glenn Fall Central School District.

Glenn Fall Central School District Proposed Budget
2005–2006

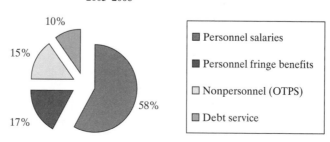

As the budget becomes more definite during the development cycle, more work is done on the budget details. Figure 8-4 provides further information on the proposed budget for the Glenn Fall School District. Note how each budget category (personnel services, fringe benefits, other than personnel services) is further defined.

Figure 8-4 Glenn Fall Central School District budget with detailed budget categories.

	A	B	C
1	**Glenn Fall Central School District No. 1**		
2	**Proposed School District Budget**		
3	**2005–2006**		
4	**Budget Category**	**Allocation**	
5	Personnel Services		
6	Salaries		
7	Teaching Staff	$29,500,000	
8	Student Support Staff	6,200,000	
9	Administrative Staff	1,900,000	
10	Plant Maintenance Staff	7,500,000	
11	SubTotal Personnel	$45,100,000	
12			
13	Fringe Benefits		
14	Health and Dental	7,500,000	
15	Retirement	1,700,000	
16	Other	3,750,000	
17	SubTotal Fringe Benefits	$12,950,000	
18	SubTotal Personnel Services	$58,050,000	
19			
20	Other Than Personnel Services		
21	Teaching Supplies/Equipment	2,600,000	
22	Student Services Supplies/ Equipment	700,000	
23	Administrative Supplies/Equipment	900,000	
24	Plant Maint. Supplies/Equipment	950,000	
25	Contractural Services	2,100,000	
26	Transportation	1,500,000	
27	Utilities	1,600,000	
28	Insurance	400,000	
29	Interfund Transfers	750,000	
30	Subtotal Other Than Personnel Services	$11,500,000	
31	Debt Service	7,000,000	
32	Total Budget	$76,550,000	

For the actual data set for Figure 8-4, go to the Companion Website at **www.//prenhall.com/picciano**

Figure 8-5 Lake Harbor School proposed budget.

	A	B	C	D	E
1		The Lake Harbor School			
2		Proposed School Budget			
3		2005-2006			1-Jul-05
4		2004-2005	2004-2005	2005-2006	Approved vs.
5		Estimated	Approved	Proposed	Proposed Budget
6		Expend. ($)	Budget ($)	Budget ($)	Change ($)
7	Category				
8	Personnel Services				
9	Teaching Staff	$1,101,966	$1,100,000	$1,200,000	$100,000
10	Student Support Staff	144,875	150,000	160,000	10,000
11	Administrative Staff	236,990	240,000	250,000	10,000
12	Plant Maintenance Staff	212,000	210,000	240,000	30,000
13	Part-Time Staff	79,777	75,000	80,000	5,000
14	SubTotal Personnel	$1,775,608	$1,775,000	$1,930,000	$155,000
15					
16	Other Than Personnel Services				
17	Teaching Supplies/Equipment	$200,667	$200,000	$210,000	$10,000
18	Student Services Supplies/ Equipment	18,990	18,000	20,000	2,000
19	Administrative Supplies/Equipment	18,900	18,000	20,000	2,000
20	Plant Maint. Supplies/Equipment	89,900	90,000	90,000	0
21	Subtotal Other Than Personnel Services	$328,457	$326,000	$340,000	$14,000
22	Total Budget	$2,104,065	$2,101,000	$2,270,000	$169,000

For the actual data set for Figure 6-1, go to the Companion Website at
www.//prenhall.com/picciano

The budget development cycle typically concludes when residents vote to approve or disapprove the school district's budget. In the case of the Glenn Fall Central School District, the vote on the budget occurred and the budget was approved. Once the budget is approved, district administrators begin the task (if they have not already done so) of allocating district funds to each school (see Figure 8-5). Lake Harbor is one of the schools in the Glenn Fall Central School district. The same basic format used for developing the district budget is used for developing the allocations. Once the budgets for the schools are established, the previous year's activity becomes less important.

SCHOOL BUDGET

The school principal generally has some discretion in implementing the budget. Nevertheless, principals have to follow certain parameters. For instance, districtwide policies about class size affect the number of full-time teaching positions allocated. Meeting state or federal government mandates for special programs may determine the type of teachers or support staff needed. Districtwide funding models for certain budget categories such as plant maintenance may be in place to ensure that buildings and facilities receive the resources needed to be safe and in good repair. To be sure that such policies are followed, the school district may require that any major changes or adjustments to the budget by the principal be approved by the district's business manager. Frequently, the school district does not allow transfers of funds from one major category (e.g., personnel services or OTPS) to another, or the district may require justifications for proposed changes.

THE CANTON ALTERNATIVE SCHOOL

The Canton Alternative School is a primary school in the Glenn Fall Central School District. The fiscal year started on July 1, 2005, and the principal, Robert Dudley, has the budget (see Figure 8-6A). The budget represents a modest increase from the previous year. For the full-time teaching staff, 30 lines, or positions, have been allocated at an average salary of $40,000 per line, for a total of $1,200,000. In establishing budgets for full-time staff, school districts frequently calculate a districtwide average salary for each position type (e.g., regular teacher, administrator, counselor) and fund the number of positions accordingly. In the following scenario, the principal uses basic budget data to make important strategic decisions for Canton.

Figure 8-6A   Canton Alternative School budget allocation.

	A	B	C	D	E
1		The Canton Alternative School			
2		School Budget			
3		2005-2006			1-Jul-05
4	Category				
5	Personnel Services	Lines/Positions	Average Salary	Category Totals	
6	Teaching Staff	30	$40,000	$1,200,000	
7	Student Support Staff	4	40,000	$160,000	
8	Administrative Staff	4	65,000	$260,000	
9	Plant Maintenance Staff	8	30,000	$240,000	
10	Part-Time Staff			80,000	
11	SubTotal Personnel			$1,940,000	
12					
13	Other Than Personnel Services				
14	Teaching Supplies/Equipment			$210,000	
15	Student Services Supplies/ Equipment			20,000	
16	Administrative Supplies/Equipment			20,000	
17	Plant Maint. Supplies/Equipment			90,000	
18	Subtotal Other Than Personnel Services			$340,000	
19	Total Budget			$2,280,000	

For the actual data set for Figure 8-6A, go to the Companion Website at
www.//prenhall.com/picciano

Figure 8-6B Canton Alternative School Budget—personnel services detail.

	A	B	C	D	E	F	G
1		The Canton Alternative School					
2		Personnel Services Detail					
3		2005-2006				1-Jul-05	
4							
5		Budget $	Number	Budget	Actual		
6	Teaching Staff	Per Line	of Lines	Allocation	Projection	Difference	
7	Regular Education Teachers (Filled)	$40,000	18	$720,000	$718,660	$1,340	
8	Special Education Teachers (Filled)	$40,000	4	$160,000	$159,430	$570	
9	Other Special Service Teachers (Filled)	$40,000	3	$120,000	$121,220	-$1,220	
10	Vacancies	$40,000	5	$200,000	$200,000	$0	
11	Subtotal			$1,200,000	$1,199,310	$690	
12	Student Support Staff						
13	Counselors (Filled)	$40,000	3	$120,000	$121,980	-$1,980	
14	Social Worker (Filled)	$40,000	1	$40,000	$39,788	$212	
15	Subtotal			$160,000	$161,768	-$1,768	
16	Administrative Staff						
17	Principal (Filled)	$65,000	1	$65,000	$110,000	-$45,000	
18	Asst. Principal - Operations (Filled)	$65,000	1	$65,000	$75,000	-$10,000	
19	Secretary (Filled)	$65,000	1	$65,000	$35,000	$30,000	
20	Vacancies	$65,000	1	$65,000	$65,000	$0	
21	Subtotal			$260,000	$285,000	-$25,000	
22	Plant Maintenance Staff						
23	Head of Maintenance (Filled)	$30,000	1	$30,000	$43,100	-$13,100	
24	Head of Custodial (Filled)	$30,000	1	$30,000	$42,500	-$12,500	
25	Maintenance (Filled)	$30,000	1	$30,000	$39,700	-$9,700	
26	Custodians (Filled)	$30,000	5	$150,000	$114,460	$35,540	
27				$240,000	$239,760	$240	
28	Subtotal			$1,860,000	$1,885,838	-$25,838	
29	Part-Time Staff			80000	$80,000	$0	
30	Total Personnel			$1,940,000	$1,965,838	-$25,838	

For the actual data set for Figure 8-6B, go to the Companion Website at
www.//prenhall.com/picciano

Mr. Dudley knows that there will be five vacancies among the full-time teaching staff and one vacancy in the administrative staff (see Figure 8-6B). The remaining positions are filled for the coming year. The average salaries for the full-time teaching staff, the student support staff, and the plant maintenance staff are close to those budgeted; however, Mr. Dudley detects a problem with the average salary ($65,000) calculated for the full-time administrators. The $220,000 salary total for the three filled administrative positions will translate into a $25,000 shortage unless a new administrator is hired for $35,000 (instead of for the average of $65,000). Salaries for administrative positions depend on responsibilities and range from $25,000 (administrative secretary) to $110,000 (principal).

Mr. Dudley's strategy for filling the personnel vacancies is to hire a high-level assistant principal and the five "best" teachers possible. Through the local principal's network, he knows that an excellent, experienced assistant principal is interested in the administrative position. She is currently earning $74,000; she would probably come to Canton for $80,000. How can the budget be adjusted to achieve his objective? Mr. Dudley has to find an additional $40,000 for the personnel services budget:

$$
\begin{aligned}
&\text{Administrative position shortfall} &&= \$25,000 \\
&\text{New, experienced assistant principal} &&= 15,000 \\
&(\$80,000 - \$65,000 = \$15,000) \\
&\text{Total} &&= \$40,000
\end{aligned}
$$

He carefully reviews the budget data and determines that $40,000 can be saved by hiring younger, less experienced teachers. He advertises the five teacher vacancies as positions with salary ranges between $25,000 and $40,000. Salaries for teachers range from $25,000 for beginning teachers to $70,000 for the most experienced teachers. Five new teachers are hired as follows:

$$
\begin{aligned}
&1 \text{ teacher } @ \$25,000 &&= \$25,000 \\
&2 \text{ teachers } @ \$30,000 \text{ each} &&= 60,000 \\
&1 \text{ teacher } @ \$35,000 &&= 35,000 \\
&1 \text{ teacher } @ \$40,000 &&= \underline{40,000} \\
&\text{Total} &&= \$160,000
\end{aligned}
$$

With a budget allocation of $40,000 for each full-time teaching position, the budget for filling the five vacancies is $200,000, hence the savings is $40,000. This amount can be applied to the full-time administrative shortfall ($25,000) and to hire a new, assistant principal ($15,000) for $80,000. Mr. Dudley could have decided to hire seasoned, experienced teachers and a younger, less experienced administrator.

These are the types of discretionary decisions that school administrators make every year. In another year, the needs of the school might be different and a different strategy would be developed. If principals have accurate and timely budget data, they are in a much better position to make such decisions.

BUDGET EMERGENCY

Assume that the fiscal year at the Glenn Fall Central School District has commenced and it is September 1, 2005. Classes will begin in a few days. The superintendent receives a telephone call from the assistant director of the state division of the budget, who indicates that because of an unexpected shortfall in state income tax revenue, state aid to all school districts will be reduced by 8%. This translates into approximately $2 million for the Glenn Fall Central district. The school district business manager does several calculations and determines the savings needed throughout the district and for each school. Canton Alternative must save

$90,000. The principal, Robert Dudley, is sent an e-mail describing the situation and requesting him to identify $90,000 in savings within the current budget. The e-mail further directs that the savings may not result in the termination of any contract with a full-time employee.

To identify $90,000 in savings, Mr. Dudley must review the budget allocation and expenditures. Figure 8-7A is a basic budget allocation and expenditure worksheet for the Canton Alternative School as of July 1, 2005, showing four columns of data: the approved budget (i.e., budget allocations), encumbrances, expenditures, and balances. As noted earlier in the chapter, schools and most governmental agencies operate on an encumbrance accounting system with monies set aside when a contract has been issued. When the services or goods are delivered and paid for, the encumbrances are reduced and the expenditures are increased. Balances are calculated by subtracting the sum of encumbrances and expenditures from the budget allocation. Figure 8-7A shows the Canton budget when the budget had just been allocated and no fiscal activity had occurred. If the state aid shortfall had been announced on July 1, 2005, Mr. Dudley would have had more available options in identifying the $90,000 savings. However, the shortfall was announced on September 1, 2005, and a good deal of expenditure activity has already occurred.

Figure 8-7B shows the same electronic spreadsheet as Figure 8-7A but with two months of activity recorded. Most full-time staff are given yearly contracts, so all funds have been encumbered for personnel services except for the part-time staff.

Figure 8-7A   Canton Alternative School budget and expenditures, July 1, 2005.

	A	B	C	D	E	F
1		The Canton Alternative School				
2		School Budget				
3		2005-2006			1-Jul-05	
4	**Category**					
5	Personnel Services	Approved Budget	Encumbrances	Expenditures	Balance	
6	Teaching Staff	$1,200,000	$0	$0	$1,200,000	
7	Student Support Staff	$160,000	$0	$0	$160,000	
8	Administrative Staff	$260,000	$0	$0	$260,000	
9	Plant Maintenance Staff	$240,000	$0	$0	$240,000	
10	Part-Time Staff	$80,000	$0	$0	$80,000	
11	SubTotal Personnel	$1,940,000	$0	$0	$1,940,000	
12						
13	Other Than Personnel Services					
14	Teaching Supplies/Equipment	$210,000	$0	$0	$210,000	
15	Student Services Supplies/ Equipment	20,000	$0	$0	$20,000	
16	Administrative Supplies/Equipment	20,000	$0	$0	$20,000	
17	Plant Maint. Supplies/Equipment	90,000	$0	$0	$90,000	
18	Subtotal Other Than Personnel Services	$340,000	$0	$0	$340,000	
19	Total Budget	$2,280,000	$0	$0	$2,280,000	

For the actual data set for Figure 8-7A, go to the Companion Website at
www.//prenhall.com/picciano

Figure 8-7B Canton Alternative School Budget and Expenditures, September 1, 2005.

	A	B	C	D	E	F
1						
2		The Canton Alternative School				
3		School Budget				
4		2005-2006			1-Sep-05	
5	Category					
6	Personnel Services	Approved Budget	Encumbrances	Expenditures	Balance	
7	Teaching Staff	$1,200,000	$1,200,000	$0	$0	
8	Student Support Staff	$160,000	$160,000	$0	$0	
9	Administrative Staff	$260,000	$260,000	$0	$0	
10	Plant Maintenance Staff	$240,000	$240,000	$0	$0	
11	Part-Time Staff	$80,000	$7,000	$5,000	$68,000	
12	SubTotal Personnel	$1,940,000	$1,867,000	$5,000	$68,000	
13						
14	Other Than Personnel Services					
15	Teaching Supplies/Equipment	$210,000	$50,000	$90,000	$70,000	
16	Student Services Supplies/ Equipment	20,000	$1,600	$2,400	$16,000	
17	Administrative Supplies/Equipment	20,000	$3,000	$1,800	$15,200	
18	Plant Maint. Supplies/Equipment	90,000	$50,000	$13,000	$27,000	
19	Subtotal Other Than Personnel Services	$340,000	$104,600	$107,200	$128,200	
20	Total Budget	$2,280,000	$1,971,600	$112,200	$196,200	

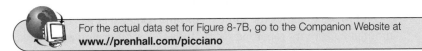

For the actual data set for Figure 8-7B, go to the Companion Website at
www.//prenhall.com/picciano

A good deal of activity has been occurring in OTPS categories as well. The balance of unencumbered and unexpended funds as of September 1, 2005 is $196,200, from which Mr. Dudley has to identify $90,000 in savings. One simple way to do this would be to calculate a percentage and apply it to each category to achieve the savings. As $90,000 represents 46% of the remaining budget ($90,000 divided by $196,200), one rational approach might be to reduce each of the part-time staff and the OTPS categories by this percentage. In doing the calculations (see Figure 8-7C), Mr. Dudley determines that this approach would not be equitable, because some categories have spent at a much more rapid rate (e.g., OTPS plant maintenance) than others (e.g., OTPS student services supplies/equipment). In addition, he does not want to reduce the part-time staff budget to the same extent as some of the OTPS categories.

Mr. Dudley reviews the balances again, makes a series of changes, and develops a second savings plan. Figure 8-7D displays and compares the new savings plan (Savings Plan 2) to the first approach (Savings Plan 1). He decides to submit Savings Plan 2 to the superintendent. Savings Plan 2 does not reduce the part-time staff as much as Savings Plan 1. To make up for this, the savings for administrative supplies/equipment and plant maintenance supplies/equipment are increased.

In this scenario, Mr. Dudley was able to consider two budget strategies and determine a way to achieve the required savings. Most likely additional strategies were possible and could have been calculated and displayed. The lesson is readily

Figure 8-7C Canton Alternative School Budget and Expenditures, new balances based on 46% savings.

	A	B	C	D	E	F	G
1							
2		The Canton Alternative School					
3		School Budget					
4		2005-2006			1-Sep-05		
5	Category					Savings Plan No. 1	
6	Personnel Services	Approved Budget	Encumbrances	Expenditures	Balance	46% Savings	New Balance
7	Teaching Staff	$1,200,000	$1,200,000	$0	$0		
8	Student Support Staff	$160,000	$160,000	$0	$0		
9	Administrative Staff	$260,000	$260,000	$0	$0		
10	Plant Maintenance Staff	$240,000	$240,000	$0	$0		
11	Part-Time Staff	$80,000	$7,000	$5,000	$68,000	$31,280	$36,720
12	SubTotal Personnel	$1,940,000	$1,867,000	$5,000	$68,000	$31,280	$36,720
13							
14	Other Than Personnel Services						
15	Teaching Supplies/Equipment	$210,000	$50,000	$90,000	$70,000	$32,200	$37,800
16	Student Services Supplies/ Equipment	20,000	$1,600	$2,400	$16,000	$7,360	$8,640
17	Administrative Supplies/Equipment	20,000	$3,000	$1,800	$15,200	$6,992	$8,208
18	Plant Maint. Supplies/Equipment	90,000	$50,000	$13,000	$27,000	$12,420	$14,580
19	Subtotal Other Than Personnel Service	$340,000	$104,600	$107,200	$128,200	$58,972	$69,228
20	Total Budget	$2,280,000	$1,971,600	$112,200	$196,200	$90,252	$105,948
21							

For the actual data set for Figure 8-7C, go to the Companion Website at **www.//prenhall.com/picciano**

Figure 8-7D Canton Alternative School Budget and Expenditures, comparison of two savings plans.

	A	B	C	D	E	F	G	H	I
1									
2		The Canton Alternative School							
3		School Budget							
4		2005-2006			1-Sep-05				
5	Category					Savings Plan No. 1		Savings Plan No. 2	
6	Personnel Services	Approved Budget	Encumbrances	Expenditures	Balance	46% Savings	New Balance	Final Savings	New Balance
7	Teaching Staff	$1,200,000	$1,200,000	$0	$0				
8	Student Support Staff	$160,000	$160,000	$0	$0				
9	Administrative Staff	$260,000	$260,000	$0	$0				
10	Plant Maintenance Staff	$240,000	$240,000	$0	$0				
11	Part-Time Staff	$80,000	$7,000	$5,000	$68,000	$31,280	$36,720	$25,000	$43,000
12	SubTotal Personnel	$1,940,000	$1,867,000	$5,000	$68,000	$31,280	$36,720	$25,000	$43,000
13									
14	Other Than Personnel Services								
15	Teaching Supplies/Equipment	$210,000	$50,000	$90,000	$70,000	$32,200	$37,800	$30,000	$40,000
16	Student Services Supplies/ Equipment	20,000	$1,600	$2,400	$16,000	$7,360	$8,640	$8,000	$8,000
17	Administrative Supplies/Equipment	20,000	$3,000	$1,800	$15,200	$6,992	$8,208	$10,000	$5,200
18	Plant Maint. Supplies/Equipment	90,000	$50,000	$13,000	$27,000	$12,420	$14,580	$17,000	$10,000
19	Subtotal Other Than Personnel Services	$340,000	$104,600	$107,200	$128,200	$58,972	$69,228	$65,000	$63,200
20	Total Budget	$2,280,000	$1,971,600	$112,200	$196,200	$90,252	$105,948	$90,000	$106,200

For the actual data set for Figure 8-7D, go to the Companion Website at **www.//prenhall.com/picciano**

available, accurate data facilitate decision making and enable school administrators to lead even in difficult budgetary situations.

SUMMARY

Timely and accurate data are essential to school administrators at the district and school levels as they make budgeting decisions. A budget is a financial plan that involves planning, receiving funds, spending funds, and analyzing results—all within a specific time period. Standards such as those developed by the Government Accounting Standards Board (GASB) assist school administers in developing budgets. Several accounting concepts are particularly important in school budgeting: encumbrances and the categories of personnel services (PS) and other than personnel services (OTPS).

Electronic spreadsheets, which allow administrators to analyze budget data based on what-if questions, are used throughout the budget cycle. Development of the budget begins at the school district level. Administrators and other officials consider details such as current expenditures and revenue, proposed expenditures and revenue, and revenue projections. At the school level, principals can exercise some discretion in implementing the approved budget at their school, but they have to follow certain parameters. Principals also must make decisions that change the school budget if there is an emergency such as a reduction in state funding for the district.

The examples of the Glenn Fall Central School District and the Canton Alternative School demonstrate data-driven decision making in budget planning and management.

Activities

1. Visit a district office or a school and meet with an administrator (e.g., superintendent, assistant superintendent, or principal) to determine how budget planning and management are done. Specifically ask how fiscal data (e.g., budget allocations or expenditures) are disseminated and who is responsible for coordinating this activity.
2. Assume you are the principal of the Canton Alternative School and have just received your budget (see Figure 8-6A) at the beginning of the fiscal year. There is a $25,000 shortfall in the administrative staff category. Your objective this year is to hire at least three top-notch, experienced teachers at salaries in the $55,000 to $70,000 range. You have five teaching vacancies and one administrative vacancy. Using the data provided in Figure 8-6B, develop a fiscal strategy to accomplish your goal.

References

Brimley, V., & Garfield, R. R. (2002). *Financing education in a climate of change*. Boston, MA: Allyn & Bacon.

Droms, W. (2003). *Finance and accounting for nonfinancial managers: All the basics you need to know*. Norwalk, MA: Perseus Publishing.

Ray, J. R., Candoli, I. C., & Hack, W. G. (2004). *School business administration: A planning approach* (8th ed.). Boston, MA: Allyn & Bacon.

Trotter, A. (2003, November 5). Budget crises may undercut laptop efforts [Electronic version]. *Education Week*. Retrieved August 14, 2003, from http://www.edweek.org/ew/ewstory.cfm?slug=10Laptops.h23&tbstoryid=59

Chapter 9

Supporting Teaching and Learning

Kate Rousmaniere (1997) in a study titled "City Teachers," commented that "testing [had taken] American schools by storm" (p. 64). The teachers she interviewed for the study talked about how confused they were by the multiplicity of tests required by local and state agencies; how the tests were incomprehensible to foreign-born students who lacked the language skills needed to pass them; and how they were too challenging for the poor urban child. One teacher lamented the "test insanity" that had overburdened the schools. Surprisingly, Rousmaniere's study is based on the testimony of 21 retired New York City teachers who were describing their experiences and the testing fervor that had gripped American public schools in the 1920s.

Today, American education has once again entered an era of standards in which testing is used to monitor student achievement and progress. And once again, the debate whether educational policies that emphasize standardized testing will improve student achievement continues. Many view testing as unjustified pressure brought on teachers and children to perform. For others, testing is the mechanism needed to hold schools accountable for the enormous investment that has been made in public education. For further discussion of this complex and impassioned issue, refer to Horn (2003), Aper (2002), or Mazzeo (2001).

The purpose of this chapter is to explore the use of data-driven decision making in the monitoring of student progress, with an emphasis on the improvement of teaching and learning. Because there will be several statistical procedures used in the examples, you may want to review Part A in Section III (Technical Support) of this book.

STATES, CITIES, DISTRICTS, SCHOOLS, CLASSES, TEACHERS, STUDENTS

One of the remarkable aspects of the current standards movement is that tests have become a common mechanism through which educators at all levels are able to communicate. State education departments have systematically designed or refined a variety of tests that are used extensively by local school districts, schools, and teachers to develop strategies for helping students to read, to do arithmetic, and to learn concepts and ideas.

Although testing has been conducted extensively for years, modern networking technology now allows many levels of the education enterprise to share, to communicate, and to take action in order to improve teaching and learning. Tests are scored rapidly at the state level; results are returned promptly to school districts and schools; and principals and teachers develop instructional strategies to meet student needs in a matter of weeks. Data files with test results are passed through digital networks from state capitals to localities and school district offices dispersed over thousands of miles. Data coordinators aggregate the data by school and by class within schools using electronic spreadsheets or statistical software programs. Principals and teachers view the records of their students on computer screens or the "old way" (i.e., on printed reports) and start planning individual programs for children who did not do well on a test.

Test data alone, however, will not improve teaching and learning. Test data need to be integrated with other data in school records and, most importantly, reviewed by teachers and other professionals who understand the curriculum and know the children involved. Teachers can then develop learning strategies for all students, but especially for those who do not meet standards or are in greatest need of assistance. Montgomery (2004) describes the assessment system in his Nebraska school district as one where instructional goals and objectives are continually reviewed and aligned with curriculum, standards, and assessments. Teachers are actively involved in all aspects of the review and alignment and are trusted by state and local education leaders to make the right decisions for their students.

Figures 9-1A and 9-1B compare student performance on an eighth-grade language arts test by school districts within a particular region of the state. The data in Figure 9-1A compare mean scale scores over a 5-year period and show both 1-year and 4-year changes. A scale score represents the number of correct answers converted to scores on a common scale so that achievement can be compared across grade levels. At the bottom of the spreadsheet, data are provided for the entire region: totals for the number of students taking the test and regionwide averages for mean scale scores and changes.

The data in Figure 9-1B are for the same population's performance levels. The performance levels are coded as follows:

- Level 1: Students do not meet the learning standards.
- Level 2: Students show partial achievement of the learning standards.

Figure 9-1A Regional school district summaries (mean scale scores).

	District	Number Tested					Mean Scale Score					One-Year Changes	Four-Year Changes
	Code	2000	2001	2002	2003	2004	2000	2001	2002	2003	2004	Mean SS	Mean SS
6	110	538	637	676	666	737	679	676.4	675.2	680.2	681.7	1.5	2.7
7	120	1716	1893	1912	1836	1891	709.6	706.5	709.3	706.1	704.7	-1.4	-4.9
8	130	1101	1127	1229	1257	1410	695	693.1	691	693.3	691.9	-1.4	-3.1
9	140	1295	1373	1131	1186	1369	683.2	675.2	682.6	679.5	679.6	0.1	-3.6
10	150	979	1014	1087	1080	1172	677.6	676.1	672.5	675.4	678.9	3.5	1.3
11	160	1998	1985	2055	2402	2441	685.6	677.3	680.2	680	679.6	-0.4	-6.0
12	170	979	957	1026	1042	1201	677.7	673.5	673.9	673.5	671.9	-1.6	-5.8
13	180	1610	1731	1726	2009	2153	685	677.2	675.4	683.4	677.1	-6.3	-7.9
14	190	1710	1769	1852	2004	2191	676.8	667.5	668.7	674.6	673.8	-0.8	-3.0
15	200	3226	3388	3344	3725	3810	683.3	678.5	683.9	680.4	680.6	0.2	-2.7
16	210	2537	2633	2723	3038	3139	691.4	684.6	682.4	683.1	680.4	-2.7	-11.0
17	220	720	841	951	1030	1014	680.9	668.1	675.5	677.8	677.6	-0.2	-3.3
18	230	1139	1207	1239	1206	1226	683.8	676.9	680.3	682.7	681.1	-1.6	-2.7
19	240	1421	1431	1390	1566	1491	681.4	677.3	686.8	679.8	691.9	12.1	10.5
20	250	1018	1128	1155	1221	1173	684.2	685.4	683.8	683.7	687.4	3.7	3.2
21	260	541	327	725	773	762	672.3	677.7	676.2	682.7	678.3	-4.4	6.0
22	270	1662	1878	1878	2007	2086	676.6	677.4	678.1	686.2	687.9	1.7	11.3
23	280	1820	1750	1651	1789	1838	691.4	684.8	686.9	686.5	686.6	0.1	-4.8
24	290	1852	2039	1992	1941	2141	678.3	676.6	670	676.4	676.8	0.4	-1.5
25	300	2633	2651	2520	2879	2962	696.6	696.8	693.8	690.4	693	2.6	-3.6
26	310	2739	2863	2931	3026	2869	710	702.9	711.1	706.1	699.1	-7.0	-10.9
27	320	2369	2556	2445	2567	2663	701.7	696.8	695.4	696.8	696.3	-0.5	-5.4
28	330	1129	1182	1150	1264	1296	681.6	672.5	679.4	682.4	678.7	-3.7	-2.9
29	340	2929	3057	3043	3354	3430	694.9	687.1	689.6	688.5	686.1	-2.4	-8.8
30	350	1954	1956	2091	2065	2150	699.6	699.6	701.3	698.6	696.7	-1.9	-2.9
31	360	1664	1716	1735	1843	1805	720.2	715	713.7	714.2	710.2	-4.0	-10.0
32	370	3142	3323	3160	3583	3686	686.6	681.3	680.6	683.9	679.8	-4.1	-6.8
33	380	1737	1881	1896	1954	1924	695.9	694.8	697	696.2	692.2	-4.0	-3.7
34	390	2342	2481	2422	2694	2812	687.3	682.8	680.7	680.3	686.5	6.2	-0.8
35	400	1875	1947	1863	2094	2159	694	687.2	687.6	688.1	686.3	-1.8	-7.7
36	410	3460	3882	3938	4313	4415	699.1	701.2	698.5	695.3	691.9	-3.4	-7.2
37	420	1473	1460	1346	1510	1576	683.4	678.2	690	687.9	682.3	-5.6	-1.1
38	430	399	506	597	680	893	648.2	630.1	645.8	652.8	644.5	-8.3	-3.7
39	440	2017	2618	1807	2137	2013	672.2	665.1	669.2	675	671.6	-3.4	-0.6
40	Total and Averages	60909	64112	64042	69240	71606	690.2	685.6	686.9	687	685.5	-1.5	-4.7

Region A – District Performance on the State Grade 8 English Language Arts Assessment
2000-2004

For the actual data set for Figure 9-1A, go to the Companion Website at
www.//prenhall.com/picciano

- Level 3: Students meet the learning standards.
- Level 4: Students exceed the learning standards.

The data show the percentages of students either meeting or not meeting the standard performance levels (data for Performance Level 2 are not provided because they represent borderline cases). At the bottom of the spreadsheet, data are provided for the entire region: totals for the number of students taking the test and regionwide average percentages and changes. These data are useful for comparing districts as well as for observing how districts progress over time. Districts that show improvement should continue to do whatever they are doing. In districts that are not improving, more aggressive action should be taken by local governing boards. Similar reports are provided for all mandated tests (e.g., mathematics, science) comparing all districts in the region. Within a district, data are provided for

Figure 9-1B Regional school district summaries (performance levels).

District Code	Number Tested					Percent in Level 1					Percent in Levels 3 & 4					One-Year Change		Four-Year Change	
	2000	2001	2002	2003	2004	2000	2001	2002	2003	2004	2000	2001	2002	2003	2004	Lev 1	Lev 3&4	Lev 1	Lev 3&4
Region A - District Performance on the State Grade 8 English Language Arts Assessment 2000-2004																			
110	538	637	676	666	737	22.5	33.4	32.2	16.7	13.4	18.8	21	17	20	24.3	-3.3%	4.3%	-9.1%	5.5%
120	1716	1893	1912	1836	1891	5.1	10.4	8.8	3.5	3.8	61.3	57.1	60.1	57.4	59.5	0.3%	2.1%	-1.3%	-1.8%
130	1101	1127	1229	1257	1410	15.3	16.5	19.7	8	8.7	40.1	37.9	33.8	34.8	37.2	0.7%	2.4%	-6.6%	-2.9%
140	1295	1373	1131	1186	1369	18.6	31	26.1	15.2	18.8	24.9	21.8	28.3	19	23.7	3.6%	4.7%	0.2%	-1.2%
150	972	1014	1007	1000	1172	25.2	31.9	35.5	33.5	10.5	10.4	20.0	10.0	16.8	21.7	4.0%	5.5%	6.9%	5.5%
160	1998	1985	2055	2402	2441	18.5	27.8	27.7	15.8	17.3	28.8	21	25.4	20.1	23	1.5%	2.9%	-1.2%	-5.8%
170	979	957	1026	1042	1201	25.8	32	31.9	20.2	26.3	19.2	18	18	13.8	15.7	6.1%	1.9%	0.5%	-3.5%
180	1610	1731	1726	2009	2153	23.6	32.5	33.7	13.3	20.7	30.6	23.5	22.3	24.5	21.8	7.4%	-2.7%	-2.9%	-8.8%
190	1710	1769	1852	2004	2191	28.2	40.5	40.3	20.4	22.9	17.3	13.6	13.2	13.4	16.4	2.5%	3.0%	-5.3%	-0.9%
200	3226	3388	3344	3725	3810	22.4	28.6	22.7	14.4	16.3	26.2	24.5	28.4	18.8	24.5	1.9%	5.7%	-6.1%	-1.7%
210	2537	2633	2723	3038	3139	12.5	22.2	25	13.4	16.2	34.9	28.9	26.7	23.6	24.7	2.8%	1.1%	3.7%	-10.2%
220	720	841	951	1030	1014	24.9	42.3	34	18.4	19.4	22.2	14	22.1	18.3	21.2	1.0%	2.9%	-5.5%	-1.0%
230	1136	1207	1239	1206	1226	18.3	27.3	25.2	10.4	14.4	25.6	19.2	22.9	21.4	23.6	4.0%	2.2%	-3.9%	-2.0%
240	1421	1431	1390	1566	1491	21.3	28	22.4	18.6	8.6	23.1	23.5	33.5	21	39	-10.0%	18.0%	-12.7%	15.9%
250	1018	1128	1155	1221	1173	20.8	23.2	24.1	15	13.3	28.4	34.2	27.1	25.6	36.5	-1.7%	10.9%	-7.5%	8.1%
260	541	327	725	773	762	34	29.7	28	9.3	16.9	13.9	19.3	17.8	20.6	21.1	7.6%	0.5%	-17.1%	7.2%
270	1662	1878	1878	2007	2086	29.6	30.9	29.3	11.5	13.1	19.4	25.2	22.8	27	35	1.6%	8.0%	-16.5%	15.6%
280	1820	1750	1651	1789	1838	14	21.7	20.9	8.8	10.1	35.7	30.6	32.9	27.1	34.6	1.3%	7.5%	-3.9%	-1.1%
290	1852	2039	1992	1941	2141	27.2	30	39.5	18.1	20.2	20.2	22.6	18	15.9	20.7	2.1%	4.8%	-7.0%	0.5%
300	2633	2651	2520	2879	2962	11.8	16.1	16.4	11.7	9	43.4	45.1	39	33.7	41.8	-2.7%	8.1%	-2.8%	-1.6%
310	2739	2863	2931	3026	2869	7.2	9.3	8.5	4.1	6.9	61.1	52.5	62	55.9	52.9	2.8%	-3.0%	-0.3%	-8.2%
320	2369	2556	2445	2567	2663	7.5	13.7	15.2	7.5	7.7	50.1	45.2	41.6	42	46.8	0.2%	4.8%	0.2%	-3.3%
330	1129	1182	1150	1264	1296	24.9	33.6	27.7	13.2	18.1	25.3	18.3	23.8	21.7	22.2	4.9%	0.5%	-6.8%	-3.1%
340	2929	3057	3043	3354	3430	12.3	23	18.6	10	12.1	41.1	33.9	35.2	31.1	31.9	2.1%	0.0%	-0.2%	-9.2%
350	1954	1956	2091	2065	2150	8.1	11.1	12	6.1	5.6	46.5	46.4	49	45	46.5	-0.5%	1.5%	-2.5%	0.0%
360	1664	1716	1735	1843	1805	2.4	5.4	5	1.2	2.8	71.8	66.5	63.6	65.2	64.8	1.6%	-0.4%	0.4%	-7.0%
370	3142	3323	3160	3583	3686	19.7	25	26.5	15.1	19.4	31.7	27.3	24.5	27.4	26.3	4.3%	-1.1%	-0.3%	-5.4%
380	1737	1881	1896	1954	1924	13.2	15.3	17.7	5.8	8.3	42.3	40.7	44.5	40.1	41.1	2.5%	1.0%	-4.9%	-1.2%
390	2342	2481	2422	2694	2812	18	23.5	26.6	16.3	12.4	31.5	28.5	24.6	20.1	33	-4.2%	12.9%	-5.6%	1.5%
400	1875	1947	1863	2094	2159	11.5	21.1	21.8	9.7	13.9	37.1	31.3	33.3	28.8	32.3	4.2%	3.5%	2.4%	-4.8%
410	3460	3882	3938	4313	4415	8.4	11.2	11.7	7.2	8.2	45.2	49.6	44.8	40.4	41	1.0%	0.6%	-0.2%	-4.2%
420	1473	1460	1346	1510	1576	24.1	32.6	23.7	12	18.5	32	28.4	39.2	32.6	32.7	6.5%	0.1%	-5.6%	0.7%
430	395	506	597	680	893	65.7	79.8	71.4	54.7	63.4	4.8	1.4	6.2	3.2	6	8.7%	2.8%	-2.3%	1.2%
440	2017	2618	1807	2137	2013	32.2	42.5	38.7	19.6	25.6	12.5	10.1	14.2	13.3	14.1	6.0%	0.8%	-6.6%	1.6%
Totals and Averages	60905	64112	64042	69240	71606	17.2	23.6	23.1	12.6	14.5	35.2	32.5	33	29.5	32.5	1.9%	3.0%	-2.7%	-2.7%

For the actual data set for Figure 9-1B, go to the Companion Website at
www.//prenhall.com/picciano

all schools so that district personnel can review the data and plan appropriate strategies (see Figures 9-2A and 9-2B).

IMPROVING TEACHING AND LEARNING

One of the most important functions of school district personnel with regard to improving teaching and learning is to provide testing data at the school building level. By doing so, they help principals, assistant principals, and teachers understand the needs of their children and act accordingly. The data must be timely, accurate, and readily available. Timeliness means that strategies can be developed before semesters and school years begin, not after they have started. Ready availability means that data are provided in electronic form and not on reams of paper. Too often, data are available to district and school administrators on computer workstations where they can be manipulated, sorted, aggregated, and disaggregated, but individual class data are printed in a "final" form for the teachers only after all this done.

Figure 9-2A School summaries (mean scale scores).

District Code	School Code	Number Tested					Mean Scale Score					One-Year Change Mean SS	Four-Year Change Mean SS
		2000	2001	2002	2003	2004	2000	2001	2002	2003	2004		
580	518	50	85	57	99	99	654.4	671.5	663	700.4	701.2	0.1%	5.7%
580	526	71	108	88	88	112	650.2	664.1	656.6	690.7	673.9	-2.5%	3.5%
580	531	71	95	87	90	86	660	690.5	674.2	678.9	669.7	-1.4%	1.4%
580	541	50	79	70	69	80	657.3	679.2	667.1	700.2	678.1	-3.3%	3.1%
580	546	62	70	84	61	62	660.3	683.8	682.1	691.4	692.6	0.2%	4.7%
580	594	57	50	62	77	65	661	682	671.8	692	682.8	-1.3%	3.2%
580	598	50	30	51	41	45	658.2	678.3	674.5	703.6	700.4	-0.5%	6.0%
580	615	64	91	80	79	93	652.1	667.5	668.8	681.7	681.4	-3.1%	1.4%
580	633	101	99	106	107	97	646.5	656.9	660.4	665.5	663.3	-0.3%	2.5%
580	659	88	89	96	108	88	665	681	675.8	664.3	665.1	0.1%	2.9%
580	662	113	123	119	106	104	667.1	679.7	678.3	673	682.7	1.4%	2.3%
580	673	115	113	124	163	153	667	675.9	677.2	683.9	682.6	-0.2%	2.3%
580	678	50	76	55	56	55	672.7	681.5	660	685.3	690.1	0.7%	2.5%
580	686	75	80	70	62	51	665.8	668.1	663.7	673.3	682.2	1.3%	2.4%
580	688	83	90	92	76	87	680.3	698.6	695	716.8	703.9	-1.8%	3.4%
580	691	54	62	58	51	51	673.6	685.9	682.5	696.2	686.7	-1.4%	1.9%
580	703	108	115	113	121	118	675.5	681.4	684.7	686.2	696.5	1.5%	3.0%
580	705	48	50	46	43	48	672.6	702.4	680.7	685	694.8	1.4%	3.2%
580	713	90	83	84	92	62	654.7	673.1	671	674.3	676.5	0.3%	3.2%
580	721	164	133	127	113	92	676.7	706.3	692.1	690.7	696.8	0.9%	2.9%
	Totals and Averages	1564	1721	1669	1702	1648	663.55	680.385	673.975	687.67	685.065	-0.0039	0.03127

For the actual data set for Figure 9-2A, go to the Companion Website at
www.//prenhall.com/picciano

Figure 9-2B School summaries (performance levels).

District Code	School Code	Number Tested					Percent Level 1					Percent Levels 3 & 4					One-Year Change		Four-Year Change	
		2000	2001	2002	2003	2004	2000	2001	2002	2003	2004	2000	2001	2002	2003	2004	Lev 1	Lev 3&4	Lev 1	Lev 3&4
580	518	50	85	57	99	99	0	2.4	0	2	0	68	80	71.9	86.9	96	-2.0%	9.1%	0.0%	28.0%
580	526	71	108	88	88	112	4.2	0.9	6.8	2.3	0.9	64.8	72.2	68.2	83	79.5	-1.4%	-3.5%	-3.3%	14.7%
580	531	71	95	87	90	86	1.4	1.1	1.1	3.3	0	69	84.2	73.6	75.6	75.6	-3.3%	0.0%	-1.4%	6.6%
580	541	50	79	70	69	80	0	0	1.4	0	0	68	88.6	84.3	95.7	83.8	0.0%	-11.9%	0.0%	15.8%
580	546	62	70	84	61	62	1.6	1.4	2.4	3.3	1.6	72.6	81.4	83.3	86.9	88.7	-1.7%	1.8%	0.0%	16.1%
580	594	57	50	62	77	65	3.5	0	1.6	0	0	77.2	92	87.1	92.2	95.4	0.0%	3.2%	-3.5%	18.2%
580	598	50	30	51	41	45	0	0	3.9	0	0	76	90	82.4	90.2	95.6	0.0%	5.4%	0.0%	19.6%
580	615	64	91	80	79	93	4.7	6.6	1.3	6.3	6.5	70.3	73.6	76.3	78.5	64.5	0.2%	-14.0%	1.8%	-5.8%
580	633	101	99	106	107	97	14.9	10.1	8.5	10.3	7.2	60.4	63.6	69.8	63.6	75.3	-3.1%	11.7%	-7.7%	14.9%
580	659	88	89	96	108	88	2.3	1.1	1	2.8	0	68.2	89.9	87.5	86.1	90.9	-2.8%	4.8%	-2.3%	22.7%
580	662	113	123	119	106	104	0.9	1.6	0	1.9	0	77	85.4	89.1	84	87.5	-1.9%	3.5%	-0.9%	10.5%
580	673	115	113	124	163	153	0	0.9	0	1.2	0	76.5	80.5	83.1	85.3	88.9	-1.2%	3.6%	0.0%	12.4%
580	678	50	76	55	56	55	2	2.6	9.1	5.4	1.8	82	81.6	69.1	83.9	89.1	-3.6%	5.2%	-0.2%	7.1%
580	686	75	80	70	62	51	0	7.5	5.7	1.6	0	77.3	75	72.9	77.4	84.3	-1.6%	6.9%	0.0%	7.0%
580	688	83	90	92	76	87	1.2	0	0	0	0	90.4	95.6	88	94.7	89.7	0.0%	-5.0%	-1.2%	-0.7%
580	691	54	62	58	51	51	1.9	0	0	0	0	83.3	88.7	94.8	94.1	92.2	0.0%	-1.9%	-1.9%	8.9%
580	703	108	115	113	121	118	3.7	4.3	4.4	4.1	1.7	81.5	84.3	85.8	84.3	90.7	-2.4%	6.4%	-2.0%	9.2%
580	705	48	50	46	43	48	0	0	0	2.3	0	79.2	98	87	88.4	91.7	-2.3%	3.3%	0.0%	12.5%
580	713	90	83	84	92	62	4.4	2.4	8.3	2.2	1.6	67.8	81.9	70.2	76.1	79	-0.6%	2.9%	-2.8%	11.2%
580	721	164	133	127	113	92	0	0	0.8	0.9	0	85.4	96.2	91.3	87.6	93.5	-0.9%	5.9%	0.0%	8.1%
	Totals and Averages	1564	1721	1669	1702	1648	2.335	2.145	2.815	2.495	1.065	74.75	84.14	80.79	84.73	86.6	-0.0143	0.0187	-0.0127	0.1185

For the actual data set for Figure 9-2B, go to the Companion Website at
www.//prenhall.com/picciano

K–12 education has reached the point where it can no longer lag behind the rest of American society in technology. Classrooms require technology for both administrative and instructional uses. Proposed improvements in teaching and learning will succeed or not depending on what goes on in the classroom. Teachers need to understand data and be able to mine the data for their particular students. Only in this way can teachers develop strategies and, most importantly, implement the changes needed to give every child the chance to succeed.

JEFFERSON MIDDLE SCHOOL

Figure 9-3 is a spreadsheet showing test results for students who took the eighth-grade, statewide language arts test in 2004 at Jefferson Middle School. Jefferson operates a sixth- through ninth-grade program in San Leon township, a growing suburb of a metropolitan area in the southeastern part of the United States. The figure shows the first 10 records of the 106 students who took the test.

Assume it is July 1, 2004, and the principal, Jane Ellen Carter, who was hired a year ago to replace a principal who had worked in the San Leon school system for 30 years, has established a committee to review the state test results and make plans for the next school year. In previous years, when results were made available by the district, the principal met and shared them with each teacher, who developed his or her own individual plans for the coming year. The new committee includes an assistant

Figure 9-3 Jefferson Middle School student data file of the results of the eighth-grade language arts test (note Microsoft Excel format).

	A	B	C	D	E	F	G	H	I	J	K
1					Jefferson Middle School						
2					Grade 8 Language Arts Test Results						
3					(Year 2004)						
4											
5			Special	Eligible	Assigned	Scale	Standard 1	Standard II	Standard III	Performance	
6	Student Id	Gender	Services	Free Lunch	Class	Score	Score	Score	Score	Level	
7	1	1	1	1	1	718	83	93	81	3	
8	2	2	1	1	3	689	72	85	63	2	
9	3	2	1	1	5	767	95	98	94	4	
10	4	2	2	1	2	697	75	88	69	2	
11	5	1	1	2	1	722	84	93	80	3	
12	6	1	1	1	2	728	87	95	83	3	
13	7	2	1	1	1	742	90	96	88	4	
14	8	2	1	1	5	770	96	98	94	4	
15	9	1	2	1	2	698	75	88	70	2	
16	10	2	1	2	3	755	93	97	91	4	

For the actual data set for Figure 9-3, go to the Companion Website at
www.//prenhall.com/picciano

principal, a teacher who is released from teaching three classes to assist in data coordination for the school, and the three eighth-grade language arts teachers. The assistant principal has decided to use the Statistical Package for Social Sciences (SPSS), because certain statistical procedures comparing **means** and **standard deviations** can be done more easily in SPSS than in a spreadsheet program. Figure 9-4A is the SPSS file layout (Variable View) that will be used for the data analysis of the test results. Figure 9-4B is a sample (first 10 records) of the actual data file (Data View) that will be used for doing the data analysis in SPSS.

Figure 9-5A is a SPSS report that provides basic information from the data file. The first part of the report is a simple frequency distribution showing the number and percentage of students in each performance level. The second part compares the means of the student scale scores by performance level. These reports provide a basic overview of student performance on the test. Eight students (7.5%) did not meet the performance standard; 32 (30.2%) students partially achieved the standard; the remaining students met or exceeded the standard. Figure 9-5B illustrates these results through a simple bar chart, also produced by the SPSS program.

In the mean scale report, the standard deviation is shown for each level in addition to the mean. The standard deviation is as important a measure as the mean. Just as the mean shows the central tendency of a group of numbers, the standard deviation shows the tendency of the group to disperse, or spread, from

Figure 9-4A SPSS file layout (Variable View) for Jefferson Middle School Student eighth-grade language arts data file.

chap8data.sav - SPSS Data Editor

File Edit View Data Transform Analyze Graphs Utilities Window Help

	Name	Type	Width	Decimals	Label	Values	Missing	Columns	Align	Measure
1	student	Numeric	4	0	Student Id	None	None	8	Right	Scale
2	gender	Numeric	1	0	Gender	{1, Female}...	None	8	Right	Scale
3	specserv	Numeric	1	0	Special Educ. Serv	{1, Gen. Educ	None	8	Right	Scale
4	eligfree	Numeric	1	0	Eligible-Free Lunch	{1, Not Eligible	None	8	Right	Scale
5	class	Numeric	8	0	Class	{1, Grade 8A}	None	8	Right	Scale
6	scalesc	Numeric	3	0	Language Arts Sca	None	None	8	Right	Scale
7	stand1	Numeric	3	0	S1- Information & U	None	None	8	Right	Scale
8	stand2	Numeric	3	0	S2 - Literary Respo	None	None	8	Right	Scale
9	stand3	Numeric	3	0	S3 - Critical Analysi	None	None	8	Right	Scale
10	level	Numeric	8	0	Performance Level	{1, 1 - Did Not	None	8	Right	Scale
11	filter_$	Numeric	1	0	level = 2 (FILTER)	{0, Not Select	None	8	Right	Scale

For the actual data set for Figure 9-4A, go to the Companion Website at
www.//prenhall.com/picciano

Figure 9-4B   SPSS file layout (Data View) for Jefferson Middle School Student eighth-grade language arts data file.

	student	gender	specserv	eligfree	class	scalesc	stand1	stand2	stand3	level
1	1	1	1	1	1	718	83	93	81	3
2	2	2	1	1	3	689	72	85	63	2
3	3	2	1	1	5	767	95	98	94	4
4	4	2	2	1	2	697	75	88	69	2
5	5	1	1	2	1	722	84	93	80	3
6	6	1	1	1	2	728	87	95	83	3
7	7	2	1	1	1	742	90	96	88	4
8	8	2	1	1	5	770	96	98	94	4
9	9	1	2	1	2	698	75	88	70	2
10	10	2	1	2	3	755	93	97	91	4

For the actual data set for Figure 9-4B, go to the Companion Website at **www.//prenhall.com/picciano**

the mean. In essence, the standard deviation expands on the information provided by the mean by identifying the range within which most scores fall. In a **normal distribution**, the distance from 1 standard deviation (*SD*) above the mean to 1 *SD* below the mean includes approximately 68% of all the scores; +2 to −2 *SD* includes approximately 95% of all scores; and +3 to −3 *SD* includes over 99% of all scores. A low standard deviation indicates that the scores are closer together. A large standard deviation indicates that there is a wide spread in the group, with more students scoring high and low.

In Figure 9-5A, the overall standard deviation is 34.96, which indicates that 68% of all of these test scores will range between 676.79 and 746.71 (+34.96 and −34.96 from the mean of 711.96). In developing a strategy for improving the test scores of this group of students, one goal would be to increase the mean of the scores while lowering the standard deviation. Increasing the mean translates into higher group performance, and decreasing the standard deviation indicates that the scores are closer to each other and that the group is moving forward as a coherent whole.

The information provided in Figure 9-5A is a first step to understanding student performance on the language arts test. To provide more insight, a greater degree of data disaggregation and analysis needs to be done. Figures 9-6A, 9-6B, and 9-6C are crosstabulations that provide the results of disaggregating performance level by

Figure 9-5A SPSS report showing a frequency distribution of performance levels and mean scale scores.

Performance Level

		Frequency	Percent	Valid Percent	Cumulative Percent
Valid	1 – Did Not Meet Performance Standard	8	7.5	7.5	7.5
	2 – Partial Achievement of Performance Standard	32	30.2	30.2	37.7
	3 – Met Performance Standard	43	40.6	40.6	78.3
	4 – Exceeded Performance Standard	23	21.7	21.7	100.0
	Total	106	100.0	100.0	

Language Arts Scale Score

Performance Level	Mean	N	Std. Deviation
1 – Did Not Meet Performance Standard	634.50	8	4.811
2 – Partial Achievement of Performance Standard	687.44	32	8.976
3 – Met Performance Standard	719.70	43	9.906
4 – Exceeded Performance Standard	757.61	23	13.197
Total	711.75	106	34.963

gender, by special education services code, and by eligible for free lunch code. Essentially, the data support these conclusions:

- Girls did better than boys.
- General education students did better than special education, English language learner (ELL), and special education/ELL students.
- Students not eligible for free lunch did better than students eligible for free lunch.

The differences between or among the groups in each of the three tables *may* all be of practical significance. A simple test of **statistical significance** can be conducted using the means of each of the three categories. Figure 9-7 shows the means of the groups within each of the categories. Figure 9-8 shows the results of a one-way analysis of variance (ANOVA), which indicates that there are statistically significant differences in mean scale scores for each of the special education services groups (.000) and the eligible for free lunch groups (.007). A statistically

Figure 9-5B SPSS-produced bar chart illustrating the frequency distribution of performance level for all students.

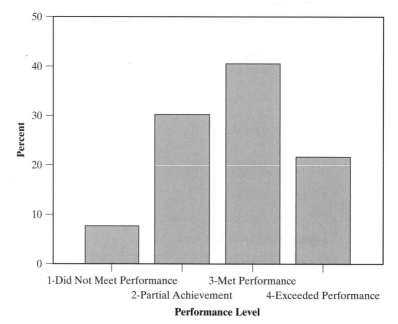

Figure 9-6A SPSS report showing a contingency table (crosstabulation) of performance levels by gender.

				Gender		
				Female	**Male**	**Total**
Performance Level	1 – Did Not Meet Performance Standard	Count		3	5	8
		% within				
		Performance Level		37.5%	62.5%	100.0%
		% within Gender		5.5%	9.8%	7.5%
	2 – Partial Achievement of Performance Standard	Count		16	16	32
		% within				
		Performance Level		50.0%	50.0%	100.0%
		% within Gender		29.1%	31.4%	30.2%
	3 – Met Performance Standard	Count		23	20	43
		% within				
		Performance Level		53.5%	46.5%	100.0%
		% within Gender		41.8%	39.2%	40.6%
	4 – Exceeded Performance Standard	Count		13	10	23
		% within				
		Performance Level		56.5%	43.5%	100.0%
		% within Gender		23.6%	19.6%	21.7%
Total		Count		55	51	106
		% within				
		Performance Level		51.9%	48.1%	100.0%
		% within Gender		100.0%	100.0%	100.0%

Figure 9-6B SPSS report showing a contingency table (crosstabulation) of performance levels by special education services code. ELL = English language learner.

			Special Educ. Services Code				
			Gen. Educ.	**Spec. Educ.**	**ELL**	**Spec. Educ. & ELL**	**Total**
Performance Level	1 – Did Not Meet Performance Standard	Count	0	2	0	6	8
		% within Performance Level	.0%	25.0%	.0%	75.0%	100.0%
		% within Special Educ. Services Code	.0%	9.5%	.0%	100.0%	7.5%
	2 – Partial Achievement of Performance Standard	Count	6	16	10	0	32
		% within Performance Level	18.8%	50.0%	31.3%	.0%	100.0%
		% within Special Educ. Services Code	9.0%	76.2%	83.3%	.0%	30.2%
	3 – Met Performance Standard	Count	38	3	2	0	43
		% within Performance Level	88.4%	7.0%	4.7%	.0%	100.0%
		% within Special Educ. Services Code	56.7%	14.3%	16.7%	.0%	40.6%
	4 – Exceeded Performance Standard	Count	23	0	0	0	23
		% within Performance Level	100.0%	.0%	.0%	.0%	100.0%
		% within Special Educ. Services Code	34.3%	.0%	.0%	.0%	21.7%
Total		Count	67	21	12	6	106
		% within Performance Level	63.2%	19.8%	11.3%	5.7%	100.0%
		% within Special Educ. Services Code	100.0%	100.0%	100.0%	100.0%	100.0%

significant difference does not exist in the means between the female and male scale scores.

A valid point might be made that the six special education/ELL student scores may be skewing the one-way ANOVA results to generate a statistically significant difference. To test this theory, a one-way ANOVA report was executed excluding the special education/ELL students from the analysis (Figure 9-9). The results still indicate a statistically significant difference (.000).

The results of the data analysis provide important information to the committee involved in developing strategies to improve teaching and learning at Jefferson Middle School. For instance, the overall strategy is to improve learning for all students, but the data indicate that a large percentage (30.2%) of the students are at

Figure 9-6C SPSS report showing a contingency table (crosstabulation) of performance levels by eligible for free lunch code.

| | | | Eligibility for Free Lunch | | |
			Not Eligible	Eligible	Total
Performance Level	1 – Did Not Meet Performance Standard	Count	2	6	8
		% within Performance Level	25.0%	75.0%	100.0%
		% within Eligible for Free Lunch Code Eligibility	2.9%	16.2%	7.5%
	2 – Partial Achievement of Performance Standard	Count	20	12	32
		% within Performance Level	62.5%	37.5%	100.0%
		% within Eligible for Free Lunch Code	29.0%	32.4%	30.2%
	3 – Met Performance Standard	Count	30	13	43
		% within Performance Level	69.8%	30.2%	100.0%
		% within Eligible for Free Lunch Code	43.5%	35.1%	40.6%
	4 – Exceeded Performance Standard	Count	17	6	23
		% within Performance Level	73.9%	26.1%	100.0%
		% within Eligible for Free Lunch Code	24.6%	16.2%	21.7%
Total		Count	69	37	106
		% within Performance Level	65.1%	34.9%	100.0%
		% within Eligible for Free Lunch Code	100.0%	100.0%	100.0%

Level 2 (very close to meeting the performance standard). The data also show that the eight students at Level 1 (did not meet the performance standard) are special education students or special education/ELL students who will in all likelihood need a good deal of individual instruction to improve their performance. At this point the committee can begin forming general insights, but it still needs more data to refine its strategy, especially with regard to the class assignments of these students during the previous school year.

Figure 9-10 is a contingency table of performance level by last year's class assignment, controlling for special educational services code. The data show that Jefferson Middle School had grouped most special education students and most ELL students into the smaller language arts classes, Classes 8B and 8D. All students in Classes 8A

Figure 9-7 SPSS report showing a breakdown of the mean scale scores by gender, special education services code, and eligibile for free lunch code. ELL = English language learner.

Language Arts Scale Score * Gender

Language Arts Scale Score

Gender	Mean	N	Std. Deviation
Female	716.47	55	34.371
Male	706.67	51	35.218
Total	711.75	106	34.963

Language Arts Scale Score * Special Educ. Services Code

Language Arts Scale Score

Special Educ. Services Code	Mean	N	Std. Deviation
Gen. Educ.	729.54	67	24.724
Spec. Educ.	690.52	21	24.572
ELL	688.00	12	16.531
Spec. Educ. & ELL	635.00	6	5.586
Total	711.75	106	34.963

Language Arts Scale Score * Eligible for Free Lunch Code

Language Arts Scale Score

Eligible for Free Lunch	Mean	N	Std. Deviation
Not Eligible	718.39	69	31.218
Eligible	699.38	37	38.506
Total	711.75	106	34.963

and 8E met or exceeded performance standards, and all but six students met or exceeded the standards in Class 8C. An important question in developing the instructional strategy is whether the special education students and the six general education students who partially achieved the performance standard would do better by receiving more individual instruction and/or by being grouped with higher performing students. The committee also examined data (see Figure 9-11) showing the class assignments of students who were eligible for free lunch and noted that a large percentage of these students were in the special education (Class 8B) and ELL (Class 8D) classes. The students eligible for free lunch who were in the general education classes (Classes 8A, 8C, and 8D) generally met or exceeded the performance standards.

During the committee's discussions, one of the teachers asked whether they should be considering any changes to the curriculum. Specifically, she was concerned with the articulation of Jefferson's language arts curriculum to state standards. To assist in

Figure 9-8 SPSS report showing one-way ANOVA of the mean scale scores by gender, special education services code, and eligible for free lunch code.

One-way ANOVA

Language Arts Scale Score by Gender

	Sum of Squares	df	Mean Square	F	Sig.
Between Groups	2,544.580	1	2,544.580	2.103	.150
Within Groups	1,25,809.042	104	1,209.702		
Total	1,28,353.623	105			

One-way ANOVA

Language Arts Scale Score by Special Education Services Code

	Sum of Squares	df	Mean Square	F	Sig.
Between Groups	7,2771.728	3	24,257.243	44.515	.000
Within Groups	5,5581.895	102	544.921		
Total	1,28,353.623	105			

One-way ANOVA

Language Arts Scale Score by Eligible for Free Lunch Code

	Sum of Squares	df	Mean Square	F	Sig.
Between Groups	8,706.485	1	8,706.485	7.568	.007
Within Groups	1,19,647.137	104	1,150.453		
Total	1,28,353.623	105			

Figure 9-9 SPSS report showing one-way ANOVA of the mean scale scores by special education services code, excluding special education/English language learner (ELL) students.

One-way ANOVA

Language Arts Scale Score by Special Education Services Code Excluding Special Education/ELL Students

	Sum of Squares	df	Mean Square	F	Sig.
Between Groups	35,303.145	2	17,651.573	30.892	.000
Within Groups	55,425.895	97	571.401		
Total	90,729.040	99			

Figure 9-10 SPSS report showing a contingency table (crosstabulation) of performance level by class, controlling for special education services codes. ELL = English language learner.

Performance Level * Class * Special Educ. Services Code Crosstabulation

Count

Special Educ. Services Code			Class					
			Grade 8A	Grade 8B	Grade 8C	Grade 8D	Grade 8E	Total
Gen. Educ.	Performance Level	2 – Partial Achievement of Performance Standard	0	0	6		0	6
		3 – Met Performance Standard	15	1	8		14	38
		4 – Exceeded Performance Standard	7	0	7		9	23
	Total		22	1	21		23	67
Spec. Educ.	Performance Level	1 – Did Not Meet Performance Standard	0	2	0	0	0	2
		2 – Partial Achievement of Performance Standard	1	13	1	1	0	16
		3 – Met Performance Standard	2	0	0	0	1	3
	Total		3	15	1	1	1	21
ELL	Performance Level	2 – Partial Achievement of Performance Standard			0	10		10
		3 – Met Performance Standard			2	0		2
	Total				2	10		12
Spec. Educ. & ELL	Performance Level	1 – Did Not Meet Performance Standard				6		6
	Total					6		6

Figure 9-11 SPSS report showing a contingency table (crosstabulation) of performance level by class, controlling for eligible for free lunch code.

Performance Level * Class * Free-Lunch-Eligibility Crosstabulation

Count

Free-Lunch-Eligibility			Class					Total
			Grade 8A	Grade 8B	Grade 8C	Grade 8D	Grade 8E	
Not Eligible	Performance Level	1 – Did Not Meet Performance Standard	0	0	0	2	0	2
		2 – Partial Achievement of Performance Standard	1	9	7	3	0	20
		3 – Met Performance Standard	12	1	6	0	11	30
		4 – Exceeded Performance Standard	5	0	3	0	9	17
	Total		18	10	16	5	20	69
Eligible	Performance Level	1 – Did Not Meet Performance Standard	0	2	0	4	0	6
		2 – Partial Achievement of Performance Standard	0	4	0	8	0	12
		3 – Met Performance Standard	5	0	4	0	4	13
		4 – Exceeded Performance Standard	2	0	4	0	0	6
	Total		7	6	8	12	4	37

answering this question, the committee looked at student performance subscore data (Standards 1, 2, and 3). Figures 9-12A and 9-12B provide a breakdown of the means for each of the subscores by special services code and by class assignment. For all groups, the lowest scores were in Standard 3 (critical analysis and evaluation). Furthermore, in all cases, Standard 3 was at least 10 points lower than Standard 2 (literary response and expression). Figure 9-13 is an excerpt of the description of

Standard 3. The teachers on the committee agreed that more work in the language arts curriculum could be done to address this standard.

DEVELOPING A PLAN

The committee at Jefferson Middle School continued to meet until the end of July. During its meetings, a good deal of discussion was dedicated to the special education and ELL programs. Committee members reviewed the individual records of a number of students in these programs and noted that many of them were close to meeting the standards. Although it would make recommendations that could benefit all students, the committee concluded that a more extensive analysis was needed for special and ELL education. At the end of July, a plan was developed with immediate and long-term objectives. The overall goal of the plan was to improve performance of all students in language arts. The plan included the following recommendations:

1. Develop a performance profile in language arts for each student to be shared with the teacher, the student, and the parents. Include performance data for other subject areas. Make the data available in electronic form on the Internet.

Figure 9-12A   SPSS report showing a breakdown of mean subscores (standards 1, 2 and 3) by special education services code. ELL = English language learner.

Special Educ. Services Code		S1 – Information & Understanding	S2 – Literary Response & Expression	S3 – Critical Analysis & Evaluation
Gen. Educ.	Mean	85.66	93.66	81.88
	N	67	67	67
	Std. Deviation	7.267	4.051	9.014
Spec. Educ.	Mean	72.19	85.10	65.76
	N	21	21	21
	Std. Deviation	8.830	7.382	9.612
ELL	Mean	69.83	82.83	60.00
	N	12	12	12
	Std. Deviation	7.709	6.191	11.740
Spec. Educ. & ELL	Mean	54.00	66.00	50.67
	N	6	6	6
	Std. Deviation	.894	.894	.516
Total	Mean	79.41	89.17	74.44
	N	106	106	106
	Std. Deviation	11.705	8.728	13.771

Figure 9-12B SPSS report showing a breakdown of mean subscores (Standards 1, 2, and 3) by class.

Class		S1 – Information & Understanding	S2 – Literary Response & Expression	S3 – Critical Analysis & Evaluation
Grade 8A	Mean	85.64	93.88	82.52
	N	25	25	25
	Std. Deviation	5.722	2.833	6.734
Grade 8B	Mean	70.44	83.88	63.62
	N	16	16	16
	Std. Deviation	8.310	7.623	8.221
Grade 8C	Mean	82.37	91.58	77.67
	N	24	24	24
	Std. Deviation	9.098	5.356	11.378
Grade 8D	Mean	62.47	75.59	54.18
	N	17	17	17
	Std. Deviation	7.534	8.024	6.483
Grade 8E	Mean	87.92	95.00	84.37
	N	24	24	24
	Std. Deviation	5.389	2.554	6.781
Total	Mean	79.41	89.17	74.44
	N	106	106	106
	Std. Deviation	11.705	8.728	13.771

2. Establish a committee in fall 2004 to consider revisions to the school report card to reflect performance and progress on state standards.
3. Address the need for teachers to have greater access to electronic student databases to monitor progress and performance.
4. Do a more extensive review of the special education and ELL programs. Consider specifically the establishment of more inclusive classes as well as more individual tutoring support.
5. Establish a committee in fall 2004 to review the eighth-grade language arts curriculum with the goal of including more activities that relate to Standard 3.
6. Provide more resources to the Resource Room (Helping Place), which provides one-on-one support for students.
7. Establish an after-school peer tutoring program on a trial basis to begin January 2005.

Ms. Carter, Jefferson's principal, endorsed the committee's recommendations and committed to doing whatever she could to provide the resources necessary for implementation.

Figure 9-13 Excerpt of the definition and characteristics of language arts Standard 3.

Standard 3: Language for Critical Analysis and Evaluation

Students listen and read to analyze and evaluate experiences, ideas, information, and issues using evaluative criteria from a variety of perspectives and recognizing the differences in evaluations based on different sets of criteria.

Students analyze, interpret, and evaluate information, ideas, organization, and language from academic and nonacademic texts, such as textbooks, public documents, book and movie reviews, and editorials.

Students assess the quality of texts and presentations using criteria related to the genre, the subject area, and the purpose (e.g., using the criteria of accuracy, objectivity, comprehensiveness, and understanding of the game to evaluate a sports editorial).

Students understand that within any group there are many different points of view, depending on the particular interests and values of the individual, and recognize those differences in perspective in texts and presentations.

Students evaluate their own work and the work of others based on a variety of criteria and recognize the varying effectiveness of different approaches.

Examples:

- Students compare a magazine article on a historical event with entries in an encyclopedia or history book.
- Students use the criteria of scientific investigation to evaluate the significance of a lab experiment.
- Students read two conflicting reviews of a popular movie and recognize the different criteria the critics used to evaluate the film.

INFORMATION OVERLOAD: A CAUTION

Administrators and teachers engaged in data-driven instruction may not be prepared to deal with the volume of data that can be generated by an information system. Herbert Simon, economist and Nobel laureate, succinctly cautioned that "a wealth of information can create a poverty of attention" (Varian, 1995, p. 200) In this chapter, the results of one test generated a number of reports that needed to be evaluated and considered carefully. Tests in other subject areas (e.g., mathematics or science) might engender a similar process or be integrated into a common planning process. To Jefferson Middle School's credit, Ms. Carter's committee agreed to work through July, so that the administrators, and especially the teachers, had time away from the normal hustle and bustle of the school year to consider carefully what data were needed and how the data could be used for improving teaching and learning. The committee's recommendations further require the development and generation of more data to monitor student progress and performance. The experienced administrator will monitor the amount of information generated, to avoid inundating staff to the point that data cannot be used effectively.

SUMMARY

American education today is in an era of standards in which testing is used to monitor student achievement and progress. Data-driven decision making can aid administrators and teachers as they work to improve teaching and learning.

Networking technology allows many levels of the education enterprise (state, district, school, class) to share test data in a timely, accurate, and readily available manner. Test data need to be integrated with other data in school records, and to be analyzed and reviewed by principals and teachers at individual schools.

Student performance on an eighth-grade, statewide language arts test was analyzed at the Jefferson Middle School using Statistical Package for the Social Sciences (SSPS) software. Results of statistical analyses (e.g., frequency distributions, means and standard deviations of scores by performance level, one-way analysis of variance) were integrated with data from the student information system. The results of analyses provided important information to a committee involved in developing strategies to improve teaching and learning at the school. The committee developed a plan with immediate and long-term objectives to improve performance of all students in language arts.

Experienced administrators monitor the amount of information generated and disseminated to avoid inundating staff with data that cannot be used effectively.

Activities

1. Visit a school district office or a school and meet with an administrator (e.g., superintendent, assistant superintendent, principal) and determine how data are being used to support instruction. Specifically, try to determine what data are available to teachers, in what form (e.g., print or on the Internet), and whether there are any issues with regard to access, timeliness, or accuracy.
2. Assume you are the principal of the Jefferson Middle School and are following up the committee's recommendations as listed in this chapter. Develop an implementation plan that includes broad cost estimates for each recommendation.
3. Assume you are the assistant principal at the Jefferson Middle School and the principal has asked you to design the format for a new individualized student performance profile. Do a search on the Internet for sample student profile forms and select two that might work as a model for Jefferson.

References

Aper, J. P. (2002). Steerage from a distance: Can mandated accountability systems really improve schools? *Journal of Educational Thought, 36*(1), 7–26.

Horn, C. (2003). High-stakes testing and students: Stopping or perpetuating a cycle of failure? *Theory into Practice, 42*(1), 30–41.

Mazzeo, C. (2001). Frameworks of state: Assessment policy in historical perspective. *Teachers College Record, 103*(3), 367–397.

Montgomery, E. C. (2004). What students need to know. In C. Glickman (Ed.), *Letters to the next president* (pp. 158–165). New York: Teachers College Press.

Rousmaniere, K. (1997). *City teachers: Teaching and school reform in historical perspective.* New York: Teachers College Press.

Varian, H. (1995). The information economy. *Scientific American, 273*(3), 200–202.

Chapter 10

Supporting Teachers and Their Professional Development

In Chapter 9, we had discussed the work of a committee of administrators and teachers who met just after the end of the school year to review student perform-ance on a statewide language arts test and to develop strategies for the coming year. The activities in which they engaged are validated by Carr and Harris (2001) in a work titled *Succeeding with Standards: Linking Curriculum, Assessment, and Action Planning*. In a chapter devoted to professional development and supervision, they provide examples of best practice. The first example, data-driven dialog, describes a collaborative model developed by Lipton and Wellman (1999) in which teachers work together and use data to gain insight into what is happening in their classrooms with the clear intention of applying their discoveries to continual improvement. Carr and Harris comment: "We cannot emphasize enough the importance of building structures and strategies for collaborative analysis of data . . ." (p. 129). In a second example of best practice, Carr and Harris (2001) refer to a model developed for high schools by Schmoker (1999) that relies on end-of-course assessment. Teachers meet immediately after the end of a course and analyze student test results; their goal is to develop a comprehensive assessment plan.

Both of these examples of best practice also refer to the professional develop-ment of teachers. Carr and Harris (2001) recognize the importance of data-driven decision processes in instructional planning and assessment of learning, but they also consider such activities as critical to professional growth. Professional devel-opment depends on respect for teachers' acquired knowledge and use of outcome data as the focus of shared dialog to expand their knowledge. This approach can be as powerful as professional development workshops, teacher evaluations, or classroom observations—perhaps even more so. To be successful, teachers' use of data-driven decision processes needs the support of confident administrators who understand the critical role that teachers play in schools and schooling. In this chapter, data-driven decision making is examined as a tool for supporting professional development activities.

SUMMATIVE AND FORMATIVE EVALUATION

One of the most important responsibilities of the school leader is the improvement of instruction. Because instruction is directly related to the quality of the teaching staff, most administrators understand the importance of evaluating staff on a regular basis and providing guidance for improvement. The need for improvement does not imply that something needs fixing or that there is a problem. Rather, most professionals recognize a need for growth throughout their career.

Administrators can choose from many approaches to evaluation. A simple summative evaluation, which is done in many schools, usually involves the observation(s) of a lesson: An evaluator observes a teacher and prepares a written commentary, the teacher and evaluator then have a follow-up discussion. A good evaluation is not simply an observation of what occurred during the lesson; it also includes suggestions for improvement. A formative evaluation might include summative evaluation activities but emphasizes suggestions for improvement leading to professional growth. In effect, the summative evaluation *summarizes* a teacher's performance, whereas the formative evaluation seeks *to form,* or to improve, the teacher's professional performance. A formative evaluation is an ongoing process throughout the school year. An administrator provides a number of opportunities for observation, for discussion, and for other situations wherein teachers can learn and grow.

The literature on formative evaluation and teacher development is extensive. An excellent source of information is the work of Charlotte Danielson (Danielson, 1996; Danielson & McGreal, 2000). Danielson and McGreal propose a holistic framework for formative teacher development that has four domains:

Domain 1: Planning and preparation. Includes comprehensive understanding of the content to be taught, knowledge of the students' backgrounds, and design of instruction and assessment

Domain 2: Classroom environment. Addresses the teacher's skill in establishing an environment conducive to learning, including the physical and interpersonal aspects of the environment

Domain 3: Instruction. Addresses the teacher's skill in engaging students in learning content and includes the wide range of instructional strategies that enable students to learn

Domain 4: Professional responsibilities. Addresses a teacher's additional professional responsibilities, including self-assessment and reflection, communication with parents, participating in ongoing professional development, and contributing to the school and district environment.

In the development of a teacher evaluation policy, program, or procedure, a holistic approach is highly recommended. In the final analysis, the development of the abilities and attitudes of teachers may be the most important direct path for the improvement of learning.

In retrospect, the example in Chapter 9 presented a situation in which teachers had the opportunity to develop professionally. A committee of Jefferson Middle School administrators and teachers met to discuss student performance on a language arts test. The purpose of the committee was to collect and analyze data and to use collective judgment and insight to develop a strategy for improving teaching and learning. At no time was this work considered a professional development activity. But what were the teachers doing? They were evaluating student performance and achievement by comparing and analyzing student characteristics (e.g., gender, need for special educational services, eligibility for free lunch). One important characteristic they considered was student class assignment. This consideration probably generated discussion on how the teachers were teaching and how their students were learning. Sharing of pedagogical knowledge and teaching approaches can become quite extensive in such situations.

One of the goals of Ms. Carter, the principal, in creating the committee was that such sharing would, indeed, happen. She hoped that in addition to developing an instructional strategy or plan, the teachers would engage each other and share their knowledge about how language arts is taught. Ms. Carter understood that teachers use a variety of techniques that sometimes work and sometimes do not work for particular students. She also had learned that the language arts faculty was a competent group of teachers who would benefit by sharing their teaching techniques with one another. During the school year, Ms. Carter had reviewed her teachers' personnel records, had observed teachers in the classroom, and had engaged teachers in follow-up discussions. In a sense, she had done her homework. She was ready to provide a situation wherein her teachers could develop professionally by working on common issues and sharing their expertise and experience.

COLLECTING PERSONNEL DATA

All schools collect personnel data on a routine basis. Applications for available positions require the submission of a curriculum vitae or a résumé. If a candidate is offered a position, an employee information or data sheet is completed and the data are entered into a computerized personnel information system. In many cases the process of professional development begins with the review of individual personnel records to determine educational background, teaching assignments, past evaluations, and so forth. At some point, the principal or a district administrator might examine data on groups of teachers (e.g., all mathematics teachers, all language arts teachers, new teachers, experienced teachers) to evaluate their abilities and effectiveness.

District and school personnel must have thorough knowledge of the procedures, processes, and guidelines that have been established for using personnel files in evaluation activities—or in any other activity. In school districts where teachers are unionized, frequently these procedures are documented as part of the collective bargaining agreement. Examples include the right of a teacher to see his or her file at any time, the schedule for and form of official observations and evaluations, and identification of those qualified to do an observation.

A major issue in recent years has been whether the results of standardized tests should be included in personnel files. A related issue is whether and how student test performance should figure in teacher evaluations. District procedures need to be followed or developed if they do not exist. For example, the city of Portland, Oregon, and the Portland Teachers Association reached this agreement:

> Student performance on district-wide and/or other standardized tests may indicate where modifications of instruction are required and the implementation of such modifications may be part of the evaluation process. However, evaluations or criticism of a teacher shall not be based specifically on the issue of comparisons of such student performances." (Nelson, 1997, http://www.lawmemo.com/arb/award/1997/127.htm)

The difficulty in using standardized test scores in teacher evaluations relates to the complexity of teaching, class assignments, and student abilities. For instance, class size is an important determinant of student performance. A large class is more difficult to teach than a smaller class, all other things being equal. The ability of students is also an important determinant of student performance. High performing students tend to continue to perform well, whereas students with special needs require support and frequently individual attention in order to pass standardized tests. If student test scores are a part of a teacher evaluation, school administrators should carefully consider whether they should be the major determinant in an evaluation.

KINGSLAND SCHOOL DISTRICT CASE STUDY

Kingsland is a modest sized school district on the West Coast. It has two comprehensive high schools, Quigley and Adams, both of which have between 70% and 80% of their students passing state standardized tests. In May 2005, the superintendent, Carol Sedona, asked each of the principals, John Killian (Quigley High School) and Joseph Simmons (Adams High School), to review their mathematics program. To assist them, the superintendent sent a report prepared by her office. The report included data (see Figure 10-1) showing that overall student performance on

Figure 10-1 Summary of student performance on Mathematics State Test (ST) comparing the 2004–2005 academic year to the previous 3 years for all math teachers at two high schools.

	Staff Id	School	Gender	Total Years of Experience	Years at Kingsland	Total Students Taking Math ST Previous 3Yrs	Total Students Passing Math ST Previous 3Yrs	No. of Students Taking Math ST 2004-2005	No. of Students Passing Math ST 2004-2005	% Pass Prev 3Yrs	% Pass 2004-2005	% Difference
			Kingsland School District									
			School Personnel High School Math Performance Analysis									
			2004-2005									
9	166367344	Quigley	M	14	14	344	290	120	92	84.30%	76.67%	-7.64%
10	102443754	Quigley	F	14	12	321	279	116	95	86.92%	81.90%	-5.02%
11	733854633	Quigley		10	10	333	276	122	93	82.88%	76.23%	-6.65%
12	133456610	Quigley	M	3	3	323	280	122	99	86.69%	81.15%	-5.54%
13	102456754	Quigley	F	7	7	320	271	113	95	84.69%	84.07%	-0.62%
14	School Averages			10	9	328	279	119	94.8	85.10%	80.00%	-5.09%
16	110243897	Adams	F	21	19	336	299	114	98	88.99%	85.96%	-3.02%
17	101996123	Adams	M	23	12	332	296	118	104	89.16%	88.14%	-1.02%
18	105324500	Adams	F	7	3	313	272	119	95	86.90%	79.83%	-7.07%
19	100348989	Adams	F	9	9	330	288	119	94	87.27%	78.99%	-8.28%
20	105321290	Adams	M	8	4	321	277	115	89	86.29%	77.39%	-8.90%
21	School Averages			14	9	326	286	117	96	87.72%	82.06%	-5.66%

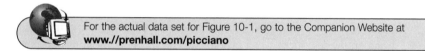

For the actual data set for Figure 10-1, go to the Companion Website at **www.//prenhall.com/picciano**

the statewide mathematics test had declined by 5.09% and 5.66% from the previous 3-year averages at Quigley and Adams, respectively. The report also showed the results for each mathematics teacher (Staff ID) at the two high schools. Dr. Sedona asked each of the principals to prepare an action plan about how he will address the issue by the end of June 2005.

Mr. Simmons, who is a new principal at Adams High School, was hired the previous year by the Kingsland School District. He had been an assistant principal and teacher in a nearby school district. Mr. Simmons reviewed the data in the report sent by the superintendent and had several meetings with two of his assistant principals. Each teacher was identified by a staff ID number, so he reviewed the personnel records of each and determined that each was a competent teacher. In examining the data in the report, he saw that the passing rates of the students of the two most experienced teachers were better than those of the less experienced teachers. He and his assistant principals decided that the five mathematics teachers at Adams would be asked to participate in planning sessions during the summer. The purpose of the sessions would be to develop a plan for improving the mathematics program. Mr. Simmons also wanted to design one or two professional development workshops on teaching mathematics. In a memorandum to the superintendent, he outlined his thoughts.

Mr. Killian, at Quigley High School, had been in the Kingsland School District for 17 years, 5 as a teacher, 5 as an assistant principal, and 7 as a principal. When he received the report from the superintendent, he reviewed the data and decided to have several meetings with his assistant principals and the mathematics teachers. He was a bit concerned that the district office might be indirectly "evaluating" teachers using the student performance on standardized tests. He also knew that a number of teachers had expressed their concern that the average class size had been increasing for the past few years and that a number of classes had grown beyond the 23-student enrollment limit for high school mathematics, science, and technology classes, established by the Kingsland Board of Education and the Kingsland Teachers Association. Mr. Killian asked one of his assistant principals to prepare a brief enrollment summary of the mathematics program for the past 4 years (see Figure 10-2), as close in format as possible to the performance summary prepared by the superintendent. The data established that enrollments had been increasing for the past 4 years and that some class sizes were higher than the 23-student maximum. Mr. Killian also knew that several mathematics classes had enrollments as high as 26 students; however, he did not think that class size alone accounted for the decrease in student performance on the state tests.

When Mr. Killian met with the mathematics teachers, they shared several of their insights. The teachers said class size was an issue, but they also indicated that the statewide mathematics tests had changed 3 years ago. Now many more of the questions on the test were word problems. The teachers thought that curriculum changes were needed in the mathematics program and that more attention was needed in language arts instruction, especially reading. They indicated that as mathematics teachers, they did not have enough time to work on the basic reading problems of some of the students. After the discussion, Mr. Killian wrote a memorandum to the superintendent that included the data in Figure 10-2 and suggested that the school district consider providing additional resources to honor the limit on class size established by

Figure 10-2 Quigley High School enrollment data comparing the 2004–2005 academic year to the previous 3 years.

	A	B	C	D	E	F	G	H	I	J	K	L	M	N
1				**Quigley High School**										
2				**Math Performance Analysis**										
3				**2004-2005**										
4														
5														
6				Total Years	Years at	No. Students Taking Math ST				Average Class Size				
7	Staff Id	School	Gender	of Experience	Kingsland	2001-200	2002-200	2003-200	2004-200	2001-200	2002-200	2003-200	2004-2005	
8	166367344	Quigley	M	14	14	112	115	117	120	22.4	23.0	23.4	24.0	1.60%
9	102443754	Quigley	F	14	12	106	108	107	116	21.2	21.6	21.4	23.2	2.00%
10	733854633	Quigley	F	10	10	110	108	115	122	22.0	21.6	23.0	24.4	2.40%
11	133456610	Quigley	M	3	3	106	106	111	122	21.2	21.2	22.2	24.4	3.20%
12	102456754	Quigley	F	7	7	105	107	108	113	21.0	21.4	21.6	22.6	1.60%
13	School Averages			10	9	108	109	112	119	21.6	21.8	22.3	23.7	2.16%
14														

For the actual data set for Figure 10-2, go to the Companion Website at
www.//prenhall.com/picciano

the Kingsland Board of Education and the Kingsland Teachers Association. He also indicated that he would like to schedule planning sessions with his mathematics teachers in July to discuss curriculum changes, as well as to study the relationship between reading ability and performance on the statewide mathematics tests. In a separate memorandum, Mr. Killian expressed his concern that the reports issued by the district office looked only at student performance as a way of evaluating teachers.

The approaches of the two principals were significantly different, even though both included additional planning. Mr. Simmons at Adams High school relied entirely on his assistant principals for insight and advice. Mr. Killian at Quigley High School, on the other hand, involved the mathematics teachers immediately. Perhaps this was because Mr. Killian was an experienced administrator, had been in the Kingsland School District a long time, and had a well-established relationship with the teachers. Mr. Killian also used data beyond that provided by the district to support his and his teachers' insights into the issue. Mr. Simmons, on the other hand, was new to the district. He did not know the organizational history of his high school and he had not yet established as close a relationship with his teachers.

After she read the two reports, Dr. Sedona recommended that the two school principals organize a series of joint meetings in July. Administrators and mathematics teachers from both high schools would convene to review the mathematics curriculum and to design any needed professional development activities. Her office would be available to assist in any way, including provision of additional data support. Dr. Sedona met with Mr. Killian to assure him that the report produced by her office was not meant as an evaluation of the teachers. She was concerned, however, about the mathematics program and wanted the principals to engage in a serious dialogue about how it could be improved.

Dr. Sedona also asked the Kingsland data coordinator, Louis Lazard, to follow up on the change in the state mathematics test and see if any relationship existed between student performance and reading abilities. Mr. Lazard decided to take a student sample from the eighth-grade language arts test scores and ninth-grade mathematics test scores for the past 5 years. He selected the eighth-grade language arts test because it contained less content (e.g., literature) than the ninth-grade English tests and focused more on language arts and reading ability. For the 5 years, he looked at the relationship of the raw scores and charted a correlation coefficient for each year as follows:

Academic year	Correlation
2000–2001	.669
2001–2002	.655
2002–2003	.734
2003–2004	.745
2004–2005	.756

Figure 10-3 Correlation of the eighth-grade language arts and ninth-grade mathematics test scores for Kingsland School District, 2000–2005.

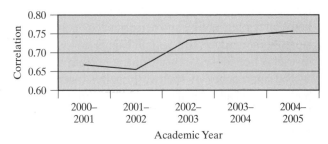

Figure 10-3 is a line graph illustrating the correlation.

Mr. Lazard concluded that there was a strong relationship between the two tests and that the relationship increased significantly 3 years ago (2002–2003) when the new mathematics test was established. He understood, however, that a correlation did not necessarily mean causality. He examined other variables and noted that other factors, such as an increase in the ELL population, might be affecting results on both tests. Without conducting a controlled, experimental research project in which a group of students was followed up over a period of time, Mr. Lazard could not establish whether a cause and effect relationship existed between reading ability and performance on the state mathematics tests. He shared his thoughts in the form of a memorandum to Dr. Sedona, who passed it along to the two principals and suggested that it might help in their discussions in July.

At the July meetings of administrators and mathematics teachers from the Adams and Quigley schools, the data from the district office as well as the Quigley data were reviewed and the two faculties shared insights. A report was issued in August that made the following major recommendations:

1. All mathematics courses should have a maximum enrollment of 23 students in accord with the agreement approved by the Kingsland Board of Education and the Kingsland Teachers Association.
2. A series of professional development workshops should be conducted in the coming year for mathematics teachers
   a. to help them update the curriculum to reflect the emphasis on word problems,
   b. to become more knowledgeable in teaching students with limited English proficiencies (English language learners), and
   c. to make greater use of technology in teaching mathematics.
3. A meeting should be scheduled with language arts teachers in middle schools and high schools to gather more information about the relationship of language arts and mathematics performance.
4. With the help of the district data coordinator, an action research project should be undertaken to examine the relationship of language arts and mathematics performance.

Dr. Sedona received the report and accepted the recommendations. She was a bit concerned about the need for a series of professional development workshops. Since coming to Kingsland, it was her impression that the resolution of many academic issues resulted in professional development activities. She favored investment in professional development and was familiar with much of the literature that supported its benefits. Nevertheless, she asked the district data coordinator whether he had any information about the effectiveness of professional development in terms of improved student performance in the Kingsland School District. She was also curious about the relationship between teaching experience and student performance.

KEEPING TRACK OF PROFESSIONAL DEVELOPMENT

In response to Dr. Sedona's request, Mr. Lazard began to assess the availability of professional development data. He was happy to find that as part of a initiative related to teacher recertification, the state had provided a small amount of funds to each school district to maintain records on formal professional development activities. The state legislature had passed regulations in 2003 requiring that all teaching licenses be recertified every 5 years. As part of the process, teachers must submit proof of enrollment in professional development programs totaling at least 300 hours. School districts were asked to verify the teachers' documentation. Hence, the districts were provided with the funds to develop and maintain professional development record-keeping files.

Figure 10-4A and 10-4B are examples of the types of data being collected and maintained. Mr. Lazard decided that he could use the summary data for each teacher (Figure 10-4B) and merge them with student performance data. He took a stratified sample of 90 teachers ($N = 90$) who taught language arts or mathematics in the district. He made sure that the sample had equal proportions of new and more experienced teachers and that all had enrolled in some staff development activity in the past 2 years. For student performance data, he decided to calculate the percentage of students passing the state standardized tests for each teacher in the sample for the 2004–2005 academic year. Figures 10-5A and 10-5B are samples of the SPSS file layout and data used for his analysis. The basic data for each teacher in the sample included the following items:

* Staff ID
* Years of teaching experience
* Subject area (1 = language arts; 2 = mathematics)
* Hours of professional development since July 2003
* Percentage (passing rate) of students passing standardized tests

Figure 10-4A Sample record layout for tracking professional development activities.

Staff ID	Name	Activity Date	No. of Hours	Type	Description
001	Jones, Karen	07-25-2003	6	Workshop	Workshop on Teaching Language Arts in an Inclusive Classroom
002	Sanders, James	07-23-2003	6	Workshop	Workshop on Teaching Language Arts in an Inclusive Classroom
003	Charles, Lynn	07-16-2005	3	Workshop	Curriculum Development in Mathematics
004	Atkins, Barry	09-30-2005	3	Workshop	Curriculum Development in Mathematics
005	Sanford, Mary	09-2005	30	Class	Graduate Course in Teaching Middle School Science
006	Skeen, Lynn	11-21-2005	6	Workshop	Using Technology in Middle School Science
007					

Figure 10-4B Sample record layout for tracking professional development activities summed and sorted by staff ID.

Staff ID/Name	Activity Date	No. of Hours	Type	Description
001/Jones, Karen	07-25-2003	6	Workshop	Workshop on Teaching Language Arts in an Inclusive Classroom
	10-23-2003	3	Workshop	Using and Preparing IEPs
	01-10-2004	6	Workshop	Understanding Learning Disabilities
	.			
	.			
002/Sanders, James	07-16-2003	6	Workshop	Curriculum Development in Mathematics
	09-2003	30	Class	Graduate Course in using Technology to Teach Mathematics
	02-22-2004	3	Workshop	Follow-up on Summer Workshop on 07-16-2003
	.			
	.			

Figure 10-5A Sample SPSS (Variable View) record layout for studying professional development and student performance.

	Name	Type	Width	Decimals	Label	Values	Missing	Columns	Align	Measure
1	staffid	Numeric	3	0		None	None	8	Right	Scale
2	yrsexp	Numeric	2	0	Years Teachi	None	None	8	Right	Scale
3	subject	Numeric	1	0	Subject Area	{1, Language	None	8	Right	Scale
4	hrsdev	Numeric	2	0	Hours of Prof	None	None	8	Right	Scale
5	passing	Numeric	4	2	Average % S	None	None	8	Right	Scale
6	expcode	Numeric	1	0	Experience C	{1, 1-5 Years	None	8	Right	Scale
7	devcode	Numeric	1	0	Hours Develo	{1, 1-10 Hour	None	8	Right	Scale
8										

chap9profdevelop.sav - SPSS Data Editor

File Edit View Data Transform Analyze Graphs Utilities Window Help

For the actual data set for Figure 10-5A, go to the Companion Website at **www.//prenhall.com/picciano**

Figure 10-5B Sample SPSS (Data View) excerpt of the data file used for studying professional development and student performance.

chap9profdevelop.sav - SPSS Data Editor

File Edit View Data Transform Analyze Graphs Utilities Window Help

1 : staffid   1

	staffid	yrsexp	subject	hrsdev	passing	expcode	devcode	var
1	1	18	1	20	79.20	3	2	
2	2	24	1	12	79.50	3	2	
3	3	4	2	12	77.40	2	2	
4	4	3	2	22	83.50	2	3	
5	5	12	1	3	77.40	2	1	
6	6	21	2	7	81.20	3	1	
7	7	20	2	3	79.60	3	1	
8	8	7	1	21	77.30	2	3	
9	9	1	1	6	81.20	1	1	
10	10	5	2	17	76.70	2	2	

Because of the need for several types of analyses, Mr. Lazard also created two **categorical variables**, also called discrete variables (see Technical Support A), that would disaggregate the sample into three groups according to years of teaching experience and hours of professional development:

Experience code
1 = 1 to 5 years of teaching experience
2 = 6 to 15 years of teaching experience
3 = 16+ years of teaching experience

Development code
1 = 1 to 10 hours of professional development
2 = 11 to 20 hours of professional development
3 = 21+ hours of professional development

To start his analysis, Mr. Lazard developed a correlation matrix; then he conducted a means comparison.

Figure 10-6 is a correlation matrix comparing the relationship of years of teaching experience, hours of professional development and student passing rate. The data show that statistically significant relationships exist between teaching experience and passing rate ($r = .311$) and hours of professional development and passing rate ($r = .280$). Although significant, these are not very high correlations; they account for approximately 9.7% (r^2, or $.311 \times .311$) and 7.8% (r^2, or $.280 \times .280$) of the variation in the variables in the sample populations. However, given that the statistical significance level is at .01, which is more rigorous than the standard .05

Figure 10-6 SPSS correlation matrix of years teaching, hours of professional development, and average percentage of students passing standardized tests (passing rate).

Correlations

		Years Teaching	Hours of Professional Development	Average % Students Passing
Years Teaching	Pearson Correlation	1	−.281 **	.311 **
	Sig. (2-tailed)	.	.007	.003
	N	90	90	90
Hours of Professional Development	Pearson Correlation	−.281 **	1	.280 **
	Sig. (2-tailed)	.007	.	.007
	N	90	90	90
Average % Students Passing	Pearson Correlation	.311 **	.280 **	1
	Sig. (2-tailed)	.003	.007	.
	N	90	90	90

** Correlation is significant at the 0.01 level (2-tailed).

level, the data are interpreted as having statistically significant relationships. The correlation matrix also indicates that there is an inverse relationship ($r = -.281$) between years of teaching experience and hours of professional development, which indicates that more experienced teachers tend to enroll in fewer hours of staff development activities.

Figure 10-7 is the output of a regression model examining the relationship of the two combined independent variables (teaching experience and professional development) to the dependent variable (passing rate). It indicates that when taken together, teaching experience and professional development represent a positive ($r = .494$) relationship to the passing rate and account for 24.4% (r^2, or $.494 \times .494$) of the variation. In essence, Mr. Lazard feels comfortable concluding that the more hours of professional development and the more years of teaching experience, the higher the students' passing rate on standardized tests.

To further test the relationship of the three variables, Mr. Lazard examined the differences in the student passing rates associated with the experience codes and the professional development codes. Figure 10-8 shows that the differences among each of the groupings are relatively small but support, to a degree, what was found with the correlation analysis. As teaching experience increases from least (1 to 5 years) to moderate (6 to 15 years) to extensive (16 years plus), the passing rates increase as well. The same is true for professional development. To finalize his interpretation, Mr. Lazard does an analysis of variance (see Figure 10-9) using the passing rate as the dependent variable and teaching experience and professional development as independent variables. The significance levels presented in the rightmost column of Figure 10-9 indicate that statistically significant differences exist when the two independent variables are combined.

Mr. Lazard summarized his findings in a brief report for the superintendent:

1. Teachers' professional development has a small but statistically significant positive relationship to students' passing rates on language arts and mathematics tests.
2. Teaching experience has a small but statistically significant positive relationship to students' passing rates on language arts and mathematics tests.

Figure 10-7 SPSS regression model showing the relationship among the three variables: years teaching, hours of professional development, and average percentage of students passing standardized tests (passing rate).

Model Summary

Model	R	R Square	Adjusted R Square	Std. Error of the Estimate
1	.494[a]	.244	.226	2.29510

[a]Predictors: (Constant), Hours of Professional Development, Years Teaching

Figure 10-8 SPSS means analysis comparing passing rate by experience code and development code.

Average % Students Passing * Experience Code

Average % Students Passing

Experience Code	Mean	N	Std. Deviation
1–5 Years Teaching	79.0900	30	2.02201
6–15 Years Teaching	80.3400	30	2.61384
16 Plus Years Teaching	80.4767	30	2.96097
Total	79.9689	90	2.60939

Average % Students Passing * Hours Development Code

Average % Students Passing

Hours	Mean	N	Std. Deviation
1–10 Hours	79.4069	29	1.55401
11–20 Hours	79.4464	28	2.74152
21 Plus Hours	80.9061	33	3.00863
Total	79.9689	90	2.60939

Figure 10-9 SPSS analysis of variance of the passing rate (dependent variable) with teaching experience code and professional development code (independent variables).

ANOVA[a,b]

			Unique Method				
			Sum of Squares	df	Mean Square	F	Sig.
Average % Students Passing	Main Effects	(Combined)	113.816	4	28.454	6.101	.000
		Experience Code	52.712	2	26.356	5.651	.005
		Hours Development Code	93.853	2	46.926	10.061	.000
	2-Way Interactions	Experience Code * Hours Development Code	127.038	4	31.760	6.809	.000
	Model		226.205	8	28.526	6.116	.000
	Residual		377.788	81	4.664		
	Total		605.993	89	6.809		

[a]Average % Students Passing by Experience Code, Hours Development Code
[b]All effects entered simultaneously

3. Combined professional development and teaching experience have a statistically significant positive relationship to students' passing rates on language arts and mathematics tests that suggest causality.

After reviewing the report, Dr. Sedona indicated to Mr. Lazard that the results of his study confirmed her intuitions.

In August 2005, the Kingsland Teachers Association sent a letter to the Kingsland Board of Education. The association requested that the district abide by the agreement that the two parties had established regarding enrollment limits, specifically enrollments in mathematics courses at Quigley High School and Adams High School. The association also asked that the board meet with it to consider setting new guidelines for all policies related to access to personnel records. A specific concern was the use of standardized test performance data, either directly or indirectly, for teacher evaluations.

SUMMARY

The professional development of teachers is recognized as important, and data-driven decision making is a tool for supporting development activities.

Administrators are responsible for the quality of the teaching staff. Among the methods they can choose for evaluating a teacher's professional performance are the simple summative process and the formative process, which involves observations and suggestions for professional growth opportunities.

All schools have policies and procedures for collecting and maintaining personnel records. The information is used in many activities, including teacher evaluation. A complex issue is whether students' scores on standardized tests should be kept in teachers' records as a means of evaluating teachers.

The Kingsland School District case study provides examples of the use of data in improving instruction and supporting professional development. In these examples, the district superintendent, high school principals and assistant principals, teachers, and a district data coordinator analyzed student performance on a statewide mathematics test and proposed plans for improving their mathematics program, including the possibility of teacher development activities.

As part of the case study, the data coordinator used SPSS software to analyze the relationship between teaching experience and student performance. Several statistical tests enabled the coordinator to provide the district superintendent with specific conclusions.

Activities

1. Visit a school or school district administrator and ask if there are policies or guidelines related to access to personnel records. Also ask if the guidelines or policies specifically address the use of student standardized test scores in teacher evaluations.

2. Collect a small sample ($N = 30$) of data on student test scores at any level. Do some simple analyses to compare performance by gender, student demographics, or school and class characteristics. Specifically consider what software to use for the analyses and what statistical procedures to follow.

References

Carr, J. F., & Harris, D. E. (2001). *Succeeding with standards: Linking curriculum, assessment, and action planning.* Alexandria, VA: Association for Supervision and Curriculum Development.

Danielson, C. (1996). *Enhancing professional practice: A framework for teaching.* Alexandria, VA: Association for Supervision and Curriculum Development.

Danielson, C., & McGreal, T. L. (2000). *Teacher evaluation to enhance professional practice.* Princeton, NJ: Educational Testing Service.

Lipton, L., & Wellman, B. (1998). *Pathways to understanding.* Guilford, VT: Pathways Publishing.

Lipton, L., & Wellman, B. (1999). *Data driven dialogue: A series for the Vermont Standards and Assessment Consortium.* Montpelier, VT. Unpublished material.

Nelson, L. (1997). Arbitration proceedings between Portland School District and Portland Association of Teachers. Citation: 1997 NAC 127. Retrieved August 28, 2003, from http://www.lawmemo.com/arb/award/1997/127.htm

Schmoker, M. (1999). Results: The essential elements of improvement. *Unpublished workshop material provided at the Association for Supervision and Curriculum Development Conference on Teaching and Learning,* Reno, NV.

Technical Support

This section provides support for understanding the technical and statistical material presented in the book. Some readers may wish to review the material before reading any of the chapters. Other readers may refer to the material as they encounter technical terms, routines, or procedures with which they are not familiar.

Technical Support A

Review of Statistical Routines Used in This Book

Statistics is a body of mathematical techniques or processes for gathering, organizing, analyzing, and interpreting numeric data. Statistics provides the basic tools of measurement, evaluation, and research. As an academic discipline, statistics has its own language, conceptual base, and applications, which require years of study to learn well. Part A reviews the statistical routines that have been used as examples in this book. It is not a complete review of statistical concepts and procedures. For more thorough discussions, refer to one or more of the many textbooks and Web sites available, including these:

Educational Research Primer by A. G. Picciano (2004) London: Continuum.

Hyperstat Online
http://davidmlane.com/hyperstat/glossary.html

Statsoft, Incorporated
http://www.statsoftinc.com/textbook/glosfra.html

STEPS—Statistics Glossary
http://www.stats.gla.ac.uk/steps/glossary/index.html

KEY TERMS

The fundamental item of data for most statistical analysis is the **variable** or **data element**. A variable is an item of data that is collected for each case in a study, and which can vary or have more than one value. Some common variables collected in education are gender, ethnicity, grade point average, and test scores. Variables can be described as continuous or categorical, depending on how many values they can contain. **Continuous variables** such as family income or a test score can contain a wide range of values. A **categorical variable** (also referred to as a discrete variable) contains a limited number of values, such as in gender or ethnicity. Certain statistical procedures are appropriate for one type of variable or the other.

Statistical significance is a basic standard used in many statistical routines. It indicates the probability of a finding having occurred by chance. It has nothing to do with importance; rather, it is simply an indication of probability. Statisticians have adopted a general standard referred to as the .05 level of statistical significance. This means that a finding has a 5% (.05) chance of occurring randomly, or that the same result would occur 1 in 20 times, assuming all other factors were equal. When a finding has a significance level of .05 or lower, it is assumed to be meaningful. Statistical significance is used in many procedures, for example, trying to determine if there is a statistically significant difference between the mean scores of girls and boys on a fourth-grade standardized reading test in a one-way **analysis of variance** (ANOVA) procedure. If the results of the one-way ANOVA show a statistical significance level of .02, the difference in the mean scores is statistically significant and meaningful. The abbreviation for statistical significance is Sig., and it appears routinely in statistical reports.

In many statistical routines, references are made to **degrees of freedom,** which indicate the number of observations or values in a distribution that are independent of each other or are free to vary. They are used with various measures to refine the results of treatments of probability or chance. For example, consider a distribution of three numbers; the numbers can vary but the sum has to equal 100. Although three separate numbers can be selected, in reality, only two numbers need be selected, because the third number is determined by the first two numbers. So if 40 and 50 are selected, the third number has to be 10. The numbers 40 and 50 are independent, but 10 is dependent on the first two numbers. In this example, there are two independent values, or two degrees of freedom. Calculating the degrees of freedom for many statistical measures can be time consuming and complex. Fortunately, most statistical software packages calculate degrees of freedom automatically. The abbreviation for degrees of freedom is df and appears routinely in many statistical reports.

DESCRIPTIVE STATISTICAL PROCEDURES

Basic descriptive procedures, specifically **frequency distributions** and **contingency tables** (also referred to as crosstabulations) are most appropriate for doing analyses on categorical variables (e.g., gender, ethnicity) or continuous variables that can be grouped into categories. For instance, family income is a continuous variable but it can be grouped into categories:

Below $10,000
$10,000–$30,000
$31,001–$50,000
$50,001–$80,000
Above $80,000

Frequency distributions and contingency tables are excellent for becoming familiar with data and identifying missing or incorrect data. They are efficient and effective because they present data in a concise format that many people are able to understand.

Frequency Distributions

A frequency distribution is a systematic arrangement of numeric values from the lowest to the highest or the highest to the lowest, with a count of the number of times each value was obtained. It also provides percentages of each of the occurrences of the values. As an example, consider the Jefferson Middle School case study in Chapter 9. A group of students completed a standardized English language arts test, and results of the test included a performance level indicator coded as follows:

Level 1: Students do not meet the learning standards.
Level 2: Students show partial achievement of the learning standards.
Level 3: Students meet the learning standards.
Level 4: Students exceed the learning standards.

It would be possible to write a paragraph describing the results; however, a simple frequency distribution table as shown in Figure A-1 clearly provides the basic information. (In all figures, SPSS means the figure was produced using the Statistical Package for the Social Sciences software.) In addition to the percentages of each value, valid percentages (excludes any missing or invalid data), and cumulative percentages are also provided. If needed, a simple bar chart can provide a picture of the distribution (see Figure A-2).

Frequency distributions can be most useful in identifying missing or incorrect data. In the example in Figure A-1, suppose one or more codes was a 0 or a 5, or any value other than 1, 2, 3 or 4. These would appear on the frequency distribution table. In the initial stages of data analysis, a good rule of thumb is to generate frequency

Figure A-1   Sample frequency distribution using SPSS.

Statistics

Performance Level		
N	Valid	106
	Missing	0

Performance Level

		Frequency	Percent	Valid percent	Cumulative percent
Valid	1 – Did Not Meet Performance Standard	8	7.5	7.5	7.5
	2 – Partial Achievement of Performance Standard	32	30.2	30.2	37.7
	3 – Met Performance Standard	43	40.6	40.6	78.3
	4 – Exceeded Performance Standard	23	21.7	21.7	100.0
	Total	106	100.0	100.0	

Figure A-2 Sample bar chart derived from a freqeuncy distribution using SPSS.

distributions for all key variables to identify any data entry errors or missing data, and then take steps to correct the problems.

Contingency Tables (Crosstabulations)

Frequency distributions are excellent for looking at one variable or data element. To compare results of two or more variables (e.g., performance level and student gender), two frequency distributions, one for females and one for males could be generated and lined up side by side. An even simpler approach is to develop a contingency table, also referred to as a crosstabulation. A contingency table is an arrangement of data in a two-dimensional classification scheme represented by rows and columns. Figure A-3 is a contingency table showing the frequencies and percentages of student performance levels by gender. The table is arranged with the data for gender in the columns and data for performance level in the rows. Contingency tables, which are common in data analysis and research, can be used with almost any type of quantitative data. Figure A-4 is a clustered bar chart illustrating the contingency table in Figure A-3.

The importance of contingency tables is that they begin the process of comparing groups to determine if differences exist. In Figure A-3, the differences in the percentages of boys and girls and their respective performance levels are negligible. In another contingency table (see Figure A-5) comparing performance level by a special education services code, differences are apparent among the four comparison groups. Note the major differences between the special education and English language learner (ELL) students who did not meet the performance standard (Levels 3 or 4) and the general education students who did not meet the standard.

Figure A-3 Report showing a contingency table (crosstabulation) of performance levels by gender using SPSS.

				Gender		
				Female	Male	Total
Performance Level	1 – Did Not Meet Performance Standard	Count		3	5	8
		% within Performance Level		37.5%	62.5%	100.0%
		% within Gender		5.5%	9.8%	7.5%
	2 – Partial Achievement of Performance Standard	Count		16	16	32
		% within Performance Level		50.0%	50.0%	100.0%
		% within Gender		29.1%	31.4%	30.2%
	3 – Met Performance Standard	Count		23	20	43
		% within Performance Level		53.5%	46.5%	100.0%
		% within Gender		41.8%	39.2%	40.6%
	4 – Exceeded Performance Standard	Count		13	10	23
		% within Performance Level		56.5%	43.5%	100.0%
		% within Gender		23.6%	19.6%	21.7%
Total		Count		55	51	106
		% within Performance Level		51.9%	48.1%	100.0%
		% within Gender		100.0%	100.0%	100.0%

MEASURES OF CENTRAL TENDENCY

Perhaps the most popular of all statistical measures are **measures of central tendency**, which include averages and other determinants of what is typical for a group of values. Of the three major measures of central tendency (**mean**, **median**, and **mode**), the mean, or the arithmetic average, is most useful in depicting what is typical for a group of values. It is used extensively within a number of other statistical formulas such as t test, analysis of variance, and regression.

Two or more means are also used to compare the differences between two or more groups, for example, pre- and post-treatment tests, male/female performance indicators, or urban/suburban/rural school characteristics. Based on the data for the Jefferson Middle School (see Chapter 9), Figure A-6 shows two tables that compare the means of student language arts scale scores by gender and by special education services code. Along with the means, the tables show the number of cases (*N*) and the standard deviation. (Standard deviation will be discussed in more depth further on.) The differences between the females and males is relatively small (almost 10 points), whereas the differences between the general education students and students in the special education services codes are large (almost 40 points). The data

Figure A-4 Clustered bar chart derived from a contingency table (crosstabulation) of performance levels by gender using SPSS.

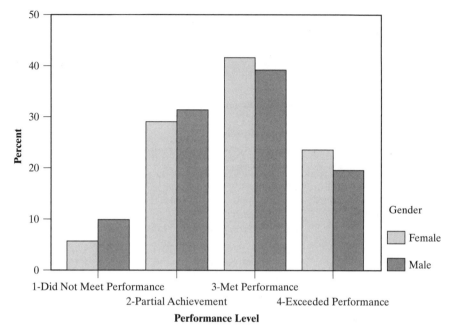

in the means tables in Figure A-6 support the data presented in the contingency tables in Figures A-3 and A-5.

In addition to observation of the differences in the means, verification of their significance can be done statistically. To do this, a procedure(s) is executed that specifically tests for the differences in the means of two or more distributions or groups. A *t* test is a test to determine the significance of the difference between the means of two and only two groups of values. Another procedure, ANOVA, can be used when there are two or more groups. Figure A-7 shows the results of a one-way ANOVA comparing the means of scale scores by gender.

The table in Figure A-7 is the result of a one-way ANOVA performed with one dependent variable (scale score) and one independent variable (gender). The final column (Sig. = .150) is the statistical significance level of the differences in the means; it indicates that there is not a statistically significant difference between the means in gender for the scale scores. For the difference to be statistically significant, the significance level would have to be .05 or lower. As it was mentioned earlier, .05 is the standard level of statistical significance.

Figure A-8 shows the results of a one-way ANOVA for more than two groups. The one-way procedure was performed with one dependent variable (scale score) and one independent variable (special education services code). The final column (Sig. = .000) is the statistical significance of the differences in the means, and it

Figure A-5 Report showing a contingency table (crosstabulation) of performance levels by special education services code using SPSS. ELL = English language learner.

			Special educ. services code				
			Gen. educ.	Spec. educ.	ELL	Spec. educ. & ELL	Total
Performance Level	1 – Did Not Meet Performance Standard	Count	0	2	0	6	8
		% within Performance Level	.0%	25.0%	.0%	75.0%	100.0%
		% within Special Educ. Services Code	.0%	9.5%	.0%	100.0%	7.5%
	2 – Partial Achievement of Performance Standard	Count	6	16	10	0	32
		% within Performance Level	18.8%	50.0%	31.3%	.0%	100.0%
		% within Special Educ. Services Code	9.0%	76.2%	83.3%	.0%	30.2%
	3 – Met Performance Standard	Count	38	3	2	0	43
		% within Performance Level	88.4%	7.0%	4.7%	.0%	100.0%
		% within Special Educ. Services Code	56.7%	14.3%	16.7%	.0%	40.6%
	4 – Exceeded Performance Standard	Count	23	0	0	0	23
		% within Performance Level	100.0%	.0%	.0%	.0%	100.0%
		% within Special Educ. Services Code	34.3%	.0%	.0%	.0%	21.7%
Total		Count	67	21	12	6	106
		% within Performance Level	63.2%	19.8%	11.3%	5.7%	100.0%
		% within Special Educ. Services Code	100.0%	100.0%	100.0%	100.0%	100.0%

indicates that there is a statistically significant difference among the scale score means of the four groups represented by the special education services code, because it is less than the .05 standard. On examining the differences between the means—especially when using control and experimental groups—the term **effect size** is sometimes used. The effect size is a secondary statistical procedure used to determine the level of significance in the difference in the means. It is calculated by taking the difference in the means of the two groups and dividing it by the standard deviation of the control group.

In the previous paragraphs, the terms **dependent variable** and **independent variable** were introduced. A dependent variable changes as a result of or in relation

Figure A-6 Two means tables of scale score by gender and scale score by special education services code using SPSS. ELL = English language learner.

Language Arts Scale Score * Gender

Language Arts Scale Score

Gender	Mean	N	Std. deviation
Female	716.47	55	34.371
Male	706.67	51	35.218
Total	711.75	106	34.963

Language Arts Scale Score * Special Educ. Services Code

Language Arts Scale Score

Special educ. services code	Mean	N	Std. deviation
Gen. Educ.	729.54	67	24.724
Spec. Educ.	690.52	21	24.572
ELL	688.00	12	16.531
Spec. Educ. & ELL	635.00	6	5.586
Total	711.75	106	34.963

Figure A-7 One-way analysis of variance table of scale score by gender using SPSS.

One-way ANOVA

Language Arts Scale Score by Gender

	Sum of squares	df	Mean square	F	Sig.
Between Groups	2544.580	1	2544.580	2.103	.150
Within Groups	125809.042	104	1209.702		
Total	128353.623	105			

Figure A-8 One-way analysis of variance table of scale score by special education services code using SPSS.

One-way ANOVA

Language Arts Scale Score by Special Education Services Code

	Sum of squares	df	Mean square	F	Sig.
Between Groups	72771.728	3	24257.243	44.515	.000
Within Groups	55581.895	102	544.921		
Total	128353.623	105			

Figure A-9 An N-way analysis of variance of the passing rate (dependent variable) with teaching experience code and professional development code (independent variables) using SPSS.

ANOVA[a,b]

			Unique method				
			Sum of squares	df	Mean square	F	Sig.
Average % Students Passing	Main Effects	(Combined)	113.816	4	28.454	6.101	.000
		Experience Code	52.712	2	26.356	5.651	.005
		Hours Development Code	93.853	2	46.926	10.061	.000
	2-Way Interactions	Experience Code* Hours Development Code	127.038	4	31.760	6.809	.000
	Model		226.205	8	28.526	6.116	.000
	Residual		377.788	81	4.664		
	Total		605.993	89	6.809		

[a]Average % Students Passing by Experience Code, Hours Development Code

[b]All effects entered simultaneously

to a change in an independent variable. An independent variable, as it changes, causes or relates to a change in another (dependent) variable. In the two previous examples, the dependent variable in each one-way ANOVA was the scale score and the independent variables were gender and special education services code. A limitation of one-way ANOVA is that it can only compare means when there is one dependent and one independent variable.

If there are two or more independent variables, an N-way ANOVA procedure can be used to compare the difference in the means. There are several different forms of ANOVA procedures. For example, a **multiple regression** is a form of ANOVA that assumes there are three or more variables: One variable is a dependent, interval, or ratio variable, and two or more variables are independent, interval, or ratio variables such as test scores, income, grade point average. Figure A-9 is the output of an N-way ANOVA procedure used in the Kingsland School District case study in Chapter 10. It was used to determine if there was a difference in the means of the passing rate on state standardized tests for the two independent variables of teaching experience code and professional development code. The statistical significance levels for each of the independent variables and for the combined variables were lower than the .05 standard.

MEASURES OF DISPERSION

Many educators place a good deal of importance on means and other measures of central tendency when doing quantitative analysis. However, measures that show

how a group of numbers spread, or disperse, are just as important. The major **measures of dispersion** are range, deviation, variance, and standard deviation.

Range is the difference between the highest and lowest values in a group of values. For example, the range of the following group of values is 40: 60, 70, 80, 90, 100. Range is calculated by subtracting the lowest value (60) from the highest value (100). The range is the simplest measure of dispersion and is useful in making an initial determination of the spread in a group of values.

Deviation is the difference (plus or minus) between a value and the mean of a group of values. For example, look again at this group of values: 60, 70, 80, 90, 100. The deviation of the value 90 in the group of values is 10, and it is calculated by subtracting the mean (80) from the value (90). The deviation is used to determine the distance of one score from the mean.

Variance is the sum of all the squared deviations from the mean divided by the number (N) of values in the group. In groups of values with an N less than 15, a statistical adjustment is made: The variance is the sum of all the squared deviations from the mean divided by $N - 1$. For example, the variance of the group of five values 60, 70, 80, 90, 100 is 250 and is calculated as follows:

Deviation of 60 from the mean (80) = $-20 \times -20 = 400$

Deviation of 70 from the mean (80) = $-10 \times -10 = 100$

Deviation of 80 from the mean (80) = $0 \times 0 = 0$

Deviation of 90 from the mean (80) = $+10 \times +10 = 100$

Deviation of 100 from the mean (80) = $+20 \times +20 = 400$

Sum of squared deviations ($400 + 100 + 0 + 100 + 400 = 1,000$) and divide by 4 ($N - 1$) = $1,000/4 = 250$

The variance is used frequently in a variety of statistical formulas (e.g., t test, ANOVA). However, because the deviations are squared, the variance value is too large in relation to the values in the group to be used as a descriptive measure. It is difficult, for example, to interpret or determine the meaning of a variance of 250 for the values of 60, 70, 80, 90, 100.

Standard Deviation is the square root of the variance, and it is the most frequently used measure of dispersion. So the standard deviation (SD) of 250 is 15.811 (the square root of the variance).

As an indication of the importance of these measures of dispersion, the t test and ANOVA procedures described earlier use the variance to calculate the significance of the differences in the means. In addition, in almost any study where the mean is used to describe a population(s), it is considered good practice to include the standard deviation.

Figure A-10   Normal, or bell-shaped, curve.

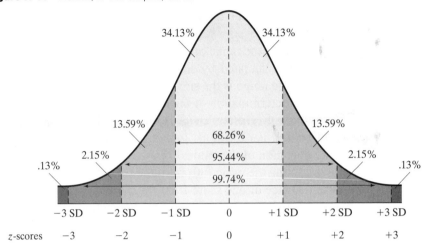

The **normal distribution**, or curve, is also based on the standard deviation of a given sample. Many years ago statisticians observed a pattern when analyzing means and standard deviations for large samples. For example, fundamental data (data not prone to bias or skewness), such as height, weight, or blood pressure, would distribute equally on both sides (plus and minus) of the mean in a bell-shaped pattern (hence, the term *bell-shaped curve*). In a normal distribution (see Figure A-10), the distance from 1 SD above the mean to 1 SD below the mean includes approximately 68% of all the scores; +2 SD to −2 SD includes approximately 95% of all scores; and +3 SD to −3 SD includes more than 99% of all scores.

When considered along with the mean, the standard deviation provides an important picture of a group of numbers. The mean indicates the average while the standard deviation indicates the dispersion, or spread, from the average. In a set of student test scores, the most desirable situation would be to have a high mean and a low standard deviation. In this case, students are scoring high (mean) and most students are very close (standard deviation) to the mean. For example, assume the results of a test indicate that the mean is 80 and the standard deviation is 5. Assuming a passing rate of 70, 95% of the students are passing. On the other hand, assume the results of the test indicate that the mean is 80 and the standard deviation is 10 (twice as large as the previous example). If the passing rate is 70, 68% of the students are passing.

MEASURES OF RELATIONSHIP

Measures of relationship examine the relationship between two or more variables or two or more sets of data. They are used extensively in correlational research. Here are three examples of descriptions of relationships: (1) Generally there is a high positive relationship, or correlation, between parents' education and students' academic achievement; (2) there is generally an inverse correlation between students' absence rates from school and academic achievement; and (3) there is no relationship between a person's height and academic achievement. A positive relationship exists when as one variable changes (becomes higher or lower), the other variable changes in the same direction. An inverse relationship exists when as one variable changes, the other variable changes in the opposite direction; or as one variable gets higher, the other variable gets lower, and vice versa. Some forms of these measures (e.g., **linear regression**) can be used to develop prediction models, for example, success in college related to high school performance.

A fundamental tenet of correlational analysis is not to assume that one variable *causes* a change in another. Correlational studies focus on relationships and not necessarily on cause and effect. However, depending on the variables being analyzed, a high correlation might indicate a cause and effect relationship.

Correlational Coefficient

Correlation is the relationship between two variables or sets of data as expressed in the form of a coefficient: +1.00 indicates a perfect positive correlation, −1.00 indicates a perfect inverse correlation; and 0.00 indicates a complete lack of a relationship. Figure A-11 represents the line diagrams for +1.00, −1.00, and 0.00 coefficients. Several different coefficients can be produced, depending on the type of variables:

- Pearson product-moment coefficient (r) is the most popular and is used with two groups of continuous variables (e.g., test scores and grade point averages).
- Spearman rank correlation coefficient (ρ, or r_s), which is a form of the Pearson product-moment coefficient, can be used with ordinal or ranked data.
- Phi (Φ) correlation coefficient, which is a form of the pearson product-moment coefficient, can be used with **dichotomous variables** (e.g., pass/fail, male/female).

Figure A-11 Line representations of correlation coefficients.

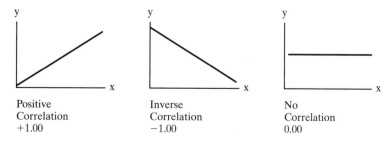

| Positive Correlation +1.00 | Inverse Correlation −1.00 | No Correlation 0.00 |

There is no simplified method for determining the magnitude of a correlation. Tests of statistical significance can be used; however, in correlational analysis, very small relationships, particularly with large samples, will be statistically significant. Some educational researchers use this convention:

Coefficient = .00 to .20—negligible correlation
Coefficient = .21 to .40—low correlation
Coefficient = .41 to .60—moderate correlation
Coefficient = .61 to .80—substantial correlation
Coefficient = .81 to 1.0—high correlation

This standard is not uniformly accepted, and researchers conducting certain types of studies may establish their own conventions. For example, in a correlational study used to establish the reliability of a standardized test, researchers might only accept as positive a coefficient that is higher than .85. Other researchers use a technique whereby they examine the square of the coefficient, where r is the coefficient and r^2 is equal to the percentage of the variation in one variable that is related to the variation in the other. An r of .5 means 25% of the variation in the variables is related (.5 squared equals .25). An r of .9 means 81% of the variation is related (.9 squared equals .81).

In published studies or reports, correlational coefficients are usually displayed as r values, for example: $r = .66$, $p < .01$ where r is the correlational coefficient and p is the level (.01) of statistical significance.

A table, or matrix, may be used to present correlations, especially if many variables are being studied. For example, in Chapter 10 (Kingsland School District), a correlation matrix (see Figure A-12) examined the relationships of three variables: years of teaching, hours of professional development, and student passing rates on standardized tests. Essentially, the data show that statistically significant relationships exist between teaching experience and passing rate ($r = .311$) and hours of professional development and passing rate ($r = .280$). Although significant, these are not high correlations, as they account for approximately 9.7% (r^2, or .311 × .311) and 7.8% (r^2, or .280 × .280) of the variation in the variables in the sample populations. However, given that the statistical significance level is at .01, which is more rigorous than the standard .05 level, the data are interpreted as having statistically significant relationships. The correlation matrix also shows an inverse relationship ($r = -.281$) between years of teaching experience and hours of professional development, which indicates that more experienced teachers tend to enroll in fewer hours of staff development activities.

Linear Regression

Linear regression uses the correlation coefficient to plot a line that illustrates the relationship of two variables, say X and Y. Specifically, linear regression attempts

Figure A-12 Correlation matrix of years teaching, hours of professional development, and average percentage of students passing standardized tests (passing rate) using SPSS.

Correlations

		Years Teaching	Hours of professional students	Average % development passing
Years Teaching	Pearson Correlation	1	−.281 **	.311 **
	Sig. (2-tailed)	.	.007	.003
	N	90	90	90
Hours of Professional Development	Pearson Correlation	−.281 **	1	.280 **
	Sig. (2-tailed)	.007	.	.007
	N	90	90	90
Average % Students Passing	Pearson Correlation	.311 **	.280 **	1
	Sig. (2-tailed)	.003	.007	.
	N	90	90	90

** Correlation is significant at the 0.01 level (2-tailed).

to show the change in Y values in relationship to changes in X values. It determines the Y intercept and the slope of the line as represented by this formula:

$$Y = a + bX$$

where Y = dependent variable; X = independent variable; b = slope of the line; and a = constant or Y intercept.

Linear regression is used in making predictions based on finding unknown Y values from known X values. In prediction studies, the Y, or dependent variable, is frequently referred to as the **criterion variable,** and the X, or independent variable, is referred to as the **predictor variable.** Here is a linear regression formula for predicting college grade point average (GPA) from known high school GPA:

$$\text{College GPA} = a + b \text{ (high school GPA)}$$

CAUTION

A researcher or data analyst must be cautious when considering the use of any predictive statistical procedure for educational purposes, because many variables influence and affect the people-intensive activities associated with education. It is not always easy to control for such variables. Predictive studies can provide direction and estimates, but they should be used carefully in any major decision-making activity.

Technical Support B

Introduction to Spreadsheet Software

Microsoft Excel, IBM Lotus 1-2-3, and Corel Quattro Pro are the most popular **electronic spreadsheet** programs. All of these programs have the same basic template and functions. If you learn one of them well, it is easy to use any of the others. This introduction is for those who are not familiar with spreadsheet software. All of these programs provide excellent help facilities that are very intuitive. Also, a number of free tutorials are available online, including these:

http://www.baycongroup.com/el0.htm
BayCon Group, Inc.

http://www.bcschools.net/staff/ExcelHelp.htm
Bay City Public Schools

http://www.usd.edu/trio/tut/excel/
University of South Dakota—Trio Program

OVERVIEW AND KEY TERMS

An electronic spreadsheet is an application program used as a tool for analysis, planning, and modeling that allows users to enter and manipulate data on a worksheet of columns and rows (see Figure B-1). Spreadsheets were designed to replace the accounting tablets or green ledger pads that were the fundamental paper documents for financial record keeping. Visicalc, developed in the 1970s, was the first popular spreadsheet program.

Spreadsheets are used extensively in the management and manipulation of numeric data. Originally, they were used in financial applications such as budgeting. Now

Figure B-1 Excel worksheet.

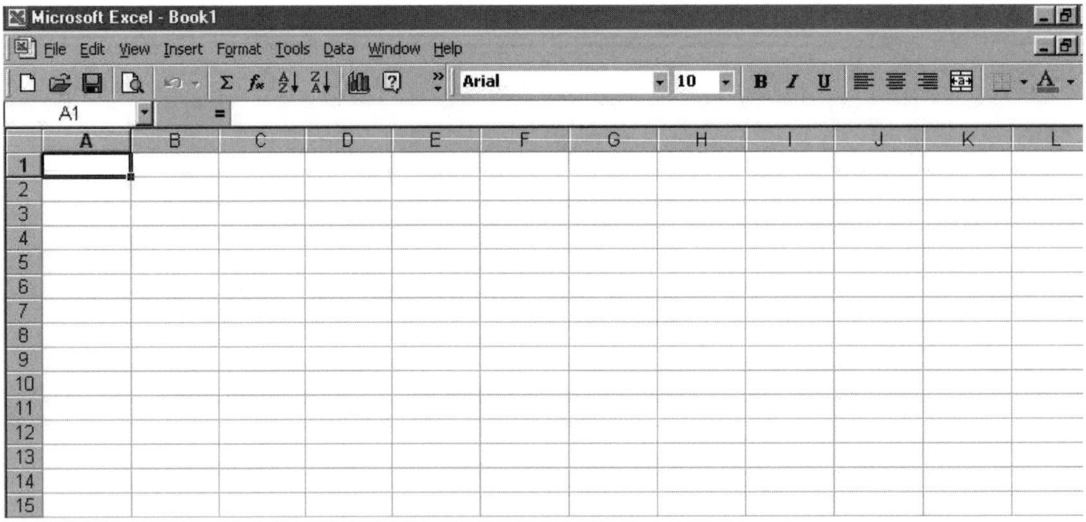

they have become popular for other data-driven decision-making activities, including student demographic analyses, enrollment projections, and facilities planning.

The following terms are commonly used in spreadsheet programs:

Worksheet: Electronic representation of a ledger sheet, divided into columns and rows; another name for the work area of a spreadsheet

Menu bar/control panel: Area above the worksheet by which you can enter commands (The menu bar in Excel functions like the Menu Bar in other Microsoft software programs)

Cell: Single location on the worksheet defined by a column and row address (e.g., C6 refers to the cell in the third column and the sixth row of the worksheet)

Cell pointer: Highlighted cell indicator that is positioned and controlled by a mouse

Cell entries: Numbers, formulas, and labels suitable to the application that are entered into the worksheet cells; types of cell entries:

- Numbers: 0 1 2 3 4 5 6 7 8 9
- Formulas and functions: mathematical operations (e.g., = A2 + A3, = B2 − B4)
- Labels: a string of literal characters, usually letters of the alphabet, that are frequently used as column and row headings (e.g., Total Budget, Enrollment, Total Personnel)

Cell entry prefixes: First character of each cell entry that determines the type of entry:

- Numbers: any digit (e.g., 0 1 2 3)
- Formulas and functions: =, SUM, AVERAGE
- Labels: any letter of the alphabet or special characters

SPREADSHEET STRUCTURE

Spreadsheets are made up of columns, rows, and cells. The COLUMN is one of the vertical spaces within the worksheet. Letters are used to designate each COLUMN'S location. In Figure B-2A, the COLUMN labeled C is highlighted.

The ROW is one of the horizontal spaces within the worksheet. Numbers are used to designate each ROW'S location. In the Figure B-2B, the ROW labeled 3 is highlighted.

The CELL is defined as the space where a specified row and column intersect. Each CELL is assigned a name according to its COLUMN letter and ROW number. In Figure B-3, the CELL labeled C4 is highlighted. When refering to a cell, always put the column designation first and the row second.

Figure B-2A Column example.

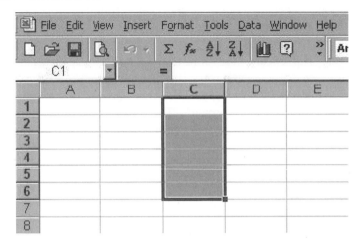

Figure B-2B Row example.

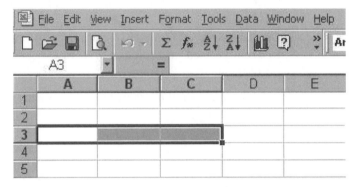

Figure B-3 Cell example.

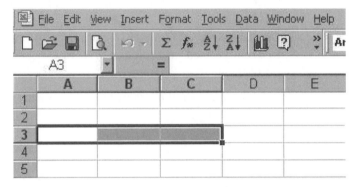

DATA TYPES AND DATA MANIPULATION

As indicated earlier, three basic types of data can be entered in a cell:

- Numbers: a number with a constant value (e.g., 4, 19, 4,689)
- Formulas and functions: a mathematical equation (e.g., =B2+B3)
- Labels: text with no numeric value (e.g., student name, gender, title)

All formulas must begin with an equals sign (=). Formulas also include a number of predefined functions. There is a list of frequently used functions, such as SUM and AVERAGE, available within Excel under the menu *INSERT* (see Figure B-4).

Spreadsheets provide all of the basic mathematical operations such as add, subtract, multiply, and divide. These are invoked by referencing their standard symbols (e.g., +, −, *, /). For example, assume that the following data have been entered:

	A	B
1	6	4
2	8	3
3	9	7

- A1 (column A, row 1) = 6
- A2 (column A, row 2) = 8
- A3 (column A, row 3) = 9
- B1 (column B, row 1) = 4
- B2 (column B, row 2) = 3
- B3 (column B, row 3) = 7

Figure B-4 Mathematical functions.

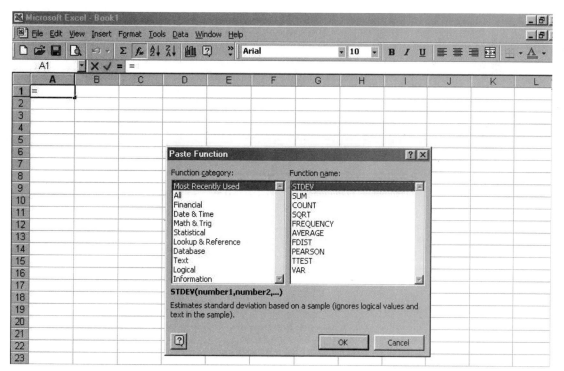

To perform a mathematical operation on any of these cells, the cells must be referenced appropriately in a new cell as follows:

Operation	Symbol	Referenced Data	Answer
Multiplication	*	= A1 * B3	42
Division	/	= A3 / B2	3
Addition	+	= B2 + A2	11
Subtraction	–	= A3 – B1	5

Sometimes when a formula or mathematical operation is entered, the same formula needs to be repeated for several different cells. For this task, the COPY and PASTE commands are available. The cell locations in the formula are "pasted" relative to the position from which they were copied.

	A	B	C
1	5	3	=A1 + B1
2	8	2	=A2 + B2
3	4	6	=A3 + B3
4	3	8	=? + ?

Cell information is copied from its relative position. In other words, in the original cell (C1) the equation was (=A1+B1). When the contents of C1 are copied and pasted into other cells, the software assumes that the operation applies to the two relative cells to the left. So the C1 equation pasted into (C2) would be (=A2+B2), and the equation pasted into (C3) would be (=A3+B3).

One of the most popular functions in any spreadsheet program is the SUM function. The SUM function takes all of the values in each of the specified cells and totals (sums) their values. The syntax is as follows:

- =SUM(first value, second value, etc.) In the first and second values, you can enter any of the following: constant, cell, range of cells.
- Blank cells return a value of zero to be added to the total.
- Text cells cannot be added to a number and will produce an error.

	A
1	50
2	100
3	200
4	Budget
5	

Notice that in A4 there is a text entry. This has no numeric value and cannot be included in a total.

Examples of the use of the SUM function follow:

Example	Cells to SUM	Answer
=sum (A1:A3)	A1, A2, A3	350
=sum (A1:A3, 100)	A1, A2, A3 and 100	450
=sum (A1 + A4)	A1, A4	#VALUE! (This is an error indicator)
=sum (A1:A2, A5)	A1, A2, A5	150

The AVERAGE function finds the arithmetic average of the specified data. The syntax is as follows: =AVERAGE (first value, second value, etc.).

	A
1	25
2	50
3	75
4	100
5	

Example	Cells to AVERAGE	Answer
=average (A1:A4)	A1, A2, A3, A4	62.5
=average (A1:A4, 300)	A1, A2, A3, A4 and 300	110
=average (A1:A5)	A1, A2, A3, A4, A5	62.5
=average (A1:A2, A4)	A1, A2, A4	58.33

The SUM and AVERAGE functions are available in a pull-down menu, as illustrated in Figure B-4.

Charts and Graphics

Frequently it is desirable to represent numeric data in graphic form. Excel has a chart program built into its main program. The Chart Wizard in the menu bar (see Figure B-5) leads users through the procedure to construct a chart from the data that has been selected.

Figure B-5   Chart Wizard menu

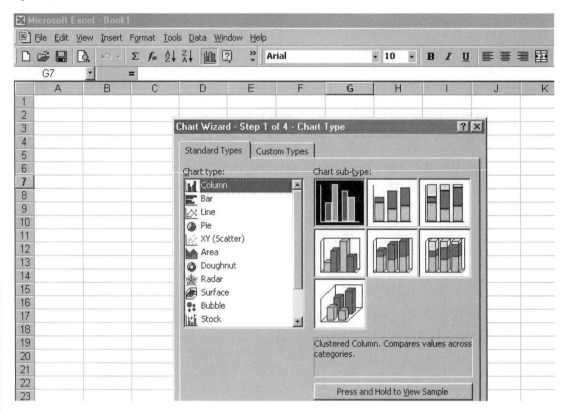

Any software program is best learned by using it, not by reading about it. This introduction was a quick overview. You are encouraged to obtain spreadsheet software and experiment with it.

Technical Support C

Introduction to the Statistical Package for the Social Sciences (SPSS)

The SPSS dataset that is used for all of the examples in Technical Support C can be found at the Companion Website at **www.prenhall.com/picciano/**

Electronic spreadsheet programs such as Microsoft Excel work well for doing simple descriptive analyses. For more sophisticated analysis, however, more powerful tools such as the Statistical Package for the Social Sciences (SPSS), the Statistical Analysis System (SAS), or the Biomedical Data Package (BMDP) are recommended. They provide most of the facilities of an electronic spreadsheet program plus additional features for doing statistical routines such as analysis of variance, regression analysis, and correlations. All of these software tools provide excellent documentation for using the features as well as guides for interpreting the results.

For the potential data analyst who is not yet comfortable with these software packages, a workshop or course may be well worth the time and effort. Without developing expertise in using these tools, educators must rely on others to analyze any substantial amount of quantitative data. Those who conduct data analysis using statistical packages know that the more familiar and comfortable the user is with the data, the more complete and accurate the analysis will be. The following sections are a brief introduction to the major features and basic formats of SPSS.

OVERVIEW

SPSS is a software package that uses pull-down menus and dialog boxes to do statistical analysis and data management. Most tasks can be accomplished simply by pointing and clicking the mouse on a desired option. In addition to the simple point-and-click interface for statistical analysis, SPSS provides the following features:

- *Data Editor:* A versatile, spreadsheet-like software system for defining, entering, editing, and displaying data
- *Output Viewer:* A feature that makes it easy to browse through results, selectively show and hide output, change the display order of results, and move presentation-quality tables and charts between SPSS and other applications
- *Graphics:* High-resolution, full-color pie charts, bar charts, histograms, scatterplots, 3-D graphics, and more
- *Data Transformations:* Features that help get data ready for analysis; for example, a user can easily subset data; combine categories; and add, aggregate, merge, split, and transpose files.

One of the most important features of SPSS is its online help facility, which includes a number of tutorials designed to help users become familiar with the software. A number of case studies provide hands-on examples using statistical procedures and interpreting the results.

SPSS provides a number of interface windows, each of which is associated with a particular SPSS file type. The most popular are listed next:

- *Data Editing Window:* Displays the contents of a data set. A data set consists of a data file and the information needed to execute SPSS routines on the data file. You can create new data sets or modify existing ones with the Data Editor. The Data Editor window opens automatically when you start an SPSS session.
- *Output Viewer Window:* Displays all statistical results, tables, and charts. The output can be edited and saved for later use. An Output Viewer window opens automatically the first time you run a procedure that generates output.
- *Syntax Window:* Allows users to access the SPSS command mode. Several advanced SPSS features are not available in the pull-down menus and can only be executed by using SPSS commands. Once SPSS commands are generated, they can be saved as separate syntax files and used over and over.
- *Script Window:* Allows users to access the SPSS scripting mode. Scripting is used to customize and automate many tasks in SPSS. Only the most serious SPSS users become familiar with this feature.

As mentioned, SPSS automatically opens up in the Data Editing window. The other windows are available by going to the File menu, Open submenu (see Figure C-1). The remainder of this section will discuss the two windows used most frequently in analyzing data in SPSS: the Data Editor and the Output Viewer windows.

THE DATA EDITOR

The Data Editor window displays the contents of the current or working data set. The Data View is arranged in a spreadsheet format that contains variables in columns and cases in rows. There are two views in each Data Editor window. The Data View, which contains data, is the sheet that is visible when you first open the Data Editor. You can access the second sheet by clicking on the tab labeled Variable View on the bottom left corner. The Variable View contains information about the data that is stored/presented in the accompanying Data View and is similar to a record layout. It contains the names of variables, their data types and widths, coding schemes, value labels, etc. Data sets that are open are called working data sets, and all data manipulations, statistical functions, and other SPSS procedures operate on these data sets.

Figures C-2A and C-2B are examples of the Data View and the Variable View, respectively, for the Chapter 10 case study about professional development (Kingsland School District). Notice that in Figure C-2A (Data View) the variable names displayed at the top of each column of data correspond exactly

Figure C-1 SPSS access/opening different windows.

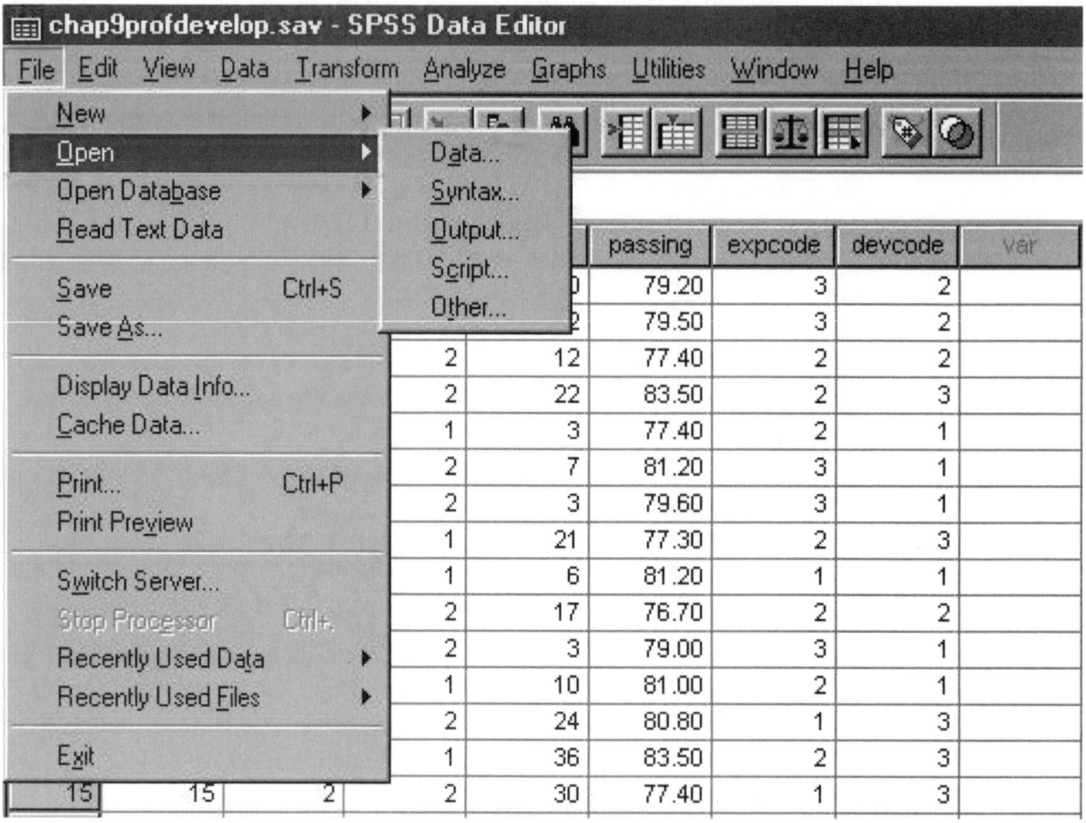

to the variable names used in the rows to describe the data in Figure C-2B (Variable View).

CREATING A DATA SET

There are several methods for creating a data set in SPSS. In the first method, you can open the SPSS program and enter data manually from a keyboard. This is an appropriate approach if the data set does not exist in electronic form (e.g., data obtained through a survey or other paper data-collection instrument). Each record for the data set will occupy one row in the Data View of the Data Editor. Before entering the data, enter the record layout (variable name, type, width, etc.) in the Variable View of the same data set. Once you have entered all of the data in the data set, save it using the File menu. Both the Data View and Variable View are saved together and are available for future analysis.

Figure C-2A Data Editor (Data View) of the Kingsland School District professional development data set.

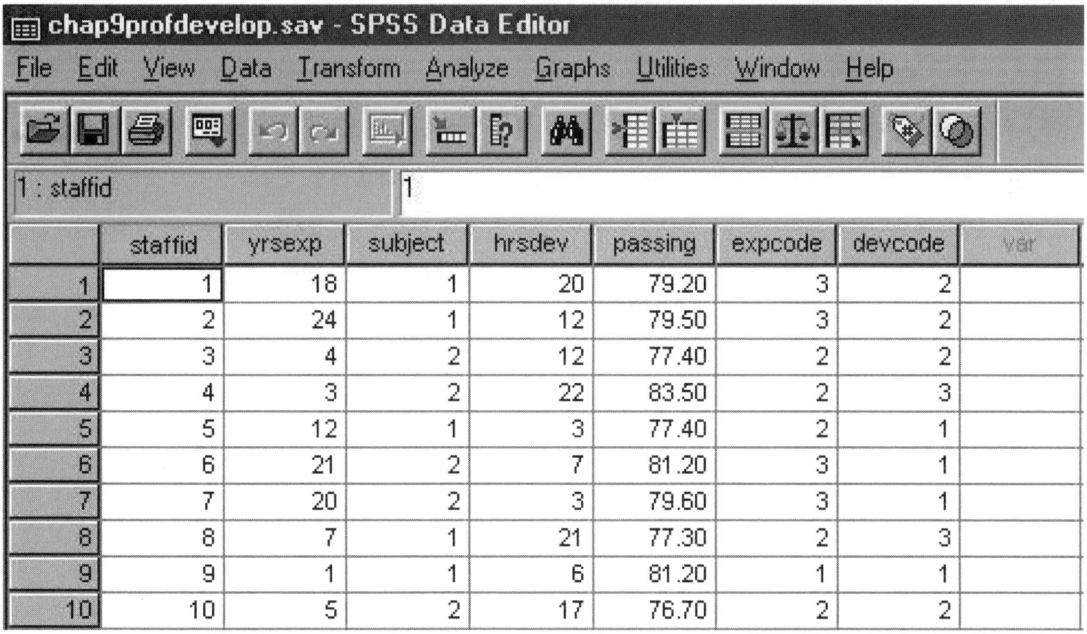

chap9profdevelop.sav - SPSS Data Editor

File Edit View Data Transform Analyze Graphs Utilities Window Help

1 : staffid 1

	staffid	yrsexp	subject	hrsdev	passing	expcode	devcode	var
1	1	18	1	20	79.20	3	2	
2	2	24	1	12	79.50	3	2	
3	3	4	2	12	77.40	2	2	
4	4	3	2	22	83.50	2	3	
5	5	12	1	3	77.40	2	1	
6	6	21	2	7	81.20	3	1	
7	7	20	2	3	79.60	3	1	
8	8	7	1	21	77.30	2	3	
9	9	1	1	6	81.20	1	1	
10	10	5	2	17	76.70	2	2	

Figure C-2B Data Editor (Variable View) of the Kingsland School District professional development data set.

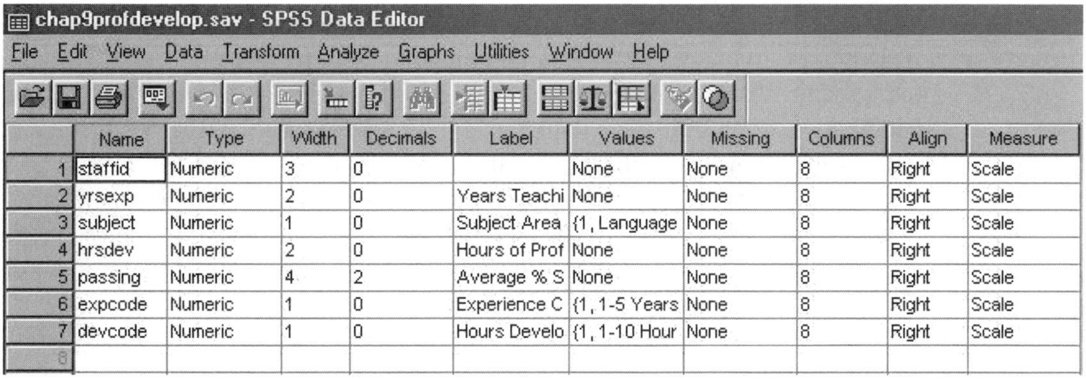

chap9profdevelop.sav - SPSS Data Editor

File Edit View Data Transform Analyze Graphs Utilities Window Help

	Name	Type	Width	Decimals	Label	Values	Missing	Columns	Align	Measure
1	staffid	Numeric	3	0		None	None	8	Right	Scale
2	yrsexp	Numeric	2	0	Years Teachi	None	None	8	Right	Scale
3	subject	Numeric	1	0	Subject Area	{1, Language	None	8	Right	Scale
4	hrsdev	Numeric	2	0	Hours of Prof	None	None	8	Right	Scale
5	passing	Numeric	4	2	Average % S	None	None	8	Right	Scale
6	expcode	Numeric	1	0	Experience C	{1, 1-5 Years	None	8	Right	Scale
7	devcode	Numeric	1	0	Hours Develo	{1, 1-10 Hour	None	8	Right	Scale
8										

The second method for creating a data set is to import an existing data set from an electronic file such as a Microsoft Excel spreadsheet. Depending on the sending file type, there are several ways that this can be done with SPSS. As an example (see Figure C-3), suppose you have a worksheet in Excel on professional development, as in the Kingsland School District data set. The simplest way to transfer these data

Figure C-3 Excel worksheet of the kingsland School District professional development data set.

	A	B	C	D	E	F	G	H
1	1	18	1	20	79.2	3	2	
2	2	24	1	12	79.5	3	2	
3	3	4	2	12	77.4	2	2	
4	4	3	2	22	83.5	2	3	
5	5	12	1	3	77.4	2	1	
6	6	21	2	7	81.2	3	1	
7	7	20	2	3	79.6	3	1	
8	8	7	1	21	77.3	2	3	
9	9	1	1	6	81.2	1	1	
10	10	5	2	17	76.7	2	2	
11	11	24	2	3	79	3	1	
12	12	14	1	10	81	2	1	
13	13	2	2	24	80.8	1	3	
14	14	13	1	36	83.5	2	3	
15	15	2	2	30	77.4	1	3	

to an SPSS file would be to copy and paste the desired cells from the Excel worksheet to a blank SPSS Data Editor window (Data View). If you do this with the Excel worksheet in Figure C-3, the result will be the data set that appears in Figure C-2A (Data View). To use this data set, after doing the copy-and-paste function, switch to the Variable View and enter manually the information for the data set (variable names, type, width, etc.). One limitation of this cut-and-paste approach is that it only works with relatively small data files that can fit on the clipboard.

(A clipboard is a temporary area in a computer's primary storage used by most operating systems for storing various types of data such as text, graphics, sound, and video. The clipboard can hold one collection of data at a time to use in a program or to cut/copy and paste data between programs.)

A third method for creating a data set in SPSS is to import a file already stored in another format such as Excel, Lotus, or Text. SPSS recognizes several formats (see Figure C-4). To do this, open SPSS and in the File menu select Open File—Data. In the dialog box provided, select the type of file you wish to use. Although SPSS does not read all file types, it does read a number of the most popular spreadsheet formats. Once you have successfully imported the file, switch to Variable View and enter manually the information (variable names, type, width, etc.) for the data set. A variation of this method for creating a SPSS data set from a file in another format is to add the SPSS variable name information into the first record of the

Figure C-4   Open File options in SPSS.

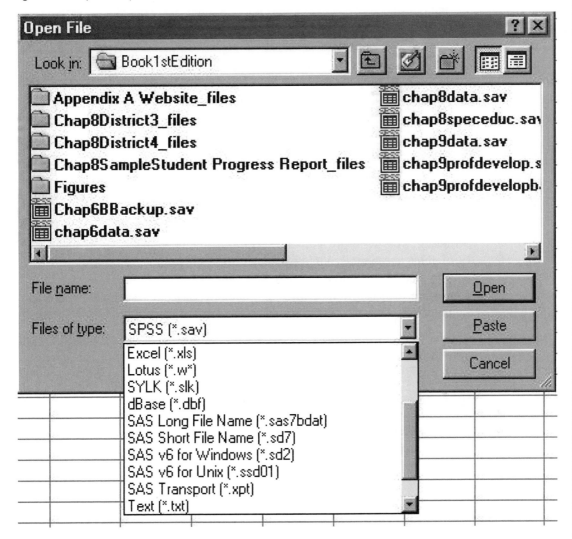

sending file. In Excel, this information would be entered into the first row of the worksheet. If you use this approach, you save the step of manually adding the variable names, type, width, and so forth. SPSS defaults to certain variable parameters based on the characteristics of the imported data.

DEFINING VARIABLES

Before describing the process for defining variables, an important distinction needs to be made between two often confused terms: *variable* and *value*. A variable is an item of data collected for each case in a study, which varies or has more than one value. Values are the numbers, names or categorical classification representing individual instances of the variable being measured. For example, a variable could be created for gender in a data set. Each individual in the data set would then be assigned a value representing her or his gender. For instance, females might be assigned the value 1, and males the value 2.

Figure C-2B provides the basic Variable View of a data set. The top row indicates the 10 items used in describing a data set:

Name: name of the variable; cannot be more than eight characters
Type: data type (e.g., numeric or string)
Width: actual width of the variable in characters
Decimals: number of decimal places (if a numeric variable)
Label: longer description of the variable name, which will appear in output
Values: descriptions of the values (e.g., a data value of 1 in a gender variable = female; a value of 2 = male)
Missing: Missing or invalid values not to be included in statistical analysis
Columns: number of columns assigned for each variable in Data View
Align: data alignment (e.g., right, left, center)
Measure: Identification of whether a numeric variable is scale, ordinal, or a nominal measure

Each of the items needs to be completed in the Variable View. If not, SPSS will default to the most common option.

TRANSFORMING DATA OPTIONS

One of the more popular features of SPSS is its ability to transform the characteristics of existing data. Figure C-5 shows the options in the Transform menu. Each

Figure C-5   Options available in the Transform menu.

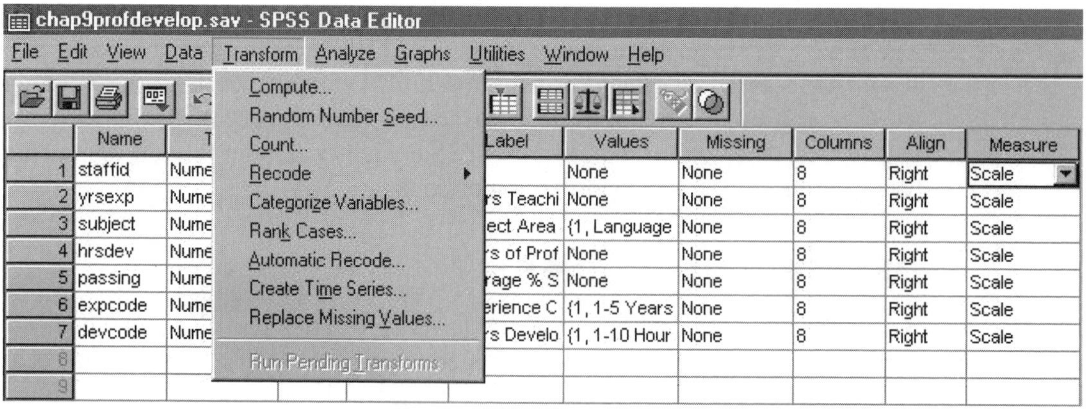

of these options provides a number of possibilities for transforming and manipulating the existing data set. All of the options cannot be explained here, but two of the most popular, Compute and Recode, will be discussed briefly.

The Compute option allows you to compute or create a new variable from the data in the existing data set. For instance, suppose you have a file containing data on each school in a school district. Among the variables in the data set are number of faculty and number of students. You could create a new variable named student/ faculty ratio by dividing the number of students by the number of faculty. The new variable would automatically be created for each record in the data set and would be available for statistical analysis.

The Recode option allows you to recode or change the values used for data analysis. For example, suppose you have a data set containing data on each student who took a standardized test. Among the variables is performance level, which is coded as follows:

Level 4: Student exceeds the learning standards.
Level 3: Student meets the learning standards.
Level 2: Student shows partial achievement of the learning standards.
Level 1: Student does not meet the learning standards.

Further, suppose you want to do an analysis that examines students who meet the standard (Level 4 or Level 3) or do not meet the standard (Level 2 or Level 1). You could recode the variable performance level as follows:

Level 4 or 3 = 2 (meets the standard)
Level 2 or 1 = 1 (does not meet the standard)

The Compute and Recode options are available via the Transform menu. To make a selection, highlight the option in the Transform menu and follow the directions in the subsequent dialog boxes. As mentioned earlier, the transform feature in SPSS is very popular. First-time users should familiarize themselves with the available options, which are fully described in the SPSS Help menu.

DATA ANALYSIS PROCEDURES AND THE OUTPUT VIEWER

Statistical procedures are executed from the Analyze menu in SPSS. Figure C-6 illustrates the main options in the Analyze menu. Most of these options have additional submenu options that provide an extensive number of statistical routines for analyzing data. In addition, several of the more sophisticated statistical routines are not available through the menus but are available in command mode. This was the case through SPSS Version 11.5; some of these command-driven routines may be made available as pull-down menus in future versions of SPSS.

Figure C-6 Options available in the Analyze menu.

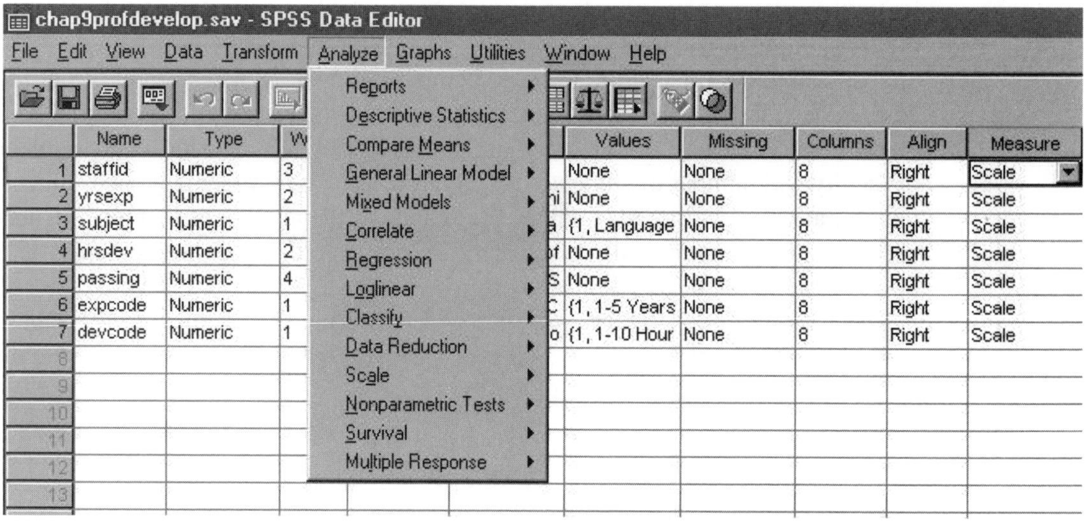

Figure C-7 Selecting the Frequencies option in the Analyze menu.

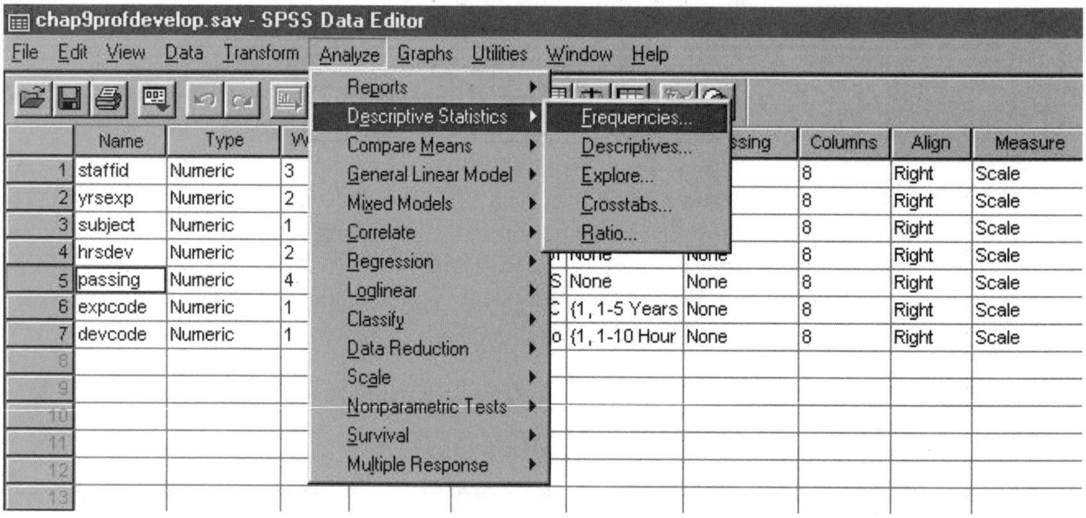

To execute an SPSS statistical routine, you must be in the Data Editor window with an open data set. Go to the Analyze menu and select the statistical routine you wish to run. For example, if you want to do a frequency distribution of one of the categorical variables (e.g., expcode; label = Experience Code) in the data set in Figures C-2A and C-2B, go to the Analyze menu, select Descriptive Statistics, then select Frequencies (see Figure C-7). A dialog box (see Figure C-8) will ask

Figure C-8 Dialog box for an SPSS frequencies routine.

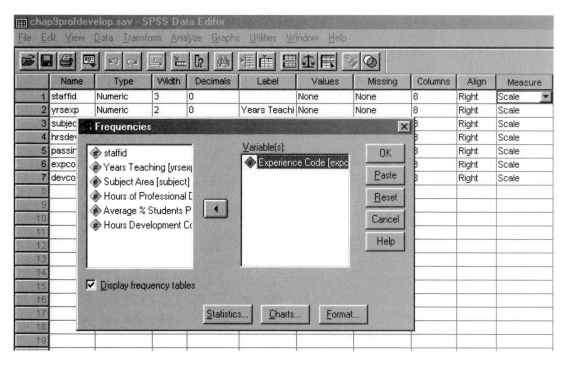

you to identify the variables you wish to use in the routine. In this example, Experience Code is selected. When you click the OK button, the requested frequency distribution will appear in the Output Viewer (see Figure C-9), which can be saved as a file, copied and pasted into Microsoft Word or other word processing software, or discarded.

As a second example, compare the means of the variable passing (label = Average % of Students Passing) in the data set in Figures C-2A and C-2B to the variable expcode (label = Experience Code). Go to the Analyze menu, select Compare Means, then select Means (see Figure C-10). A dialog box (see Figure C-11) will appear asking you to identify the variables you wish to use in the routine. For this example, select Average % of Students Passing and Experince Code. When you click the OK button, the requested means comparison table appears in the Output Viewer (see Figure C-12). The means comparison table can be saved as a file, copied and pasted into Word or other word processing software, or discarded.

As a third example, do a correlation of the variable yrsexper (label = Years Teaching) and the variable passing (label = Average % of Students Passing) in the data set in Figures C-2A and C-2B. Go to the Analyze menu, select

Figure C-9   Sample output for an SPSS frequencies routine.

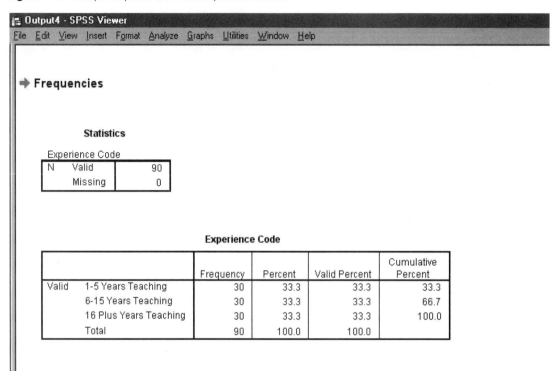

Figure C-10   Selecting the Means option in the Analyze menu.

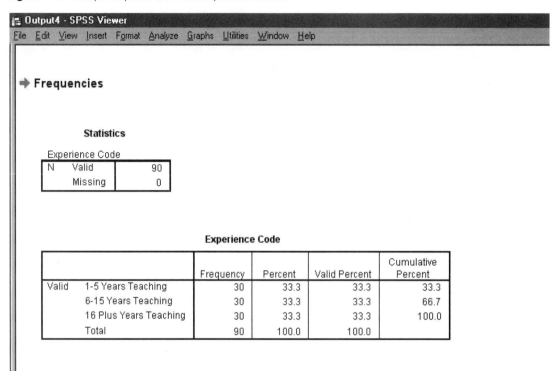

Figure C-11 Dialog box for an SPSS means routine.

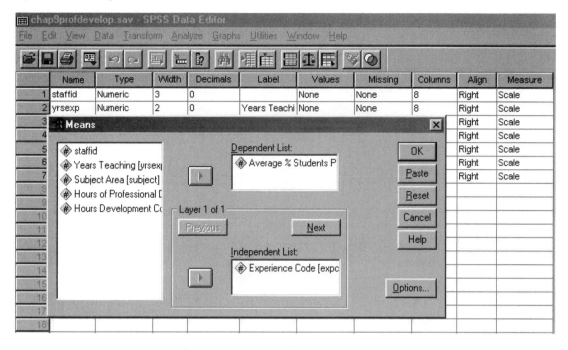

Figure C-12 Sample output for an SPSS means routine.

➤ **Means**

Case Processing Summary

	Cases					
	Included		Excluded		Total	
	N	Percent	N	Percent	N	Percent
Average % Students Passing Experience Code	90	100.0%	0	.0%	90	100.0%

Report

Average % Students Passing

Experience Code	Mean	N	Std. Deviation
1-5 Years Teaching	79.0900	30	2.02201
6-15 Years Teaching	80.3400	30	2.61384
16 Plus Years Teaching	80.4767	30	2.96097
Total	79.9689	90	2.60939

Figure C-13 Selecting the Correlate option in the Analyze menu.

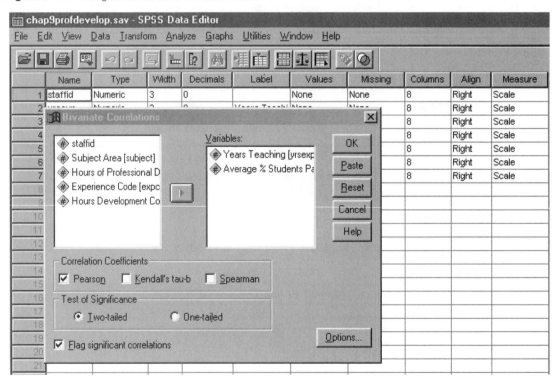

Figure C-14 Dialog box for an SPSS correlate routine.

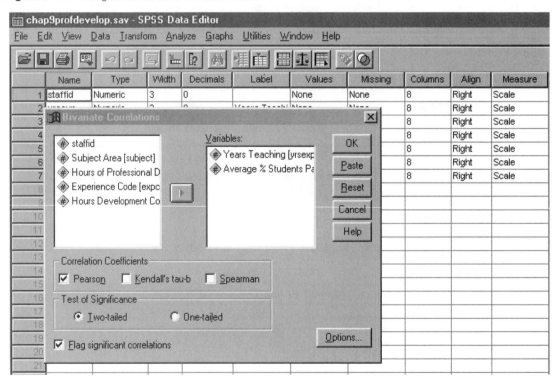

Figure C-15 Sample output for an SPSS correlate routine.

➤ **Correlations**

Descriptive Statistics

	Mean	Std. Deviation	N
Years Teaching	11.46	8.205	90
Average % Students Passing	79.9689	2.60939	90

Correlations

		Years Teaching	Average % Students Passing
Years Teaching	Pearson Correlation	1	.311**
	Sig. (2-tailed)	–	.003
	N	90	90
Average % Students Passing	Pearson Correlation	.311**	1
	Sig. (2-tailed)	.003	–
	N	90	90

**Correlation is significant at the 0.01 level (2-tailed).

Correlate, then select Bivariate (see Figure C-13). A dialog box (see Figure C-14) will appear asking you to identify the variables you wish to use in the routine. For this example, select Years Teaching and Average % of Students Passing. When you click the OK button, the requested Pearson correlation table will appear in the Output Viewer (see Figure C-15). The correlation table can be saved as a file, copied and pasted into Word or other word processing software, or discarded.

GRAPHS AND CHARTS

SPSS contains a complete set of graphics capabilities. The options are available in the Graphs menu (see Figure C-16). To construct a chart or graph, select one of the options and follow the directions in the dialog box. For example, say you want to produce a bar chart for the categorical variable devcode (label = Hours Development) in the data set in Figures C-2A and C-2B). Go to the Graphs menu

Figure C-16 Options available in the Graphs menu.

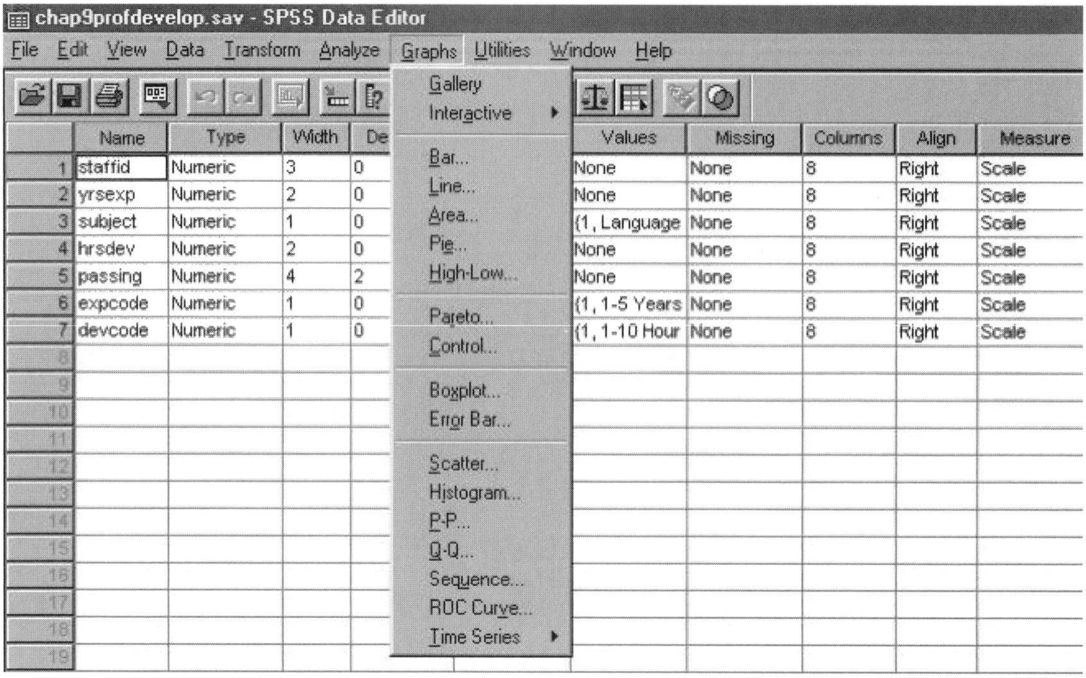

Figure C-17 Selecting the Bar option in the Graphs menu.

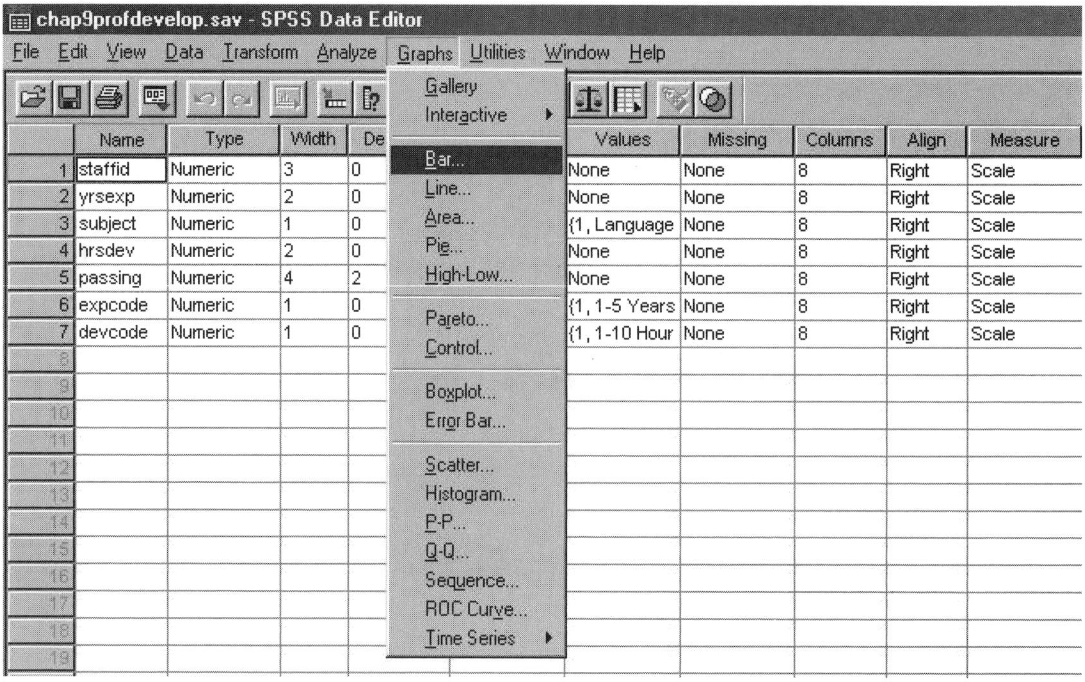

Figure C-18 Selecting Simple bar chart in the first dialog box.

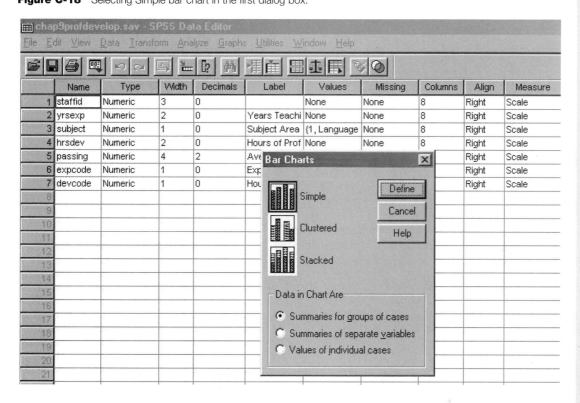

and select Bar (see Figure C-17). A dialog box (see Figure C-18) will appear asking you to identify the type of bar chart you want. For this example, select a simple bar chart. A second dialog box (see Figure C-19) will appear asking for the variable you wish to use in the chart. For this example, select Hours Development. When you click the OK button, the requested bar chart will appear in the Output Viewer (see Figure C-20). The bar chart can be saved as a file, copied and pasted into Word or other word processing software, or discarded.

SPSS can be learned only by using it, not by reading about it. This introduction was a quick overview. You are strongly encouraged to obtain the software and experiment with it.

Figure C-19 Selecting a variable for the bar chart in the second dialog box.

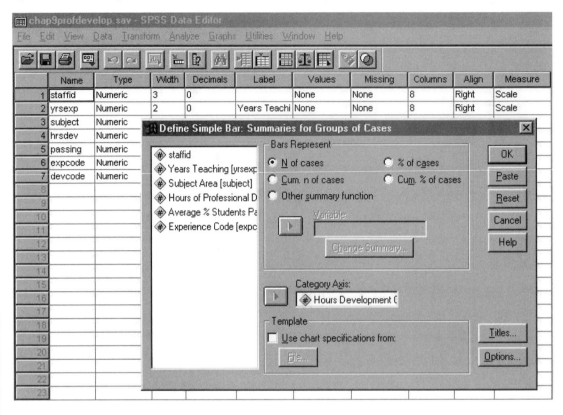

Figure C-20 Sample output for an SPSS bar chart routine.

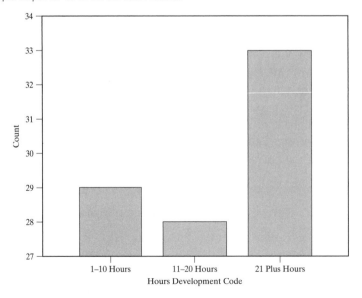

Technical Support D

Database Management Terms and Sample Outline

The primary definition of a database is a collection of files in which data can be created, updated, and accessed. However, a more modern definition requires that data files be interrelated, or integrated, so that data can be accessed easily across all files and redundancy of data be kept to a minimum. The basic concept of databases involves the management of data in an increasingly more complex hierarchy. The members of this hierarchy, from least to most complex, are the character, the data element, the data record, the data file, and the database. These terms are defined as follows:

A *character* consists of a single letter of the alphabet (A through Z), a single digit (0 through 9), or a single special character (e.g., $, %, +). A *data element*, also referred to as a *data field*, groups these characters to represent characteristics of a person, place, or thing. Examples of data elements are birth date, gender, father's name, family income, grade, course number, and room number. A *data record* consists of a collection of related data elements for a single entity (person, place, or thing). Examples of data records are the payroll record of an individual employee, the inventory record of a single piece of scientific equipment, or the transcript record of an individual student. A *data file* is a collection of related data records. For example, the records of all employees compose a personnel file, and the records of all students compose a student file.

A *database* is a collection of data files and records. The term can be applied to a single collection of files such as a student database or personnel database. It can also be applied to multiple collections of files such as a school district's database, which could include student, personnel, course (or curriculum), financial, and facilities files. A *database management system* is a package of computer programs that allows the user to create, maintain, and access the data on a database. Examples of database management systems include Oracle (Oracle Corp.) for large computer systems and Access (Microsoft Corp.) for small computer systems.

STUDENT DATA ELEMENT OUTLINE

The following student data element outline from the U.S. Department of Education lists recommended data elements to be maintained by school districts for all students. This outline comes from the National Center for Education Statistics (NCES) Student Data Handbook, which is a 310-page document describing all aspects of building a student information system. Further information, including all coding schemes, is available online:

http://nces.ed.gov/pubs2000/2000343.pdf
http://nces.ed.gov/ccd/

Data Element Outline

The following entries outline the organization of the section titles, categories, and data elements (with the data element numbers), as well as their definitions, included in this handbook.

A. PERSONAL INFORMATION

Section A, Personal Information, includes information about a student's personal, family, and demographic status.

Entity Uses: Student, Parent/Guardian, Employer, Sibling(s) or Other School-Age Children Living in Student's Household, Responsible Adult of Student's Household, Other Adult Living in Student's Household, Sponsor, Emergency Contact

Name–A word or series of words by which a subject is known and distinguishable.

0010	First Name
0020	Middle Name
0030	Last/Surname
0040	Generation Code/Suffix
0050	Personal Title/Prefix
0060	Alias
0070	Former Legal Name
0080	Last/Surname at Birth
0090	Nickname
0100	Tribal or Clan Name
0110	Name of Individual
0120	Name of Institution

Background Information–Personal information about (and particular to) an individual, organization, or institution.

0130	Identification Number
0140	Identification System
0149	Hispanic or Latino Ethnicity
0150	Race
0160	National/Ethnic Origin Subgroup
0170	Sex
0180	Birthdate
0190	Birthdate Verification
0200	City of Birth
0210	County of Birth
0220	State of Birth
0230	Country of Birth Code
0231	Name of Country of Birth
0232	Born Outside of the United States
0240	First Entry Date (into the United States)
0250	Citizenship Status
0260	Country of Citizenship
0270	English Proficiency
0280	Language Type
0290	Language Code
0291	Name of Language
0292	Languages Other Than English
0300	Religious Background

0310	Minor/Adult Status
0315	Homelessness Status
0320	Migratory Status
0330	Migrant Classification Subgroup
0340	Migrant National Certificate of Eligibility (COE) Status
0350	Migrant Residency Date
0360	Migrant Last Qualifying Move (LQM) Date
0361	Migrant Last Qualifying Arrival Date (QAD)
0362	Migrant To Join Date

Address/Contact Information–Information that can be used to direct communication to an individual, organization, or institution.

0369	Address Type
0370	Street Number/Name
0380	Apartment/Room/Suite Number
0390	City
0400	County
0410	State
0420	Zip Code
0430	Country
0440	Complete Permanent Address
0460	Communication Status
0461	Communication Number Type
0470	Communication Number
0489	Electronic Mail Address Type
0490	Electronic Mail Address
0520	Zone Number
0530	Residence Block Number
0540	Other Geographical Designation
0550	Public School Residence Status
0560	Non-Resident Attendance Rationale
0570	Dwelling Arrangement
0580	Dwelling Ownership
0590	Head of Household

Family Information–Information about the student's family condition and responsibilities.

0600	Marital Status
0610	Financial Dependency
0620	Number of Dependents
0630	Family Income Range
0640	Economic Disadvantage Status
0641	Eligibility for National School Lunch Program
0642	Participation in National School Lunch Program
0650	Family Public Assistance Status
0660	Relationship to Student
0670	Life Status
0680	School/Local Education Agency Status
0690	Occupation
0700	Employment Status

0710	Employer Type
0720	Highest Level of Education Completed

B. ENROLLMENT

Section B, Enrollment, includes data about a student's entrance or re-entrance into the institution in which he or she receives instruction (including instruction in school or by correspondence), about his or her membership (including attendance, absence, tardiness, and early departure), and about his or her exit from school (including transfer, withdrawal, and death).
Entity Uses: Student, School, Local Administrative Unit (LAU)

School Information–The identification of the school(s), educational institution(s), and corresponding agencies that a student previously attended, currently attends, concurrently attends, or is transferring to attend.

0730	Enrollment Status
0740	Lowest Grade Level
0750	Highest Grade Level
0760	School Administration
0770	School Type

Entrance Information–Information concerning the entrance or re-entrance of a student into a school or other educational institution. This includes a description of the status of a student when he or she is admitted to an institution and a classification of his or her entry.

0780	Admission Date
0790	Admission Status
0800	Entry Date
0810	Cohort Year
0820	Entry Type
0830	Entry Level
0840	Full-Time/Part-Time Status
0841	Full-Time Equivalent (FTE) Status
0850	Day/Evening Status
0860	Boarding Status

Tuition And Fee Information–Information concerning situations in which the receipt of a payment is required for instruction, services, privileges, or the use of equipment, books, or other goods.

0870	Tuition Payment Amount
0871	Fee Payment Type
0880	Fee Amount
0920	Total Cost of Education to Student
0930	Tuition Status
0940	Payment Source(s)

Financial Assistance–The monetary support in form of scholarships, grants, prizes, or awards received by a student from a source other than his or her parent/guardian, spouse, or own resources to help meet the student's educational expenses.

0950	Financial Assistance Qualifier
0960	Financial Assistance Type
0970	Financial Assistance Descriptive Title

0980   Financial Assistance Source
0990   Financial Assistance Amount

Membership Information–Information indicating the period of time a student's name is on the current roll of a class or school while the school is in session regardless of his or her presence or absence. A student is a member of a class or school from the date he or she enters until his or her name is withdrawn from the rolls (or after a pre-set number of consecutive days of absence based on state or local laws or regulations). During this period, the student is either present or absent on each day or half day during which school is in session.

1000   Number of Days of Membership

Attendance Information–Information concerning a student's presence, absence, and tardiness in a class or school. Attendance is the presence of a student on days when school is in session.

1010   Daily Attendance Status
1011   Number of Days in Attendance
1012   Number of Days Absent
1013   Number of Tardies
1020   Class Attendance Status
1030   Released Time

Exit/Withdrawal Information–Information concerning a student who exits or withdraws his or her membership in a class, grade, or school during the regular school term or between regular school terms for known or unknown reasons. Membership usually is terminated after excessive consecutive days of absence other than for prolonged illness, upon the completion of school work, transfer to another school, dropping out/discontinuing school, or death.

1040   Exit/Withdrawal Date
1050   Exit/Withdrawal Status
1060   Exit/Withdrawal Type
1070   Death Date
1080   Death Cause
1090   Illness Type
1100   Expulsion Cause
1110   Expulsion Return Date
1120   Discontinuing Schooling Reason
1130   Compulsory Attendance Status at Time of Discontinuing School
1140   Residence After Exiting/Withdrawing From School
1150   Information Source

Non-Entrance Information–Information recorded under this heading concerns individuals residing in the local education agency boundaries who: 1) are of compulsory school attendance age or are of school census age (if these limits are greater); and 2) have not entered any public school during the current regular school session and are not classified as discontinuers or dropouts.

1160   Reason for Non-Entrance in Local Elementary and Secondary School

C. SCHOOL PARTICIPATION AND ACTIVITIES

Section C, School Participation and Activities, includes information about all aspects of a student's activities in school, including classes the student takes, their outcomes, and graduation information.
Entity Uses: Student, School, Counselor, Homeroom Monitor, Class, Teacher

Session Information–Included in this section is information about the type and length of a session for which class and performance information are recorded.

1170	Session Type
1180	Session Beginning Date
1190	Session Ending Date
1200	Total Days in Session
1201	Number of Hours in School Day

Course Information–Information about the organization of subject matter and related learning experiences provided for the instruction of students on a regular or systematic basis, usually for a predetermined period of time (e.g., a semester or two-week workshop).

1210	Organization
1220	Course Code System
1221	Course Code
1222	Elementary Subject/Course
1230	Instructional Level
1231	State University Course Requirement
1240	Descriptive Title
1250	Period
1260	Time Element
1270	Principal Medium of Instruction
1271	Language of Instruction
1280	Location of Instruction/Service
1290	Location of Instruction/Service Description
1300	Credit Type Offered
1310	Number of Credits Attempted
1320	Repeat Identifier
1330	Number of Credits Received
1340	Reporting Means
1350	Reporting Method
1360	Grade Assigned
1370	Grade Value Qualifier

Grading Period Information–Information about the prescribed span of time that serves as the unit for which student performance is assessed. A grading period may be interrupted by one or more vacations.

1380	Grading Period Beginning Date
1390	Grading Period Ending Date
1400	Total Days in Grading Period

Performance Information—Information about the performance of a student in courses during a given school grading period, session, school year, or career.

1410	Credits Attempted: Given Grading Period
1420	Credits Attempted: Given Session
1430	Credits Attempted: Given School Year
1440	Credits Attempted: Cumulative
1450	Credits Received: Given Grading Period
1460	Credits Received: Given Session
1470	Credits Received: Given School Year

1480	Credits Received: Cumulative
1490	Grade Points Received: Given Grading Period
1500	Grade Points Received: Given Session
1510	Grade Points Received: Given School Year
1520	Grade Points Received: Cumulative
1530	Grade Point Average (GPA): Given Grading Period
1540	Grade Point Average (GPA): Given Session
1550	Grade Point Average (GPA): Given School Year
1560	Grade Point Average (GPA): Cumulative

Progress Information–Information about the nature of a student's progress for each school term.

1570	Promotion Type
1580	Non-Promotion Reason

Honors Information–Information about the nature of the academic distinctions or other honors received by a student.

1590	Honors Information Code
1591	Honors Description
1592	Class Rank
1593	Total Number in Class
1594	Percentage Ranking

Activity Information–Information about a student's participation in cocurricular or extracurricular activities under the sponsorship and/or direction of the school (e.g., student organizations, intramural and interscholastic athletics, publications, band, orchestra, and service activities).

1600	Activity Title
1601	Activity Code
1602	Activity Description
1610	Activity Type
1611	Name of Activity Sponsor
1612	Activity Involvement Beginning Date
1613	Activity Involvement Ending Date
1614	Amount of Activity Involvement

Graduation Information—Summary information about the student's completion of graduation requirements, diploma received, and honors received.

1621	Diploma/Credential Type
1622	Diploma/Credential Award Date
1623	Diploma/Credential Level and Honors
1624	Diploma/Credential and Honors Description
1625	Non-Course Graduation Requirement Code
1626	Non-Course Graduation Requirement Date Met
1627	Non-Course Graduation Requirement Scores/Results

D. NON-SCHOOL AND POST-SCHOOL EXPERIENCE

Section D, Non-School and Post-School Experience, pertains to the activities and work experience of a student outside of his or her school. These activities may or may not be sponsored by the school or

under the guidance or supervision of staff members. This section also includes information about training received outside of the school, honors and recognitions granted, offices and positions held by the student, and academic and occupational plans of the student when he or she finishes school.
Entity Uses: Student, Employer, Postsecondary Institution

Non-School Activity Information–Information about participation in non-work activities which are neither sponsored by the school nor under the guidance or supervision of staff members. This may include information about the various offices and positions held by the student including information on travel, hobby, and other special interests and abilities.

1630	Non-School Activity Code
1631	Non-School Activity Description
1632	Non-School Activity Sponsor
1633	Amount of Non-School Activity Involvement
1640	Non-School Activity Beginning Date
1650	Non-School Activity Ending Date

Institutional/Organizational Information–Information about any organization for which an individual works and/or any postsecondary institution that he or she attends.

Work Experience–Information about paid or unpaid work performed by a student.

1670	In-School/Post-School Employment Status
1680	Experience Type
1690	Work Type
1700	Program of Study Relevance
1710	Employment Permit Number
1720	Employment Permit Certifying Organization
1730	Employment Permit Description
1740	Employment Permit Valid Date
1750	Employment Permit Expiration Date
1760	Employment Start Date
1770	Employment End Date
1780	Number of Hours Worked Per Work Week (Monday–Friday)
1790	Number of Hours Worked Per Weekend
1800	Employment Recognition

Post-School Education/Training–Information in this category concerns a student's aspirations and plans for post-school vocation, training, and education.

1810	Post-School Training or Education Subject Matter
1820	Education Planned
1830	Post-School Recognition

Other Post-School Information–Information in this category pertains to other post-school experience not mentioned above.

1840	Career Objectives
1850	Military Service Experience
1860	Voting Status
1870	Other Post-School Accomplishments

E. ASSESSMENT

Section E, Assessment, contains information regarding assessment conducted on a student. It includes assessment purpose, administration, response, and scoring.

Entity Uses: Assessment, Evaluator

Assessment Information–The general classification of an assessment administered to a student based upon the anticipated use of the information it provides. This also includes information that identifies the assessment.

1880	Purpose
1890	Assessment Type
1900	Assessment Title
1910	Assessment Content
1920	Subtest Type
1930	Level (for which Designed)
1940	Grade Level when Assessed
1950	Copyright Date

Administrative Issues–This category contains information relating to the administration of an assessment to a student.

1959	Non-Participation Reason
1960	Administration Method
1970	Administration Form
1980	Response Form
1990	Administration Language
2000	Special Accommodation
2010	Administration Date
2020	Location
2030	Position

Score/Results Reporting–This category contains information about assessment results, the manner in which they are presented, and factors which may influence their interpretation.

2040	Assessment Reference Type
2050	Norm Group
2060	Norm Year
2070	Norming Period
2080	Score Range
2090	Reporting Method
2100	Score Results
2110	Score Interpretation Information
2120	Reporting and Documentation

F. TRANSPORTATION

Section F, Transportation, concerns the transportation of students to and from school and school-related activities.

Entity Uses: Student, Transportation Contact, Transportation Vehicle

Transportation Information–Identifies information about a student's transportation needs and services received.

2130	Transportation Status
2140	State Transportation Aid Qualification
2150	Transportation at Public Expense Eligibility
2160	Special Accommodation Requirements

Transportation Contact–The individual who is responsible for a student's transportation to and/or from school or the person who receives the individual at a bus stop or other location.

Distance/Time Information–Information about the distance and time a student must travel to school.

2170	Distance From Home to School
2180	Total Distance Transported
2190	Length of Time Transported

Vehicle Information–Information about the different types of vehicles used to transport a student.

2200	Ownership/Type
2210	Route Description
2220	Run Description
2230	Stop Description

G. HEALTH CONDITIONS

Section G, Health Conditions, includes information concerning various aspects of a student's current physical condition, health history, evaluations, physical limitations, and health care provider.
Entity Uses: Student, Health Evaluation, Health Care Provider

Identifiers–This category includes a student's health record identification number, descriptive measurements of height and weight, and identification of hair and eye colors, and outstanding birthmarks that might be recorded over a period of time.

2240	Height
2250	Weight
2260	Hair Color
2270	Eye Color
2280	Birthmark
2290	Blood Type

Oral Health–The condition of an individual's mouth or oral cavity; more specifically the condition of the hard tissues (i.e., teeth and jaws) and the soft tissues (i.e., gums, tongue, lips, palate, mouth floor, and inner cheeks). Good oral health denotes the absence of clinically manifested disease or abnormalities of the oral cavity.

2300	Number of Teeth
2310	Number of Permanent Teeth Lost
2320	Number of Teeth Decayed
2330	Number of Teeth Restored
2340	Occlusion Condition
2350	Gingival (Gum) Condition
2360	Oral Soft Tissue Condition
2370	Dental Prosthetics
2380	Orthodontic Appliances

Maternal and Pre-Natal Condition–The condition as well as the type and extent of medical care received by a student's mother prior to the birth of the student.

2390	Initial Pre-Natal Visit (Gestational Age)
2400	Total Number of Pre-Natal Visits During Pregnancy
2410	Total Weight Gain During Pregnancy

Conditions at Birth–Information regarding the health and/or other medical conditions observed or measured at a student's birth.

2420	Weight at Birth
2430	Gestational Age at Birth
2440	Health Condition at Birth

Health History–A record of an individual's afflictions, conditions, injuries, accidents, treatments, and procedures.

2450	Diseases, Illnesses, and Other Health Conditions
2460	Medical Treatment
2470	School Health Emergency Action
2480	Injury
2490	Substance Abuse
2500	Routine Health Care Procedure Required at School
2510	Health Condition Progress Report
2520	Health Care History Episode Date

Medical Evaluations–A record of diagnostic examinations an individual may undergo for identification or evaluation of a medical process or condition.

2530	Evaluation Sequence
2540	Medical Examination Type
2550	Medical Examination Instrument Description/Title
2560	Medical Examination Date
2570	Uncorrected Score/Results
2580	Corrected Score/Results
2590	Medical Examination Unit of Measure
2600	Blood Pressure
2610	Overall Diagnosis/Interpretation of Vision
2620	Overall Diagnosis/Interpretation of Hearing
2630	Overall Diagnosis/Interpretation of Speech and Language
2640	Service Alternatives
2650	Corrective Equipment Prescribed
2660	Corrective Equipment Purpose
2670	Diagnosis of Causative Factor (Condition)
2680	Condition Onset Date

Disabling Conditions–Current health conditions (e.g., orthopedic, neurological, cardiac, or respiratory) that have been identified by a health care provider or other qualified evaluator and may incapacitate an individual in any way.

2690	Primary Disability Type
2691	Qualified Individual with Disabilities under Section 504 of the Rehabilitation Act
2692	Qualified Individual with a Disability under the Individuals with Disabilities Education Act (IDEA)

2693   Qualified Individual with Disabilities under the Americans with Disabilities Act
2700   Disability Level
2710   Secondary Disability Type
2720   Tertiary Disability Type

Medical Laboratory Tests–Instances in which specific medical laboratory tests are applied to determine the condition or functionality of bodily parts or systems or to identify diseases and abnormalities.

2730   Blood Test Type
2740   Tuberculosis Test Type
2750   Medical Laboratory Procedure Results

Immunizations–Instances in which an individual is protected or immunized against specific diseases by inoculation or vaccination, or by having previously contracted a disease.

2760   Immunization Type
2770   Immunizations Mandated by State Law for Participation
2780   Immunization Date
2790   Immunization Status Code

Nutrition–Information about an individual's dietary habits, needs, and limitations.

2800   Special Diet Considerations

Referrals–The act of directing an individual to a qualified health care provider for medical assistance, health, evaluation, or information.

2810   Referral Purpose
2820   Referral Cause
2830   Referral Date
2840   Referral Completion Date
2850   Referral Completion Report

Limitations on School Activities–The circumstance or situation in which an individual's participation in the regular school program is modified or precluded.

2860   Limitation Description
2870   Limitation Cause
2880   Limitation Beginning Date
2890   Limitation Ending Date

Health Care Provider–A professional individual with the responsibility to provide any of a variety of health care services to a student.

2900   Provider Type
2910   Provider Specialty
2920   Provider Authority
2930   Referral Status

Other Health Information–Information about an individual's medical or health requirements that are not otherwise addressed above.

2940   Emergency Factor
2950   Related Emergency Needs

2960	Insurance Coverage
2970	Health Care Plan
2980	Hospital Preference
2990	Medical Waiver
3000	Religious Consideration
3010	Other Special Health Needs, Information, or Instructions

H. SPECIAL PROGRAM PARTICIPATION AND STUDENT SUPPORT SERVICES

Section H, Special Program Participation and Student Support Services, includes information concerning student participation in support, enrichment, and special assistance programs as well as early childhood programs (not limited to special needs populations) available through federal, state, or local agencies, public or private schools, and for-profit, non-profit or other community-based organizations. Services may be instructional or non-instructional in nature and may be provided in school or other-than-school facilities. Also contained in this section is information about student eligibility identification and determination, program modification rationale, types of supplementary programs provided, service delivery, and monitoring efforts.

Entity Uses: Student, Evaluator, Program/Service, Service Provider

Identification Procedure–A description of the procedures used to identify a student as eligible for student support services or special assistance programs in early childhood, elementary or secondary education. These programs supplement regular services offered by a school. Eligibility is based upon characteristics of the status or condition of the student, his or her family, or their community, as mandated by program criteria.

3020	Identification Procedure
3030	Identification Results
3040	Participation Eligibility Indicator
3050	Program Participation Reason
3060	Program Participation Identification Date

Early Childhood Program Participation–Information about a child's care, education, and/or services from birth to enrollment in kindergarten (or first grade if kindergarten is not available). Programs include care, education, and/or services provided by a parent/guardian, by a relative other than a parent/guardian, and by a non-relative. Location, sponsorship, and funding of care, education, and/or services are also addressed.

3070	Caregiver/Early Childhood Program Provider
3080	Caregiver/Early Childhood Program Setting
3090	Family Day Care Status
3100	Caregiver/Early Childhood Program Description
3110	Early Childhood Program Sponsorship
3120	Early Childhood Program Funding Source
3130	Early Childhood Program Components
3131	Early Childhood Special Education Setting
3132	Early Childhood Program Focus

Individualized Education Program Information–Information regarding efforts made to develop, implement, and revise an Individualized Education Program (IEP) or other individualized programs for students requiring such services.

| 3140 | Individualized Program Type |
| 3150 | Individualized Program Date Type |

3160   Individualized Program Date
3170   Number of Minutes per Week Included

Special Program and Student Support Service Participation–Information regarding the student's participation in one or more special programs after an identification process has been completed.

3180   Special Assistance Program Name
3190   Benefit Type
3200   Program Funding Source
3210   Instructional Program Service Type
3220   Student Support Service Type
3230   Transitional Support Service Type
3240   Service Description

Special Program/Services Delivery–The prescribed and planned arrangement in which programs/services are provided, including the location, setting, funding, and timing.

3250   Care/Service Frequency
3260   Care/Service Day Status
3270   Care/Service Intensity
3280   Care/Service Duration
3290   Care/Service Beginning Date
3300   Service Setting

Service Provider–The individual or organization responsible for administering the program/service.

3310   Service Provider Type

Monitoring Procedure–A description of the procedures used to monitor the participation and progress of a student enrolled in special programs or student support services that are in place of or in addition to normal services offered by the school.

3320   Monitoring Method
3330   Remarks

Program Exit–Information regarding the termination of a student's program services.

3340   Care/Service Ending Date
3350   Program Exit Reason

I. DISCIPLINE

Section I, Discipline, contains information regarding student discipline, including the nature of an offense, type of disciplinary action, dates of disciplinary action, and the individual administering the disciplinary action.

Entity Uses: Student, Disciplinarian

Nature of Offense–Information under this category contains data elements relating to the description and severity of the offense.

3360   Incident Type
3361   Convicted Offense
3370   Incident Description
3380   Incident Occurrence Date

3390	Incident Occurrence Location
3391	Offense/Incident Occurrence Time

Disciplinary Action–Information in this category relates to the type and extent of disciplinary action taken by authorities.

3400	Disciplinary Action Type
3410	Disciplinary Action Description
3420	Disciplinary Action Status
3430	Disciplinary Action Beginning Date
3440	Disciplinary Action Ending Date
3450	Disciplinary Action Authority

Technical Support E

Internet Resources for Data-Driven Decision Making

The SPSS dataset that is used for all of the examples in Technical Support E can be found at the Companion Website at **www.prenhall.com/picciano/**

American Association of School Administrators
http://www.aasa.org

American Association for Supervision and Curriculum Development
http://www.ascd.org

American Federation of Teachers
http://www.aft.org

Collaborative Inquiry Uses Data to Get Results
Hands On! Spring 2001, TERC
http://www.terc.edu/handsonIssues/s01/ready.html

Common Core of Data
National Center for Education Statistics, U.S. Department of Education
http://nces.ed.gov/ccd/index.asp

Data-Driven Decision Making
Technology Information Center for Administrative Leadership
http://www.portical.org/matrix1.html

Data-Driven Decisions
The School Administrator Web Edition, April 2001, The American Association
    for School Administrators
http://www.aasa.org/publications/sa/2001_04/contents_april2001.htm

Data-Driven School Improvement
Johnson, J. ERIC Digest, No. 109, 1997. Educational Research Information
    Center (ERIC) Clearinghouse on Educational Management
http://www.ed.gov/databases/ERIC_Digests/ed401595.html

Data-Driven Success
Liddle, E. Electronic School, March 2000
http://www.electronic-school.com/2000/03/0300f3.html

Data Inquiry and Analysis for Educational Reform
Wade, H. H. ERIC Digest, No. 153, 2001. ERIC Clearinghouse on
    Educational Management
http://eric.uoregon.edu/publications/digests/digest153.html

Databases Can Help Teachers with Standards Implementation
Bernhardt, V. L. Education for the Future Initiative, 2000
http://www.educationadvisor.com/ocio2001/DatabasesCanHelp.pdf

Educational Policy Publications: Data-Driven Decision Making
North Central Regional Educational Laboratory, 2000
http://www.ncrel.org/policy/pubs/dddm.htm

Education Trust
http://www.edtrust.org/main/main/index.asp

Education Week on the Web: Special Reports and Series
http://www.edweek.org/sreports/special_reports_full_list.html

EDsmart Incorporated
http://www.edsmartinc.com

Grow Network
http://www.grownetwork.com/

Improving School Board Decision Making: The Data Connection
The National School Boards Foundation
http://www.schoolboarddata.org/index.htm

Improving Teaching and Learning with Data-Based Decisions: Asking the
    Right Questions and Acting on the Answers
Protheroe, N. ERS Spectrum, 2001. Educational Research Service
http://www.ers.org/spectrum/sum01a.htm

just4kids
http://www.just4kids.org/

Kids Count
Annie E. Casey Foundation
http://www.aecf.org/kidscount/

Learning to Use Data to Get Results
Barron, P., Behrends, C., & Feeney, J. 2002. ENC Focus 9(1). Eisenhower
    National Clearinghouse
http://www.enc.org/focus/pd/document.shtm?input=FOC-002596-index

McDowell Foundation
Educators as Researchers
http://www.mcdowellfoundation.ca/main_mcdowell/current/
    resources_for_teacher_researchers.htm

National Association of Elementary School Principals
http://www.naesp.org

National Association of Secondary School Principals
http://www.nassp.org

National Center for Education Statistics (NCES)
U.S. Department of Education
http://nces.ed.gov/

National Education Association
http://www.nea.org

National Parent Teachers Association (PTA)
http://www.pta.org

No Child Left Behind Information Web Site
http://www.ed.gov/nclb/landing.jhtml?src=pb

Resources for Data-Driven Decision Making
National Staff Development Council
http://www.nsdc.org/library/research.cfm

School, District, and State Report Cards
Northwest Regional Educational Laboratory. March 2002
http://www.nwrel.org/planning/reports/rptcards/

School Reform by the Numbers
The Focused Reporting Project, Jefferson County, KY. Spring 2000
http://www.middleweb.com/CSLVfinal/CSLVfinall.html

Schools and Staffing Survey
National Center for Education Statistics, U.S. Department of Education
http://nces.ed.gov/surveys/sass/

Shared Accountability
Strategies for School System Leaders on District Level Change, 7 (1).
    May 2000. The Panasonic Foundation in collaboration with American
    Association of School Administrators
http://www.aasa.org/issues_and_insights/technology/May2000_Strategies.pdf

Socrates Data System
Center for Resource Management, Inc.
http://www.crminc.com/socrates/Page2.htm

The Nation's Report Card
National Assessment of Educational Progress (NAEP), National Center
    for Education Statistics, U.S. Department of Education
http://nces.ed.gov/nationsreportcard/

Teachers and Students as Action Researchers: Using Data Daily
Cooper, C. & Cromey, A. Learning Point, Summer 2000. North Central
    Regional Educational Laboratory
http://www.ncrel.org/info/nlp/lpsu00/resrch.htm

Thinking About Tests and Testing: A Short Primer on "Assessment Literacy"
Bracey, G. W. American Youth Policy Forum in cooperation with the National
  Conference of State Legislatures
http://www.cse.ucla.edu/CRESST/Files/BraceyRep.pdf

The Toolbelt: A Collection of Data-Driven Decision-Making Tools for
  Educators
North Central Regional Educational Laboratory
http://www.ncrel.org/toolbelt/index.html

This Goes on Your Permanent Record: Data Warehousing
Deck, S. CIO Magazine, December 2000
http://www.cio.com/archive/110100/permanent.html

Tools for Accountability
Annenberg Institute for School Reform
http://www.annenberginstitute.org/Toolbox/index.html

Tools for Using Data to Drive Decisions: An Evaluation Template
Jurs, S. June 2002, Southeastern Regional Vision for Education (SERVE)
http://www.serve.org/_downloads/June2002.pdf

Using Data to Improve Schools: What's Working
American Association of School Administrators
http://www.aasa.org/cas/UsingDataToImproveSchools.pdf

Glossary

Analysis of covariance. (ANCOVA) Statistical procedure that compares the means of two or more groups. ANCOVA assumes there are more than two variables: One variable is a dependent, interval, or ratio variable, and two or more variables are a combination of independent, nominal, interval, or ratio variables.

Analysis of variance. (ANOVA) Statistical procedure that compares the means of two or more groups to determine if any differences between the means are statistically significant.

Categorical variable. Variable such as gender or ethnicity that contains a limited number of values. Also referred to as a discrete variable.

Cause-effect relationship. Relationship between two or more variables in which one or more variables effect another variable.

Character. Letter, numeral, or special character such as a comma or exclamation point that can be represented by one byte, or unit, of computer storage.

Client-server system. Distributed data communications system in which computers perform two important functions, either as "clients" or "servers." The client function makes requests for data (e.g., files) from the server, which locates the data on the data communications system and processes the request for the client.

Cluster sample. Type of sample in which the entire population is divided into groups, or clusters, and a random sample of these clusters is selected. All subjects in the selected clusters are then included in the sample.

Contingency table. Arrangement of data in a two-dimensional classification scheme represented by a series of rows and columns.

Continuous variable. Variable such as a test score or salary that contains a wide range or unlimited number of values.

Control group. Group of subjects in an experimental study who do not receive an experimental treatment.

Converted score. Score that is derived from a raw score and represented in another form that is more easily understood. For example, a percentile ranking is derived from a z score.

Correlation coefficient. Decimal number between -1.00 and $+1.00$ that indicates the degree to which two variables are related.

Criterion variable. In prediction studies, the variable that is predicted by another variable. Also referred to as the dependent variable.

Crosstabulation. *See* contingency table.

Data-driven decision making. Use of data analysis to inform when determining courses of action involving policy and procedures. Note that data analysis is used *to inform* not replace the experience, expertise, intuition, judgment, and acumen of competent educators.

Data disaggregation. Use of software tools to break data files down into various characteristics. For example, a software program is used to select student performance data on a standardized test by gender, by class, by ethnicity, or by other definable characteristics.

Data element. Grouping of characters (letters of the alphabet, numerals, special characters) to represent some specific data characteristic of a person, place, or thing. Examples are a person's name, street address, and gender. Also referred to as a data field or data item.

Data element dictionary. Table used to identify the content and coding schemes used for all the data elements in a database. The term *data element dictionary* is also used for a document that identifies the content, definitions, and coding schemes used for all data elements in a database.

Data field. *See* data element.

Data file. Collection of related data records. Examples are a personnel file of all personnel records or a student file of all student records.

Data item. *See* data element.

Data mining. Frequently used term in research and statistics that refers to searching or "digging into" a data file for information to understand better a particular phenomenon.

Data processing. General term used for the systematic processing (storing, manipulating, sorting, etc.) of data on computer systems.

Data record. Grouping of related data elements for a single entity such as a person, place, or thing. Examples are a personnel record, inventory record, and financial record.

Data structure. Method by which data are organized in a database.

Data warehousing. Computerized database information system that is capable of storing and maintaining data *longitudinally*, that is, over a period of time.

Database. Collection of data files and records.

Database management system (DBMS). Package of computer programs that allows users to create, maintain, and access the data on a database.

DBMS. *See* database management system.

Decision making. Generally defined as choosing between or among two or more alternatives. However, in a modern school organization, decision making is an integral component of more encompassing management processes such as academic planning, policymaking, and budgeting.

Degrees of freedom. Mathematical concept used with various measures such as *t* tests, analysis of variance, and chi-square tests to refine the results of probability or chance in determining statistical significance. It indicates the number of observations or values in a distribution that are independent of each other or are free to vary.

Dependent variable. Variable that changes as a result of or in relation to a change in an independent variable. In prediction studies it is also referred to as the criterion variable.

Deviation. Difference (distance plus or minus) between a value and the mean of a group of values.

Dichotomous variable. Categorical variable that has only two possibilities (e.g., gender).

Digital. Related to digits. Computers are considered digital because all data and instructions are represented as binary digits.

Discrete variable. *See* categorical variable.

Downloading. In a computer network, the process of transferring a copy of a file from one computer, generally referred to as a central file server, to another, requesting computer.

Effect size. Secondary statistical procedure used to determine the level of significance in the difference in the means. It is calculated by taking the difference in the means of the two groups and dividing it by the standard deviation of the control group.

Electronic spreadsheet. Application programming software that provides the user with an electronic grid of rows and columns similar to a ledger worksheet. It is used extensively for budgets, forecasts, projections, and other number-based applications. Examples are Excel and Lotus 1-2-3.

Encumbrance. In school finance, a commitment or contract to pay for goods or services.

Environmental scanning. Term used in planning that means engaging in activities to provide information outside of an organization or on the external environment.

Experimental group. Group in an experimental study that receives the experimental treatment.

Frequency distribution. Systematic arrangement of numeric values from the lowest to the highest or the highest to the lowest, with a count of the number of times each value was obtained.

Hardware. Physical components of a computer system such as the central processing unit, printer, monitor, and keyboard.

HTTP. *See* hypertext transfer control protocol.

Hypertext transfer control protocol (HTTP). The most commonly used protocol on the World Wide Web. It runs in conjunction with TCP/IP.

Idiographic research. Method that involves the study of one or a few subjects, often over a long period of time.

Independent variable. Variable which, as it changes, relates to or causes a change in another (dependent) variable. In prediction studies, it is also referred to as the predictor variable.

Internet. Network of networks that provides the basic protocol standard for allowing data communications systems to link themselves together throughout the world.

LAN. *See* local area network.

Likert scale. Named for Rensis Likert, scale used in surveys and questionnaires to simplify responses by providing from three to seven options in a consistent format (e.g., very dissatisfied, dissatisfied, no opinion, satisfied, very satisified).

Linear regression. Use of correlation coefficients to plot a line illustrating the linear relationship of two variables, *X* and *Y.*

Local area network (LAN). Connection of computer equipment using data communications over a limited geographic area such as a room, building, or campus.

Longitudinal study. Study that looks at phenomena over a period of time.

Mean Arithmetic average of a group of numbers.

Measures of central tendency. Averages or values that represent what is typical for a group of values. Three of the most popular measures of central tendency are the mean, median, and mode.

Measures of relationship. Statistical measures that show a relationship between two or more paired variables or two or more sets of data. The most common statistical measure of relationship is the correlation coefficient.

Measures of dispersion (or spread). Statistical measures that show contrasts or differences in a group of values. The most common measures of spread are range, deviation, variance, and standard deviation.

Median. Midpoint in a group of values, above and below which half of the values fall; a measure of central tendency.

Mode. Value in a group of values that occurs most often; a measure of central tendency.

Multiple regression. Form of analysis of variance that assumes there are three or more variables: One variable is a dependent, interval, or ratio variable, and two or more variables are independent, interval, or ratio variables such as test scores, income, and grade point average. It is frequently used to develop prediction models.

Network. Group of computer devices connected by a data communications system. Two major types of networks are local area networks (LANs) and wide area networks (WANs).

Non-tax-levy funds. In school finance, funds that are derived from private individuals, corporations, or special-purpose government programs.

Nomothetic research. Research that involves the study of large groups, often on one occasion.

Normal curve (normal distribution). Distribution of values in a variable in which most values are near the mean and all values cluster around the mean in a symmetrical, bell-shaped pattern. In a normal distribution, the distance from 1 standard deviation (SD) above the mean to 1 SD below the mean includes approximately 68% of all the values; +2 SD to –2 SD includes approximately 95% of all values; and +3 SD to –3 SD includes more than 99% of all values.

Normal distribution. *See* normal curve.

Other Than Personnel Services (OTPS). In school finance, a budget category that refers to things such as supplies, textbooks, equipment, and contracts to repair or to replace facilities.

OTPS. *See* Other Than Personnel Services.

Pearson product-moment coefficient (r). Most popular form of correlation coefficients used with two groups of continuous variables (e.g., test scores and grade point averages).

Percentile rank. Converted score that shows the point in a distribution below which a given percentage of scores fall. For example, if a score of 65 is at the 70th percentile, then 70% of the scores fall below 65.

Personnel services. In school finance, a budget category that refers to expenditures for people (e.g., employees, full time or part time).

Predictor variable. In prediction studies, the variable that predicts another variable. Also referred to as the independent variable.

Protocol. General term used for a set of rules, procedures, or standards used to exchange information in data communications. Examples of such rules are a code or signal indicating the beginning of a message, a code or signal indicating the end of a message, and a code or signal indicating that a device is busy with another task. Computer manufacturers have established various protocols for exchanging information on their equipment.

Query language. User-friendly language that enables users to retrieve and display data from a database.

Random sampling. Process of selecting a sample such that all the subjects in a population have an equal chance of being selected.

Range. Measure of spread or dispersion, which is the difference between the highest and lowest values in a group of values.

Relational database. Database structure that uses a table to relate or link one data element with another data element.

Reliability. Degree to which a standardized test consistently measures what it is supposed to measure.

Sample. Smaller group of individuals or cases that is representative of a larger population.

SAS. *See* Statistical Analysis System.

Scientific method. Procedure for problem solving used in most disciplines that consists of four steps: defining a problem; stating a main question or hypothesis; collecting relevant data; and analyzing the data to answer the question or test the hypothesis.

Significance level. *See* statistical significance.

Software. Computer programs and instructions that direct the physical components (hardware) of a computer system to perform tasks.

SPSS. *See* Statistical Package for the Social Sciences.

Standard deviation. Most frequently used measure of spread or dispersion determined by calculating the square root of the variance.

Statistical Analysis System (SAS). Comprehensive software system designed to perform statistical analysis and data management.

Statistical Package for the Social Sciences (SPSS). Comprehensive software system designed to perform statistical analysis and data management.

Statistical significance. Indication of the probability of a finding having occurred by chance; the general standard referred to as the .05 level of statistical significance indicates that the finding has a 5% (.05) chance of not being true and, conversely, a 95% chance of being true.

Statistics. Body of mathematical techniques or processes for gathering, organizing, analyzing, and interpreting numeric data—the basic tools of measurement, evaluation, and research.

Stratified sample. Type of random sample that attempts to include representative proportions of certain characteristics (e.g., gender, ethnicity, income levels) of the larger population.

System. Group of interrelated parts assembled to achieve some common goal or end. The three major components of most systems are input, process, and output. Examples of systems are computer systems, ecological systems, economic systems, political systems, and school systems.

Tax-levy funds. In school finance, funds derived directly from taxes levied on citizens (e.g., property taxes or income taxes).

TCP/IP. *See* Transmission control protocol/Internet protocol.

Transmission control protocol/Internet protocol (TCP/IP). Standard protocol used on the Internet. Originally developed by the U.S. Department of Defense.

t test. Parametric test used to determine the significance of the difference between the means of two groups of values.

Triangulation. Multipronged approach to data collection that attempts to use one or more data collection techniques to verify data collected by another technique.

Validity. Degree to which a standardized test measures what it is supposed to measure.

Variable. Item of data collected for each case in a study, and which varies, or has more than one value.

Variance. Commonly used measure of spread or dispersion calculated by the sum of all the squared deviations from the mean divided by the number (N) of values in the group.

Uploading. In a computer network, process of transmitting a copy of a file from a computer to a central file server.

WAN. *See* wide area network.

Wide area network (WAN). Connection of computer equipment using data communications over a widespread geographic area such as a town, city, or country.

World Wide Web. Protocol and file format software incorporating hypertext and multimedia capabilities for use on the Internet.

WWW. *See* World Wide Web.

Index